ALASKA

R·E·A·D·E·R

THE

ALASKA
R·E·A·D·E·R

Voices from the North

EDITED BY
ANNE HANLEY AND CAROLYN KREMERS

FULCRUM PUBLISHING
GOLDEN, COLORADO

Library of Congress Cataloging-in-Publication Data
The Alaska reader : voices from the north / edited by Anne Hanley and Carolyn Kremers.
    p. cm.
Includes bibliographical references.
ISBN 1-55591-555-8 (pbk.)
    1. American literature—Alaska. 2. Alaska—Literary collections. I. Hanley, Anne. II. Kremers, Carolyn, 1951- III. Title.

PS571.A4A425 2005
810.8'032798—dc22

                                                            2005012687

Printed in the United States of America
0 9 8 7 6 5 4 3 2 1

 Editorial: Haley Groce, Kay Baron, Faith Marcovecchio
   Design: Patty Maher
Cover image: Caribou at sunset on Anaktuvuk Pass, Alaska © 2000 by
             Nick Jans

Fulcrum Publishing
16100 Table Mountain Parkway, Suite 300
Golden, Colorado 80403
(800) 992-2908 • (303) 277-1623
www.fulcrum-books.com

CONTENTS

INTRODUCTION

My first introduction to Alaska was through a story.

When I was six, my aunt gave me a children's picture book about the Serum Run to Nome. It inspired me to line up all the footstools in front of our big recliner in my East Coast living room, thereby making a dog team and sled. I spent many happy hours riding the recliner and shouting commands to my footstools.

When I was in my mid-twenties, I picked up a paperback of John Muir's *Travels in Alaska* at a flea market. The old man behind the table asked if I'd been to Alaska. I was amused. Who had ever actually been to Alaska? Nobody I knew. It turned out that he had been stationed there during World War II. He always wanted to return, but never made it. "Go now," he urged, "before you get too old." He talked me out of buying the Muir book because he said it was worn and ugly. "Come back next week and I might have something for you."

I was curious enough to go back. As soon as he saw me, he pointed to a cardboard box. Inside was a ten-volume first edition of Muir's complete works bound in fawn-colored leather with the titles stamped in gold. Each volume was illustrated with hand-painted watercolors and the first volume had Muir's autograph on the frontispiece. The only books of comparable quality that I had ever seen were locked behind mesh screens in the Rare Books Room at the Boston Public Library. I could keep the books, he said, for an indefinite loan.

As soon as I finished the *Travels in Alaska* volume, I passed it on to my husband. We were living in San Francisco at the time and he was completing his medical residency. He read the book and then showed me an ad in a medical journal: "Doctor wanted. Fairbanks, Alaska." He was kidding of course. Or was he? We had just migrated from the East

Coast to the West Coast and were already too far from home as far as our families were concerned. The Bay Area offered mild weather, natural beauty, and a rich cultural environment. Still, the ad stuck in our minds. We decided Alaska might be fun for a year.

Twenty-eight years later, we still live in Fairbanks in the land-locked Interior of the state, hundreds of miles from Muir's majestic coastal mountains. We don't even own one dog let alone a dog team, but I still credit the picture book and Muir's *Travels in Alaska* with laying the groundwork for our decision to move to Alaska. Stories linked to a place with mythic overtones resonate deep in the unconscious.

In Jungian psychology, north is the direction of the unknown. That makes it both dangerous and thrilling. Outcasts are banished to the North, but if they are willing to die to their old selves and re-create themselves anew, the North offers redemption. If they are poor, they can get rich (fur, gold, oil, fast-food franchises). If they are weak, the North offers ordeals for strength training and character building.

In cultures that depend on the weather and on the movements of animals, stories are more than entertainment. They convey vital infor-mation. In oral traditions, like those of many Alaska Natives, a story is told to a particular audience for a particular purpose. It might warn, or comfort, or instruct a young person in the proper method of hunting. In an oral tradition, each telling of a story is a dynamic exchange between the storyteller and the listener.

Two years ago when I began writing a newspaper column on Alaska writers, I realized that I was not well informed about Alaskan literature. Carolyn Kremers, who was teaching "Literature of Alaska and the Yukon Territory" at the University of Alaska Fairbanks, was kind enough to loan me books by Alaskan writers from her personal library and to suggest writers I might consider for my columns.

In July 2004, Carolyn and I did a two-week backpacking trip in Gates of the Arctic National Park as members of the first "Artists in Residence" program sponsored by the park service. When we got together to plan the food for the trip, I observed the careful way she counted and recounted the Pilot crackers. She had a mathematical approach for determining the proper amount of food—so many grams for each of us per day—while I was more of an "eyeball" cook. ("That looks like about the right amount. Toss it in.") Our reading styles were similar to our trip-planning styles. Where I was spontaneous, she was deliberate. I immediately loved a piece of writing or hated it. Carolyn took her time before deciding, but once she'd made up her mind, she was sure of her reasons. She waged a well-planned, unrelenting campaign to convince me to include Native stories in their original languages. I introduced her to a few writers, like Arlitia Jones and Phoebe Newman. In the end we educated each other.

We began by looking at as many anthologies of Alaskan writing as we could find. That exercise made me despair. What could we possibly assemble that would say something about Alaska that hadn't already been said?

As soon as I started reading the first chapter of Seth Kantner's novel *Ordinary Wolves*, I knew that my misgivings were unfounded. Here was a writer giving voice to a reality I never knew existed. Kantner, who grew up in a sod house on the tundra, tells his story from the point of view of a child with the same background. *Ordinary Wolves* proved to me that there was uncharted territory left to explore in Alaskan writing.

Once Carolyn and I started reading, the stacks of books we had to consider seemed overwhelming. In the end, however, deciding on the final selections was easy. We simply chose what we could not bear to leave out. I was pleased that so many poets made the final cut. Their voices are fresh and vital, worthy of a wider audience.

After we had our pile of final choices, we looked them over to see what themes they suggested to us. We were intrigued to find that a good number were by children of people who came to Alaska with a dream. What does Alaska look like to these "Children of Dreamers"? The selections in "Taking Risks, Confronting Consequences" explore why people take risks when the consequences could be fatal. In "Transformations," storytellers play at shape-shifting. "Naming and Unnaming" examines the compulsion to name. "Finding Self and Spirit" contains tales of inner journeys. "Feminine and Masculine Unbound" looks at gender roles in Alaska where survival sometimes offers unique opportunities to break out of stereotypes.

"Alaska as a Parable for the Future" poses the question: If the Circumpolar North proves to be the canary in the mine for changes brought about by global warming, how will the people of Alaska cope with those changes? Who will be the heroes in this new, frontline struggle?

I have always been impressed at the range of skills possessed by Alaskans. My neighbor can mend a fence, fix a generator, sing a complicated aria, worm a dog. One of my husband's patients, an old miner, demanded to watch while a pacemaker was inserted into his chest because he wanted to know how to take out "the goll darn thing" if he ever decided he no longer wanted to avail himself of its services. Looking over the writers represented in this anthology, I see hunters, trappers, teachers, pilots, scientists, fishermen and fisher-women, a stone mason, a sled builder, a former governor, a meat cutter. If I were marooned in a one-room cabin for a whole winter, I would choose these people to be with me, not only because they could keep the fire going and put food on the table, but also because they could sustain my soul. If, come spring, the river in front of the cabin suddenly opened, I'd have no qualms about climbing into a leaky rowboat with these writers. Not only would they have the skills to keep the boat afloat, they would have the experience—and vision—to give me hope no matter how close we were to sinking. These writers have rich lives full of real adventures. I'd follow them anywhere. I hope this anthology will lead you to journey farther with these extraordinary people.

Anne Hanley
Alaska State Writer Laureate 2002-2004

PART I

Children of Dreamers

ORDINARY WOLVES

Seth Kantner

 In the bad mouse year—two years after magazines claimed a white man hoofed on the moon—Enuk Wolfglove materialized one day in front of our house in the blowing snow and twilight of no-sun winter. His dog team vanished and reappeared in the storm. Abe stood suddenly at the window like a bear catching a scent. "Travelers!" He squeezed out his half-smoked cigarette, flicked it to the workbench, wiped ashy fingers on his sealskin overpants. We kids eyed the cigarette's arc—we could smoke it later, behind the drifts, pretend we were artists like him.

"Poke up the fire?" Abe grinned like an older brother, our best friend, no dad at all. "And hide the vanilla." His head and broad shoulders disappeared as he squirmed into his shedding caribou-calfskin parka. He banged the door to break the caribou-skin stripping loose and jumped into the storm.

Jerry pocketed the cigarette. He glanced up through his eyelashes. "I'll share," he mumbled. Iris and I paced the floorboards, excited about travelers. We were barefoot and red toed. It was getting dark, and stormy, or we'd all have dressed in parkas and hurried outside. Jerry lowered a log into the barrel stove. He got the second log stuck and had to wrench it back out, sparky and smoking. "Goddamn son of a biscuit!" he said, practicing with Abe absent. He was tall and ten—twice my age—and had the good black hair. Also, he remembered cities and cars and lawns, red apples on trees—if that stuff was true. Jerry left the draft open until flames licked the pipe red and smoke leaked out the cracks. He tracked down each spark, wet his finger, and drowned it. He wiped his finger on a log, peered at it, and wet it again. Abe was spanking-strict about fire. That, and no whining.

"It's Enuk Wolfglove!" Iris said. "Only one traveler!" Through the flapping Visqueen window we watched Abe and the man hunching against the wind, chaining the dogs in the willows near our team. Enuk lived west, downriver in Takunak village, but like wind he came off the land each time from a different direction. Iris squinted, myopically counting his dogs. Abe would be too generous, offering too much fish and caribou off our dogfood pile that needed to last until Breakup. Iris felt bad if our dogs got narrow and had to eat their shit. She was eight now, black hair too, and with blue eyes—but they were weak. She had gotten snowblind, the spring before last when she didn't wear her Army goggles on the sled back from the Dog Die Mountains. Someday, Abe meant to mailorder glasses.

I broke a chunk of thin ice off the inside of the window and sucked it. "How come they hitchin' 'em there?" The ice tasted like frozen breath and wet caribou hair.

Jerry peered over our shoulders. "You're talking Village English. Company isn't even off the ice." His voice was tight. People made him nervous. People made all of us nervous, except Iris. Our family lived out on the tundra. Abe had dug a pit, old Eskimo style, and built our igloo out of logs and poles, before I even grew a memory. Eskimos wouldn't live that way anymore, but for some reason we did. The single room was large, sixteen by sixteen, and buried to the eaves in the protective ground. In the back, over our beds, trees reached into the soil on the roof, and in the storms we heard their roots groaning, fighting for their lives out in the wind. Our walls and roof Abe insulated with blocks of pond sod. In the sod, mice and shrews rustled and fought and chewed and built their own homes, siphoning off warmth and mouthfuls of our food and winnowing it down to tiny black shits. Abe had escaped something, roads and rules possibly. Little things didn't bother him; Abe liked his meat dried, cooked, raw, or frozen. He didn't mind fly eggs on it—as long as the tiny maggots weren't moving.

Once we had a mom. She wasn't coming back. That's what Iris said she told Jerry the day she flew away. She had a twelve-string guitar and apparently liked music more than caribou and bears and a moss roof that leaked. She'd left us alone with none of those thousand warm things children with mothers don't count. Abe never talked about it. He never painted it. Her leaving was the back wall of my memory.

Iris scraped at the ice on the window with her fingernails inside her sleeve. Her bony elbows stuck out of her shirt. "They're chaining below the willows so the drifts won't bury his dogs." She flitted away to hang our parkas on pegs over the wood box, push *mukluks* and clothes tighter into the corners and under our bunks. Caribou hairs clung to all our clothes. She whisked hair and Abe's plane shavings and sawdust into dirt corners with a goose wing.

The north wind swept the open tundra and howled into the spruce on the bank where our sod home was buried in the permafrost. The skylight shuddered. Snow laced over the riverbank. The gray wool of moving snow hid the horizons. Overhead the frozen sky purpled with night, and above the wind and frantic branches clung watery stars. Out under the ice, the wide Kuguruk River flowed past the door, through the arctic part of Alaska that our mail-order schoolbooks called *barren icy desert*. That shamed me, that quick, throwaway description flung from the far rich East, printed in the black-and-white validation of a textbook. My protests only made Abe shrug.

The homemade Visqueen window shivered and whacked. The men chopped a frozen caribou for the dogs. The dogs ripped the skin off the meat and swallowed chunks. They guarded the skin, pinning it down with their claws. When the last bone and meat crystal was sniffed off the snow, they chewed the hair off the skin, ate the skin. Then they curled up to protect their faces and feet.

We heard the men trudging through the drift, up on the eave, down into the trench to the door. The snow squeaked as Abe shoveled, then pounded on the skin door. "Chop the ice along the bottom! Hear me?" Jerry scrambled for the hatchet. "Now get back!" Torn by wind and muffled by the skins, his voice came in mad. I hid behind the water barrel. Abe and Enuk surged in out of the swirling snow. Ovals of frozen skin and drifted-on ice whitened their faces. I stared, longing for frostbite, the scars of heroes. Abe pulled his hood back and his curly yellow hair sprang out; his turquoise eyes shone above his bearded face. "Windy."

"*Alappaa* tat wind." Enuk was a few inches shorter than Abe. His wide face was stiff, his goatee iced. The men grinned and shook snow off their parkas and whipped snow off their *mukluks*. They eased ice off their whiskers. Iris danced barefoot between them, smiling and scooping up snow to throw in the slop bucket. I wished I could move like her, light and smiling. Behind the water barrel I stood on the dirt and the damp mouse turds, excited at having company.

Enuk's gaze swung and pinned me down. "Hi Yellow-Hair! Getting big! How old?" His face was dark and cold-swollen.

Travelers all carried names for me, like the first-class mail. None were the ones I wanted. I inched out beside the blasting stove, my eyes down. "Five." It was hard to look at Enuk—or any traveler—in the eyes after seeing no people for weeks. It was hard to speak and not run and hide again. Enuk's frost-scarred face betrayed mysteries and romantic hard times that drew a five-year-old boy with swollen dreams. He was muscled in the forearms in the way of a skinned wolverine. He didn't eat most store-bought food, except Nabob boysenberry jam. When he was out hunting with his dog team and snowshoes he carried a can of jam. He'd chop it open and—after dried meat, or frozen meat, or cooked meat—around his campfire he'd suck on chips of frozen jam. He also carried his little moosehide pouch. Inside were secrets; once he'd let us hold gold nuggets, lumpy, the diameter of dimes. We handed them back and they disappeared in the folds of leather. The day I turned old I was going to be Enuk. Small discrepancies left footprints in my faith, such as the fact that he was Eskimo and I seemed to be staying *naluaġmiu*. But years lined up ahead, promising time for a cure.

Our last human visitor had been Woodrow Washington, a month before. Woodrow had a mustache and one tooth on the bottom, one on top. They didn't line up. Not near. His closest worldly ties were with the bottle, and that left him narrow and shaky. Though he hunted like everyone, his concentration and shots tended to stray. When he showed up, Jerry always hid the vanilla. Sober, he was nice and extra polite. "Tat Feathers boy, he suicide." Woodrow had brought news and stayed only long enough for warmed-up breakfast coffee. "He use double-barrel, backa their outhouse. You got fifty dollar? I sure need, alright?" Abe gave him the money. Abe leaned on his workbench and rubbed his ears. Harry Feathers was—or had been—a shambling teenager with blinky eyes and acne. He talked to Abe when Abe was snacking our sled dogs in front of Feathers's post office. It seemed as if maybe nobody else listened to Harry.

Woodrow had been disappointing company. We had only what money was in the Hills Bros can, but I blamed him more for not spending the night. And not bringing our first class.

Jerry served boiled caribou pelvis, in the cannibal pot, and pilot crackers, salmon berries, *qusrimmaq*, and the margarine that travelers had left—without the coloring added. Abe didn't allow something for nothing; yellow dye was poison; the color of food was nothing. We all carried sharp sheath knives forged out of old chisels and files and used them to cut at the fat and meat on the pelvis bone. Afterward, for a while I forgot my shameful blue eyes and yellow hair when Enuk leaned back on the bearskin couch. He hooked his thumb under his chin. His gaze slid away, beyond the leaning logs of the back wall. His pleasant face might have said *aarigaa taikuu*, but what he did say was, "Tat time it blowing same like tis, up Jesus Crick I kill my dowgs." I wiped my greasy hands on my pants and climbed onto his words as if they were a long team to pull me away to the land of strength and adultness.

He whittled a toothpick out of a splinter of kindling. He let the chips spin into the darkness under the table to mix with the caribou hairs and black mouse turds that carpeted our hewn floorboards. Eskimos weren't like Franklin and Crazy Joe or other *naluaġmius* who occasionally came upriver; Enuk's story was just to fill the night and he wasn't afraid to let silence happen between words. Time was one bend of open water to him and he hunched comfortable on the bank, enjoying what the current carried.

With the stick, Enuk picked his teeth. He had most of his teeth, he said, because he never liked "shigger" or "booze." I didn't know what booze meant and was scared to ask, vaguely convinced it might be something frilly that city women ordered out of the first half of the Sears catalog. I sat on the chopping-block stump and stared up into his face.

Abe threw a log into the stove. Sparks hissed red trails up around his shaggy head and flicked into darkness against the low ceiling poles.

The poles around the five-gallon-can safety hung with dust tendrils from past smoke. Smoke and the oily odor of flame spread in the room. Abe filled a kettle, making hot water for tea. Mice and shrews rattled spoons on the kitchen boards.

"Wind blow plen'y hard tat night I get lost. Freeze you gonna like nothing." Enuk nodded at our bellied-in plastic sheeting windows behind his head, white and hard with drifted snow. A dwindling line of black night showed at the top. "My lead dowg, he been bite my dowgs. Al'uv'em tangle in'a willows. I leave 'em, let'um bury. I sleep in ta sled, on *qaatchiaq*. Tat night I never sleep much."

He chuckled and glared. "You listen, Yellow-Hair? Can't see only nothing too much wind." Enuk's bottom lip was thick and dark and permanently thrust out. I laughed, shy, and slapped my grubby red feet on the cold floor and tried to push out my too-thin lip.

In the corner on Abe's spruce-slab bed, Jerry and Iris lay on his caribou-hide *qaatchiaq* playing checkers. "Rabies," Jerry murmured. "His story's going to have rabies."

She pinched him. "It's your turn." A shrew ran on the floor. Enuk's black eyes followed it. He picked up the block of kindling and waited. Behind the wood box shrews whistled.

Jerry dragged a moose-antler checker over her pieces. The tops of his were marking-penned black, Iris's red. "Kay then. King me." They wore corduroy pants. The corduroy ridges were eroded off the knees, thighs, and butts. Iris had two belt loops cinched together with twine to keep her too-big pants up. Abe didn't encourage us to change clothes more than once a month. More than twice a month put a burden on everybody. He wouldn't say no, but the house was low and one room—the only place to get out of the weather for miles—and the faintest disapproval could hang in the air.

The corner posts of Abe's bed were weather-silvered logs, the tops bowled from use as chiseling blocks and ashtrays. Above the foot of his bed, his workbench was messy with empty rifle brass, pieces of antler and bone, rusty bolts, wood chips, and abandoned paintings, the canvas and paper bent and ripped by his chisels and heavy planes. Abe Hawcly was a left-handed artist. He was also our dad. But we kids didn't know to call him anything generic or fatherly, only Abe. Travelers called him that. By the time we realized what normal people did, years had hardened into history. Calling him Dad felt worse than shaking hands.

"Enuk. Here." Abe slid a mug across the uneven boards to the middle of the table. He rubbed his sore knee and sat and rolled himself a cigarette with one hand. "Kids, don't worry about schoolwork tonight." He waved his match out. Two joints of his ring finger had been swallowed by a whaling winch in Barrow. His hands were thick and red, paint dried in the cracks. They carved faces on scraps of firewood and drew whole valleys lurking with animals on cardboard boxes.

"Ah, *taikuu*." Enuk slurped the scalding tea that would have seared a kid's mouth into mealy blisters. "My dowgs be funny tat night. Lotta growl."

Another night passed in his story.

"How old were you?" My words tumbled away like a fool's gloves bouncing downwind. Blood stung my cheeks. Interrupting seemed worse than pissing your pants in front of the village schoolhouse.

"Hush, Cutuk," Jerry said. Iris giggled and pretended to bite her nails, both hands at once. Abe had a piece of caribou-sinew string in his fingers, and he began pulling loops though loops. A lead dog formed. He turned the wick down on the lamp. Storytelling shadows stretched farther out from the moldy corners. The wind gusted. The door was half buried. I pictured those yellow metal nuggets. Wondered if they were in Enuk's pocket, and how young he'd been when he found the first one.

Enuk sipped. "Cutuk, you gonna be hunter?" He flicked my arm, unaware of the stinging power of his thick fingers. Tears flooded my eyes. "Tat's good. You got one 'hol life. Tat's plen'y. Gonna you be tired if you alla time try hurry."

Abe smiled. He pulled a string. In his hands the lead dog vanished.

I shrank low and twisted broken threads in the knees of my pants. At least he'd used my Eskimo name. Clayton was my white name—a mushy gray one. I had taught my ears not to hear it, until people learned it didn't work. *Cutuk* meant fall. Not fall when the berries were ripe and the bears were fat enough—fall like dropping down out of a tree without planning. Except in Iñupiaq it was spelled *katak*; but none of us or Enuk had known the spelling. The way Iris sounded it out had stuck. It was no first-pick name, misspelled and not even easy to say, but Enuk bestowed it on me before I could campaign for a better one. So I justified it into greatness by pretending it had special come-from-behind potential.

"Night time, still snowing I hear lotta growl. First light gonna I dig t'em dowgs. Right there, blood in'a snow. When I fin' my leader, tat one try bite." He ran his fingers through his shoulder-length hair. One of his ears had a hole up near the top as small as a goose's windpipe. Gray hairs curled through. "Five dowgs. Good size dowg team back then time, not much food on ta country. Not like now gonna t'em white guy dowgfed in'a bag. I shoot three before it turn dark. Right there I know tat gonna be real bat. Tat was nineteen…nineteen thirty-something, before Kennedy and Hitler fight. Could be I'm twenty-five tat time.

"Cutuk. Peoples got not much shells tat time not like now. I got jus' only one shell. I go 'head shoot t'em last two dowgs."

The glory of Enuk's words melted under a warm spell of reality. I pictured my pup Ponoc, grinning his sloppy puppy grin—he collapsed under the boom of a rifle. Blood sprayed Ponoc's silver face and ran out a red hole, steaming into the snow like the last rabid fox Abe had shot. The corners of my throat grew wet and needed to swallow.

"How many nights I wait. Even I make spear from spruce. Then I see hills. Right there," Enuk shrugged, grinned, and gestured, his huge fingers cutting straight across his other palm, angling up, "I take off on snowshoe. No dowgs. Could be they already let me gonna crazy. I see wolv'reen. Right there. Real close. No ammo in ta pocket. Long time ago gonna plenty hard time we always have. No ammo in ta pocket."

Enuk sat for a minute, then shuffled over and dumped his coffee grounds in the slop bucket by the door. The grounds plopped on the dishwater frozen in the bottom. He reached up to a peg behind the stove for his parka and *mukluks*. Reminiscence no longer softened his face; the telling was over—the story, like old stories I'd heard at the Wolfgloves' house in Takunak, started in the middle and ended somewhere along where the storyteller grew tired.

Enuk shook water droplets out of his wolf ruff. I tried to contemplate the way I knew grown-ups did, to poke at his words with sharpened thoughts. I wondered if he'd restart the tale the following night—or in a year. I felt I should comprehend something profound about shooting dogs, but I couldn't get past thinking that the books on the shelf over Abe's bunk, the soapy dishwater and coffee grounds in the slop bucket—and our team sleeping buried down by the river— all were blatant proof that we owned too much, lived too comfortably. I needed tougher times to turn me Eskimo.

Our low door was built from split spruce poles, insulated with thick fall-time bull caribou hides nailed skin-out on both sides. The hinges were *ugruk* skin. "Better chop the bottom loose," Abe suggested. He reached in the wood box for the hatchet. Enuk pounded with his big fists until the condensation ice crumbled. He yanked inward. The wind and swirling snow roared, a hole into a howling world; the wind shuddered the lamp flame. A smooth waist-high white mirror of the door stood in his way. Chilled air rolled across the floor. Enuk leapt up and vanished over the drift into the night gusts.

Chunks of snow tumbled down. I had a flash of memory— summertime, green leaves. Enuk, and a strange man. The man had combed hair. And a space between his teeth that he smiled around and showed us how to spit through. He cradled an animal in calico cloth. *A baby porcupine!* The man seemed to be Enuk's son Melt. But how could that be? Melt was mean and smiled like indigestion. Mixed up behind my eyes was that baby porcupine dead in a cotton flour sack, a ski plane taking off, and me crying, unable to convey the tragedy of my blue Lego spiraling to the bottom of the outhouse. These memories seemed valuable, as unreplaceable as that Lego had been, but the roar of the wind sucked my concentration into the dark.

Abe scratched snow aside trying to close the door again. "Need to use the pot?" he asked.

Iris did and I did, and we hurried. There was nowhere to hide— it was how Abe had first explained the word *vulnerable*—with Enuk coming back momentarily. Breaking trail to the outhouse would have involved digging out the door, getting all dressed in overpants and parkas, finding our way, digging out the outhouse door, trying not to crap on our heavy clothes. Then tracking snow in the house; wet furs; trying to get the door closed again; firing up the stove. Abe didn't encourage any of it. Embarrassment counted as nothing. It mattered to him as much as the color of margarine.

Abe slammed the door, and again. His hair and the collar of his flannel shirt were floured with snow. He grinned. "Glad I don't have to go to work in the morning."

"What he gonna do?" I asked, instantly ashamed of the excess of Village English in my voice.

"Check the dogs." Jerry clacked checkers together, matter-of-factly. "Abe, can an animal catch rabies and get those symptoms in one night?"

"Maybe not. That virus takes a couple weeks to infect your nervous system." Abe picked up the book he'd been reading that morning—*The Prophet*—turned it over, peered at the spine thoughtfully, and put it back down. Abe eyed his thumbnail and bit it. "I had to shoot a rabid moose that charged in the team, long time ago, in the Helpmejack Hills."

"Does a person forget their friends?"

Iris crossed her eyes. "Jerry'll never skin another fox's face."

"I bonked that rabid one that scared you," Jerry growled, "chewing the door. You were going to stay inside until Abe got home."

A second rabid fox had screamed insults to our sled dogs and snarled in the window at his warped reflection. After that incident my imagination encountered them all winter, during the bad-mouse year, foam dripping off their narrow black lips. Nights mice and shrews streaked across my pillow and gnawed at my caribou-hide *qaatchiaq*, and I lay awake doubly frightened that something as invisible and unaccredited as mouse spit could carry such consequences.

Jerry chewed his cheeks, cataloging Abe's answers. Jerry remembered poems, songs, definitions. I believed that he wanted to be the healthiest, the smartest, and the best, in case our mom came back. He was all that, and had black hair—things that I thought should come to him with smiles.

Iris's eyes flashed. "Guys, I say that's what happened six years ago. Abe caught rabies! He thought he was walking to the store in Chicago to buy tobacco, next thing he noticed a new baby, lots of snow, and us kids gathering *masru*. He's maybe still got 'em."

I looked down, ashamed; I hadn't seen a city. Jerry didn't smile. "You win." He rolled up the birchbark checkerboard, with every other square peeled to make the board pale white and brown. Under the dull roar of the wind, in the leftover silence, I had a sudden flash—Jerry was thinking our mother may have caught rabies.

A gust shook the stovepipe. Abe shut the draft on the fire, lit a candle to place by his bed. He pissed in the slop bucket. He rubbed his knee. "One of you kids lay Enuk out a *qaatchiaq.*" Steam rose out of the bucket. I stood up, rattling the lamp on the table, disturbing the shadows.

The door burst open. Enuk jumped in. A thought startled me: *Would a person tell if he had been bitten?* People might run away. Someone would stand across a valley and sink a bullet in your head. What if a dog bit me and died later; would I have the courage to tell? Enuk rubbed his hands together close to the stove. He grabbed my neck from behind. He laughed near my ear. "What you're laying out *qaatchiaq* for, Yellow-Hair? You gonna *nallaq*? Nice night, le's go hunt!"

★

Two days passed. The wind fell away and Abe shoveled out the door entrance. We climbed up the snow trench into a motionless thirty-below day. The old marred snowdrifts had been repaired and repainted. A scalloped white land stretched to the riverbanks, across the tundra to the orange horizon. The cold sky seemed crystalline, dark blue glass, in reach and ready for one thrown iceball to bring it shattering down.

In our parkas and *mukluks*, we kids ran back and forth examining the new high drifts and sliding off cornices. Abe helped Enuk find his sled and they dug at it. The snow was hard, and it chipped and squeaked under their shovels. They iced the sled runners with a strip of brown bear fur dipped in a pan of warm water. They were careful not to get any water on their *mukluks*. Iris and I stood together while Abe and Enuk harnessed his seven dogs. Jerry stayed in the safety of our dog yard. He mistrusted strange dogs. Often they snapped at him, though he never lost his temper and clubbed dogs with shovels or rifle stocks the way other people did. I vowed when I grew big enough to handle huskies I wouldn't miss a chance to help a traveler hitch up.

Enuk stood on the runners with one foot on the steel claw brake, his hands in his wolf mittens holding the toprails. The dogs lunged against their towlines, yelping to run. Our dogs barked and scratched the snow. There was little room left in the yowling for last words with company. Enuk said something and nodded north. We stepped close. "Next time, Cutuk? Be good on ta country." He swept away, furrowing snow to dust with his brake.

We hurried out on the river to watch him become a black speck and disappear far off downriver. Dark spruce lined the far riverbank. In my mind I could see the village and barking dogs and the people there, and Enuk's grandchildren, Stevie and Dawna Wolfglove, with their mother, Janet, to kiss them and make caribou soup with yellow seashell noodles.

Jerry kicked snow. Abe put his hand awkwardly across my shoulder. I flinched. Abe and Jerry and I didn't touch—unless it was rough, tickling or king-of-the-hill wrestling over a cornice. Abe turned toward the house. "If the trail stays firm…" He wiped his nose. He liked us to be happy, and we usually stayed that way for him. "Maybe next month if the trail's okay, we'll go to town? Nice to have a traveler, wasn't it?"

I tried to ignore the splinters of comfort at the thought of people. I was going to be a hunter; the toughest hunters traveled alone. I kept my mouth shut and broke the tiny tears off my eyelashes. Abe hated whining. He believed that excess comfort was damaging, that whininess was contagious. Stern lines would gather at his mouth and grooves would form above the bridge of his nose. "You an Everything-Wanter now?" he'd growl. And then I would wish for my mother with her black hair and flashing eyes.

But the truth that made me squirm?—she'd left me few memories. All I was certain I remembered of her was that man January Thompson, a fat Outsider, a wolf bounty hunter with a blue and gold airplane on skis, bouncing on the ice, lurching into the sky. I pretended a memory but in the tiny honest slice of my mind I knew I had cannibalized whole hindquarters off Jerry's stories. Jerry was almost five when they left the lower States. "We came in Abe's blue truck," he'd say. "The license plates said North to the Future. You were almost three, Iris. 'Member?" That was all. But it stung. That history didn't include me. The Hawcly past before the Arctic was another planet, a sunny place of Sunkist lemons and green grapes drying into raisins—instead of meat drying into meat—a place that I'd never walked and couldn't put roots to even in memory.

Jerry once told how my mother had a yellow car, with a built-in radio. I wondered why so many of the stories had cars. Did all the cars have radios? When he related these things, Iris and I squeezed together on the bearskin couch, curious about that stranger down in the States who wasn't coming back, but somewhere still lived. It was all strange, but seemed normal, too, the way she was a fairy tale that kept fogging over, while Enuk, even vanished downriver, stood in my life as sharp as a raven in the blue sky.

Abe and Jerry and Iris tramped up to the house. I lingered in the dog yard, playing with Ponoc and the others. They stared downriver, howling occasionally, forlorn and dejected about not following Enuk's team. It was a chance to play with the dogs without getting scratched and licked off my feet. I ruined it by slipping Ponoc a stray chip of frozen moose off the snow near the dogfood pile. Sled dog brains kept to narrow, well-packed trails of thought, and food lay at the end of all the trails. They howled and gestured with their noses, wagging and protesting the inequitable feeding. My heart grew huge for them, my happy-go-lucky friends, always delighted to see me, prancing and tripping over their chains. How endless the land would be without their companionship.

Suddenly I saw the dog yard empty, the strewn gnawed bones, the yellow pissicles and the round melted sleeping circles, all drifted white; only the chain stakes remained stabbing out of the snow like gray grave markers. A mouse ran out from under the meat pile, dropped a turd, and disappeared down a round hole. I backed away from the lunging dogs. Maybe they were already infected.

Ponoc bit a wad of caribou hair off his stomped yard and tossed it playfully in the air. His pink tongue flicked between his teeth, his mouth muddy with hairs. I spat between my teeth. Maybe in my huge future I would have to shoot a whole team of my own dogs. The thought of the years ahead flooded hot in my chest. I raced up to our igloo, to my brother and sister and father, there eating *paniqtuq* and seal oil and red jam. Food that would make me Eskimo.

1972: MOVING TO ALASKA TO OPEN A MEAT SHOP

ALASKA OR BUST
—bumper stickers along the Alcan

Arlitia Jones

Outside Whitehorse the truck's front axle blew
apart. Somewhere before the border, over-
loaded, the trailer tongue snapped in two.
We slept in the ditch with mosquitoes and burned
the mangled tires of freight trucks that passed
us going eighty. We were amazed by fireweed.
We ate the flesh of grayling and char and played
card games we'd learned back home where we
would never be anything but the poor kids.
When Hanford shut down, whole town went tits up,
the packinghouse closed. Iowa Beef forced
the mom-and-pops out. But we had hope.
The pipeline workers ate prime rib and filet.
Christ, it rained like a bastard that first day.

SNOBS

Jean Anderson

 Darrin is sitting off to the side, on the floor. Not under the skylight in the public library's waiting area, not on one of the shiny wooden benches scattered among the delicate indoor trees, but here in the shadows next to the tray filled with brochures. He's waiting to be picked up after school where she told him to wait, yes. But here he can see his mother before she sees him. Here he can think, which he needs to do, maybe figure out how to tell her.

And there she is suddenly, too soon. Though late as always of course, ten minutes late, wearing her new used parka and looking breathless—red-cheeked, harried, her face somber and serious as usual while she struggles through the big glass double doors with the stack of books and the records she's returning.

He guesses his mother must be the only woman left in the world who still checks out—listens to, actually *plays*—the library's ancient phonograph records. Poets reading their own poems, black disks she spins in her classes and also listens to herself, frozen in place sometimes while she washes the dishes at night, listening before she begins grading papers. On the few nights she's not teaching, that is.

"Other teachers buy tapes, Mom, or CDs." He told her that about a month ago. Because he saw the tapes in a catalog she got in the mail: *Poets Speak*. But she said no, of course. Tapes would be too expensive, that was the reason. He knew it even though she didn't say it: *ochen dorogova*—very expensive, in Russian. She's trying to learn that from the big old shiny-black records, too: Russian. "For Siberian students, dear," an interest she's added since he lived with her last, a year ago.

"The library's recordings are perfectly good, Darrin," she said last month, turning the cheap paper catalog around and around in her hands. She was trying hard not to frown, he could tell. "Wouldn't the world be a better place if we all shared things, honey? If we'd use up what we have that's still good before we rush out to buy new?"

She even carries his old portable record player to her classes, the one his grandparents gave him for Christmas when he was a little kid. She doesn't have time to drive to campus, she says, find parking and pick up a phonograph—often broken anyway—then repeat the entire process to return it. Which seems to him no reason at all. No reason for an adult to carry a child's record player covered with red and yellow beach-ball stuff like wallpaper. Besides, she doesn't allow herself to "waste gas," since she teaches not on campus but in town, at the army post or else out at the air force base. And "wasting gas," he knows it, just means money again: *ochen dorogova.*

Darrin sighs, grits his teeth, squeezes his eyes closed for a minute before he stands up and walks toward her, and he's not quite dragging his backpack. He's being careful about that. They've already quarreled twice since he arrived from Juneau about his habit of dragging things.

But why does she make him *feel* like dragging things? Even his feet? That's the issue as far as he's concerned. *Why?* Why does *his* mother buy used coats that look nearly as bad as the one she's just worn out?

"Oh, honey," she says, seeing him at last, "give me a hand, will you? Grab these records before I drop them?"

And one of her students—of course—is rushing up to them from some place. Popping out of the woodwork Dad would call it: "Here, Dr. Taylor, let me help." The student is hush-voiced as they all are around his mother. Reverent, like somebody breathlessly saying a prayer they've worked hard to memorize.

So Darrin only grabs a few of the books, while the student—who has long dirty hair and a bad case of acne, as the hushed-voiced ones always do seem to have, either or both—fumbles to take the records. Darrin hates it when they call her "Dr. Taylor." Because most of the time she stops right then, on the spot, to correct them. Blocking the path and so on, telling them her dissertation "isn't quite complete."

Not saying she can't afford to leave Fairbanks and go Outside to work on it. Maybe never will be able to afford it, ever, which he knows is the truth. Saying only that she's isn't really Dr. Taylor yet. *Just yet.* That's how she usually puts it: "Just yet." The same when they say "Professor." She's actually an adjunct faculty member, she tells them, her voice so achingly precise. Not a professor: "Ms. Taylor will do just fine."

He hates the way she smiles when she says it, her face so damned pure. Glowing, almost radiant—*beatific*, he thinks that's the word; he came across it in one of her dictionaries. As if "being paid *nothing* to teach class after class, year after year," which he heard her sobbing about, crying into the telephone to his grandmother one day last week, saying: It's just—so *wrong*, Mom. So abusive. So demeaning and hurtful." Well, smiling as if all that is just what she's dreamed of and longed for forever while she talks with one of her students.

But she doesn't say any of it this time.

"Rodrigo, I'd like you to meet my son Darrin." She says that to the student instead. And Darrin nods politely, trying not to let his eyes wander over the student's strange-looking clothes and puzzling yellowish skin, while his mind bounces the odd-sounding name like a basketball added to all the rest: Native? But what? Tlinget? Asian and African, maybe? But then why Rodrigo? Maybe Filipino? Surely not a Siberian?

"Rodrigo is a chess player too, Darrin," she's saying.

And Darrin is suddenly ashamed of himself. Ashamed of his own clunky and uncontrolled mind—a racist's mind? His thoughts probably prove he's at least some kind of major snob-in-training.

And snobs are what his mother hates most. He doesn't know how many times he's heard her proclaim it, thousands probably. And he *does* agree in a way. Totally, maybe. But—face it—he does *not* want to be forced into playing chess with this head-bobbing person who reminds him of a bookend in his grandparents' bedroom in Juneau. Good God, no!

"Neat," he says instead, trying to smile at the student, hoping with a splash of her own phrasing to please his mother for once. Rodrigo is smiling back painfully.

The bookend is what's left of a pair, Gramma's told him—a little ceramic man who looks like a pale Anglo version of an Oriental, a China boy thought up by a Whiteman. The tiny ceramic head sways constantly, bobbing up and down any time anybody gets anywhere near the bookend. He can't imagine two of them, ever. He thinks somebody probably broke the other one to put it out of its misery—and now here's this real-live Rodrigo, still bobbing his head.

It's all too much, suddenly. His mother studying Russian from the library's old records, even using his wornout record player to play them. Then this shabby student. And the fact that he can't go to the dentist this year. He *will not.* Will *not* tell his mother about his new aching cavity, since he knows she has no medical coverage. He'll suffer silently, wait till next year with Dad, when he'll be covered again.

And of course he won't tell her what he's been thinking. He *won't,* dammit, *will not* tell her that he's homesick. That he wants to go back to Dad this year. That he'd rather be back home with Dad and his new family. *Home*—that's how he's begun to think of it.

No, he'll tough it out this year, here, in the junior high he hates, watching TV alone nights while she's out teaching. Trying to focus on his homework in the tiny living room where she sleeps on the couch so he can have her bedroom. Listening to those scratchy Russian records pouring out from the steamy kitchen, or to poets nobody ever heard of intoning their odd-sounding words. Riding in her wornout Honda, hoping it won't break down or drift off into a snowbank. Thinking about eating more than doing it since he knows how little money she has.

Thinking about being laid back, cozy, sprawled in an easy chair in front of the big TV at Dad's, eating popcorn, staring into the fire, drinking juice or pop, pigging out, joking with his step-brother—*next year.* Being an ordinary American again, with parents who have real jobs that pay real money. Parents who let you buy new clothes rather than garage-sale specials. Who let you go to a movie rather than borrowing old ones—"classics"—from the library. Or to the dentist.

Because all that *is* what he wants, he sees it now. To be a *real* American, a snob, at Dad's. How can he tell her it's only October and already he'd rather be there? In Juneau with Dad and his new family?

Well, he won't, dammit. He'll keep on doing what he's doing, just as she will. Walking stiffly ahead carrying borrowed books. Walking behind this weird-looking kid called Rodrigo who's probably only one of the eighty or so she's teaching English to this semester for five dollars an hour, some of them probably far worse off than this one.

He wants her to quit, to leave, to stop wearing her "Kick Me" sign. That's what he heard her say once, a joke, to a fat woman, Barb, that she introduced, in the hallway at her apartment, as "my colleague."

But she won't leave. He thinks she'll stay here forever suffering silently, putting one foot in front of the other, smiling falsely and pretending not to be a snob—just as he's doing now. But as soon as he thinks this, he knows he's wrong. She'll do something else entirely. She'll shame him in some new way he can't even imagine yet.

And he says it again, just to push that thought from his mind, but slightly louder: "Chess, huh? Neat."

FIRE

Linda Schandelmeier

Father,
the night I was five,
sparks
shooting from the roof

you punched
out a window,
thrust my cloth bed
through glass,
I rocked out of sleep
into snow.

Sparks
like stars the night
asks for,
beautiful in their fever,
I saw a few
inside me.

What you saved me
for, your hand
covering my mouth
sour smell of your thighs
my hair in the dirt.

You call up the dark
so you can build
your fire,
the husk of my body
glowing orange
behind us.

ROAD SONG

Natalie Kusz

On January 10, only Hobo met me at the bus stop. In the glare from school-bus headlights, his blue eye shone brighter than his brown, and he watched until I took the last step to the ground before tackling me in the snow. Most days, Hobo hid in the shadow of the spruce until Mom took my bag, then he erupted from the dark to charge up behind me, run through my legs and on out the front. It was his favorite trick. I usually lost my balance and ended up sitting in the road with my feet thrown wide out front and steaming dog tongue all over my face.

Hobo ran ahead, then back, brushing snow crystals and fur against my leg. I put a hand on my skin to warm it and dragged nylon ski pants over the road behind me. Mom said to have them along in case the bus broke down, but she knew I would not wear them, could not bear the plastic sounds they made between my thighs.

No light was on in our house.

If Mom had been home, squares of yellow would have shown through the spruce and lit the fog of my breath, turning it bright as I passed through. What light there was now came from the whiteness of snow, and from the occasional embers drifting up from our stovepipe. I laid my lunchbox on the top step and pulled at the padlock, slapping a palm on the door and shouting. Hobo jumped away from the noise and ran off, losing himself in darkness and in the faint keening dog sounds going up from over near the Horners' house. I called, "Hobo. Come back here, boy," and took the path toward Paul's, tossing my ski pants to the storage tent as I passed.

At the property line, Hobo caught up with me and growled, and I fingered his ear, looking where he pointed, seeing nothing ahead there but the high curve and long sides of a Quonset hut, the work shed the Horners used also as a fence for one side of their yard. In the fall, Paul and Kevin and I had walked to the back of it, climbing over boxes and tools and parts of old furniture, and we had found in the corner a lemmings' nest made from chewed bits of cardboard and paper, packed under the curve of the wall so that shadows hid it from plain sight. We all bent close to hear the scratching, and while Paul held a flashlight I took two sticks and parted the rubbish until we saw the black eyes of a mother lemming and the pink naked bodies of five babies. The mother dashed deeper into the pile and we scooped the nesting back, careful not to touch the sucklings, for fear that their mama would eat them if they carried scent from our fingers.

It seemed that we had spent most of the fall looking out just like that for shrews and lemmings. Oscar and Vic had cats, and Paul and Kevin had three German shepherds, and one or another of them usually found a rodent to play with. Oscar's cats would catch a shrew in their teeth, holding tight to skin behind its neck until its eyes swelled out and it stopped breathing. The boys and I squeezed the cats' jaws, screaming, "You're not even *hungry*," until the teeth parted and the shrew dropped into our palms. If we were fast enough, it was still alive, and we pushed its eyes back in and let it go. The dogs worried a lemming in their mouths, dropping it out on occasion and catching it back into the air, over and over again until it couldn't move and was no longer any fun. When we caught the dogs doing this, we beat their ears with walking sticks, but usually we were too late and had to bury the thing under moss.

The dogs were loud now beyond the Quonset, fierce in their howls and sounding like many more than just three. Hobo crowded against my legs, and as I walked he hunched in front of me, making me stumble into a drift that filled my boots with snow. I called him a coward and said to quit it, but I held his neck against my thigh, turning the corner into the boys' yard and stopping on the edge. Paul's house was lit in all its windows, Kevin's was dark, and in the yard between them were dogs, new ones I had not seen before, each with its own house and tether. The dogs and their crying filled the yard, and when they saw me they grew wilder, hurling themselves to the ends of their chains, pulling their lips off their teeth. Hobo cowered and ran and I called him with my mouth, but my eyes did not move from in front of me.

There were seven. I knew they were huskies and meant to pull dogsleds, because earlier that winter Paul's grandfather had put on his glasses and shown us a book full of pictures. He had turned the pages with a wet thumb, speaking of trappers and racing people and the ways they taught these dogs to run. They don't feed them much, he said, or they get slow and lose their drive. This was how men traveled before they invented snowmobiles or gasoline.

There was no way to walk around the dogs to the lighted house. The snow had drifted and been piled around the yard in heaps taller than I was, and whatever aisle was left along the sides was narrow, and pitted with chain marks where the animals had wandered, dragging their tethers behind. No, I thought, Kevin's house was closest and out of biting range, and someone could, after all, be sitting home in the dark.

My legs were cold. The snow in my boots had packed itself around my ankles and begun to melt, soaking my socks and the felt liners under my heels. I turned toward Kevin's house, chafing my thighs together hard to warm them, and I called cheerfully at the dogs to shut up. Oscar said that if you met a wild animal, even a bear, you had to remember it was more scared than you were. Don't act afraid, he said, because they can smell fear. Just be loud—stomp your feet, wave your hands—and it will run away without even turning around. I yelled "Shut up" again as I climbed the steps to Kevin's front door, but even I could barely hear myself over the wailing. At the sides of my eyes, the huskies were pieces of smoke tumbling over one another in the dark.

The wood of the door was solid with cold, and even through deerskin mittens it bruised my hands like concrete. I cupped a hand to the window and looked in, but saw only black—black, and the reflection of a lamp in the other cabin behind me. I turned and took the three steps back to the ground; seven more and I was in the aisle between doghouses, stretching my chin far up above the frenzy, thinking hard on other things. This was how we walked in summertime, the boys and I, escaping from bad guys over logs thrown across ditches: step lightly and fast, steady on the hard parts of your soles, arms extended outward, palms down and toward the sound. That ditch, this aisle, was a river, a torrent full of silt that would fill your clothes and pull you down if you missed and fell in. I was halfway across. I pointed my chin toward the house and didn't look down.

On either side, dogs on chains hurled themselves upward, choking themselves to reach me, until their tethers jerked their throats back to earth. I'm not afraid of you, I whispered; this is dumb.

I stepped toward the end of the row and my arms began to drop slowly closer to my body. Inside the mittens, my thumbs were cold, as cold as my thighs, and I curled them in and out again. I was walking past the last dog and I felt brave, and I forgave him and bent to lay my mitten on his head. He surged forward on a chain much longer than I thought, leaping at my face, catching my hair in his mouth, shaking it in his teeth until the skin gave way with a jagged sound. My feet were too slow in my boots, and as I blundered backward they tangled in the chain, burning my legs on metal. I called out at Paul's window, expecting rescue, angry that it did not come, and I beat my arms in front of me, and the dog was back again, pulling me down.

A hole was worn into the snow, and I fit into it, arms and legs drawn up in front of me. The dog snatched and pulled at my mouth, eyes, hair; his breath clouded the air around us, but I did not feel its heat, or smell the blood sinking down between hairs of his muzzle. I watched my mitten come off in his teeth and sail upward, and it seemed unfair then and very sad that one hand should freeze all alone; I lifted the second mitten off and threw it away, then turned my face back again, overtaken suddenly by loneliness. A loud river ran in my ears, dragging me under.

My mother was singing. *Lu-lee, lu-lay, thou little tiny child*, the song to the Christ Child, the words she had sung, smoothing my hair, all my life before bed. Over a noise like rushing water I called to her and heard her answer back, Don't worry, just sleep, the ambulance is on its way. I drifted back out and couldn't know then what she prayed, that I would sleep on without waking, that I would die before morning.

She had counted her minutes carefully that afternoon, sure that she would get to town and back, hauling water and mail, with ten minutes to spare before my bus came. But she had forgotten to count one leg of the trip, had skidded up the drive fifteen minutes late, pounding a fist on the horn, calling me home. On the steps, my lunchbox had grown cold enough to burn her hands. She got the water, the groceries, and my brother and sisters inside, gave orders that no one touch the woodstove or open the door, and she left down the trail to Paul's, whistling Hobo in from the trees.

I know from her journal that Mom had been edgy all week about the crazed dog sounds next door. Now the new huskies leaped at her and Hobo rumbled warning from his chest. Through her sunglasses, the dogs were just shapes, indistinct in windowlight. She tried the dark cabin first, knocking hard on the windows, then turned and moved down the path between doghouses, feeling her way with her feet, kicking out at open mouths. Dark lenses frosted over from her breath, and she moved toward the house and the lights on inside.

"She's not here." Paul's mother held the door open and air clouded inward in waves. Mom stammered out thoughts of bears, wolves, dogs. Geri grabbed on her coat. She had heard a noise out back earlier— they should check there and then the woods.

No luck behind the cabin and no signs under the trees. Wearing sunglasses and without any flashlight, Mom barely saw even the snow. She circled back and met Geri under the windowlight. Mom looked toward the yard and asked about the dogs. "They seem so hungry," she said.

Geri looked that way and then back at my mother. "No. Paul's folks just got them last week, but the boys play with them all the time." All the same, she and Mom scanned their eyes over the kennels, looking through and then over their glasses. Nothing seemed different. "Are you sure she isn't home?" Geri asked. "Maybe she took a different trail."

Maybe. Running back with Geri behind her, Mom called my name until her lungs frosted inside and every breath was a cough. She whistled the family whistle my father had taught us, the secret one he and his family had used to call one another from the woods in Nazi Germany. *"Dodek, ty-gdzie,"* the tune went. "Dodek, where are you?" She blew it now, two syllables for my name, high then low, then a lower one, quick, and another high slide down to low. Her lips hardly worked in the cold, and the whistle was feeble, and she finished by shouting again, curling both hands around her mouth. "Come on," she said to Geri. "Let's get to my cabin." The three younger children were still the only ones home, and Mom handed them their treasure chests, telling them to play on the bed until she found Natalie. Don't go outside, she said. I'll be back real soon.

Back at the Horners', Geri walked one way around the Quonset and Mom the other. Mom sucked air through a mitten, warming her lungs. While Geri climbed over deeper snow, she approached the sled dogs from a new angle. In the shadow of one, a splash of red—the lining of my coat thrown open. "I've found her," she shouted, and thought as she ran, Oh, thank God. Thank, thank God.

The husky stopped its howling as Mom bent to drag me out from the hole. Geri caught up and seemed to choke. "Is she alive?" she asked.

Mom said, "I think so, but I don't know how." She saw one side of my face gone, one red cavity with nerves hanging out, scraps of dead leaves stuck on to the mess. The other eye might be gone, too; it was hard to tell. Scalp had been torn away from my skull on that side, and the gashes reached to my forehead, my lips, had left my nose ripped wide at the nostrils. She tugged my body around her chest and carried me inside.

VITAL SIGNS

I had little knowledge of my mother's experience of the accident until many months afterward, and even then I heard her story only after I had told mine, after I had shown how clearly I remembered the dogs, and their chains, and my own blood on the snow—and had proven how little it bothered me to recall them. When I said I had heard her voice, and named for her the songs she had sung to me then, my mother searched my face, looking into me hard, murmuring, "I can't believe you remember." She had protected me all along, she said, from her point of view, not thinking that I might have kept my own, and that mine must be harder to bear. But after she knew all this, Mom felt she owed me a history, and she told it to me then, simply and often, in words that I would draw from long after she was gone.

She said that inside the Horners' cabin she had laid me on Geri's couch, careful not to jar the bleeding parts of me, expecting me to wake in an instant and scream. But when I did become conscious, it was only for moments, and I was not aware then of my wounds, or of the cabin's warmth, or even of pressure from the fingers of Paul's grandfather, who sat up close and stroked the frozen skin of my hands.

Geri ordered Paul and Kevin to their room, telling them to stay there until she called them, and then she stood at Mom's shoulder, staring down and swaying on her legs.

Mom looked up through her glasses and said, "Is there a phone to call an ambulance?"

Geri was shaking. "Only in the front house, kid, and it's locked." She held her arms straight toward the floor, as if to catch herself when she fell. "Karla should be home in a minute, but I'll try to break in." She tugged at the door twice before it opened, and then she went out, leaving my mother to sing German lullabies beside my ear. *When morning comes*, the words ran, *if God wills it, you will wake up once more*. My mother sang the words and breathed on me, hoping I would dream again of summertime, all those bright nights when the music played on outside, when she drew the curtains and sang us to sleep in the trailer. Long years after the accident, when she felt healed again and stronger, Mom described her thoughts to me, and when she did she closed her eyes and sat back, saying, "You can't know how it was to keep singing, to watch air bubble up where a nose should have been, and to pray that each of those breaths was the last one." Many times that night she thought of Job, who also had lived in a spacious, golden land, who had prospered in that place, yet had cried in the end, "The thing that I so greatly feared has come upon me." The words became a chant inside her, filling her head and bringing on black time.

The wait for the ambulance was a long one, and my mother filled the time with her voice, sitting on her heels and singing. She fingered my hair and patted my hands and spoke low words when I called out. Paul's grandfather wept and warmed my fingers in his, and Mom wondered where were my mittens, and how were her other children back home.

Geri came back and collapsed on a chair, and Karla, her sister-in-law, hurried in through the door. Geri began to choke, rocking forward over her knees, telling Karla the story. Her voice stretched into a wail that rose and fell like music. "It's happening again," she said. "No matter where you go, it's always there."

Karla brought out aspirin and gave it to Geri, then turned and touched my mother's arm. She whispered, "She's remembering her boy." She said that as soon as Geri was quiet, she would leave her here and fetch my siblings from the trailer.

"Thank you," Mom told her. "I'll send someone for them as soon as I can." She looked at Geri, wishing she had something to give her, some way to make her know that she was not to blame here; but for now Mom felt that Geri had spoken truth when she said that sorrow followed us everywhere, and there was little else she could add.

The ambulance came, and then everything was movement. I drifted awake for a moment as I was lifted to a stretcher and carried toward the door. I felt myself swaying in air, back and forth and back again. Paul's whisper carried over the other voices in the room, as if blown my way by strong wind. "Natalie's dying," he said; then his words were lost among other sounds, and I faded out again. A month later, when our first-grade class sent me a box full of valentines, Paul's was smaller than the rest, a thick, white heart folded in two. Inside, it read: "I love you, Nataly. Pleas dont die." When I saw him again, his eyes seemed very big, and I don't remember that he ever spoke to me anymore.

It was dark inside the ambulance, and seemed even darker to my mother, squinting through fog on her sunglasses. She badgered the medic, begging him to give me a shot for pain. The man kept working, taking my pulse, writing it down, and while he did, he soothed my mother in low tones, explaining to her about physical shock, about the way the mind estranges itself from the body and stands, unblinking and detached, on the outside. "If she does wake up," he said, "she'll feel nothing. She won't even feel afraid." When Mom wrote this in her journal, her tone was filled with wonder, and she asked what greater gift there could be.

CORRECTING THE LANDSCAPE

Marjorie Kowalski Cole

"...evolution did not intend trees to grow singly. Far
more than ourselves they are social creatures, and no
more natural as isolated specimens than man is as a
marooned sailor or hermit."

—John Fowles, *The Tree*

 Sandra Leasure, M.D., a widowed physician and subscriber
to my weekly newspaper, the *Fairbanks Mercury*, came
home one September afternoon to her house on the
Chena River where she had lived for twenty years, a few miles outside
of Fairbanks. She sat down at her kitchen table, turned her head as
usual to take in the river and shrieked. She jumped up and shouted in
her empty house, "What happened to the trees?"

Across the river the mixed spruce-birch forest had disappeared,
chewed up by heavy machinery. Chopped and splintered wood
covered the ground. She looked over a sheared wasteland to the
George Parks Highway. The highway had been there for years, behind
the trees; suddenly it was almost in her living room.

Sandra stared at the revision of her landscape and after awhile
reached for the telephone and called us. It may seem an odd choice,
to call a small weekly newspaper rather than, say, the Mayor's office
or the Department of Planning and Zoning, but, she told me later, "I
had to make an instant decision and I didn't want to hear a
spokesperson." Instead, she happened to get me, the editor and
publisher, just putting down my pen from crossing out half of an
editorial that wasn't going well.

"Up and down the bank," she told me. "The shock of my life. The trees are gone."

I like Doctor Leasure. When I took over this newspaper a year and a half ago, she responded immediately to our call for subscribers and donors. Not only that but she was a nice doctor; my sister Noreen and I had seen her a couple of times, before she retired. Kind of woman you felt chivalrous toward, although she'd managed fine on her own in Alaska for several decades. I didn't know what to say about the trees being cut, except that for starters I'd drive on over and take a look.

I stuck my head into the newsroom to see if anyone would like to come along.

My sister Noreen, chief reporter, supply officer and adviser, was fixed in front of a computer screen. She hammered on the keys as though it made a difference how hard you hit them. Her blue eyes had gone ice cold; she chewed her lips. Must be working up that interview with a marine biologist on the long-term effects of the *Exxon Valdez* oil spill. I looked around for someone else.

A journalism student from the university, hired by Noreen to sell display ads for us, stood nearby noting something on the dummy that lay on the light table. Gayle Kenneally was a quiet Alaskan native woman, one of those older students who have lived awhile before they decide to finish a degree. A single mother, I think Noreen told me. I didn't know Gayle well at all, she stopped in with a couple of ads twice a week and rarely spoke, but she seemed like pleasant company. I'd seen her with a camera. Maybe she needed a subject for her photography class.

"Ms. Kenneally," I said, a bit on the hearty side as I stepped into the room, "a story's come up. Maybe. Bring your camera today?"

She had three blue lines tattooed on her chin, above them a shy and pleasant smile. Freckles. Mixed heritage, like the rest of us.

"Yeah, I can come along," she agreed.

"Grab an extra can of film." I waved toward the supply cupboard. We operated hand to mouth at the *Mercury*, but so rarely did our own photography that I knew there'd be film left from Noreen's last shopping trip.

Then my Honda wouldn't start right away; that car gave me nothing but trouble. It wasn't going to make it through the winter. Gayle didn't say a word.

On Doctor Leasure's own two acres, every birch tree was wrapped in chicken wire to discourage the beavers. But across the river, wood was scattered as though it had been through a grinder. The emptiness that faced us made no sense. Robbed of context, you couldn't even get angry. I stood there trying to see the land as it might have looked a day before: impossible. The look in Doctor Leasure's face, however, was unmistakable. She was moving from shock to grief. Those trees weren't coming back.

Gayle and I drove over the highway bridge and parked to walk over the cut ground. Splinters covered the earth like a suffocating blanket. Not a thing was standing. It smelled strong and pungent, but nothing moved.

This time of year in the woods, yellow leaves fill the air at a touch of wind. They float right off the trees at every shiver of wind as the whole place strips down for winter. But here nothing moved, and the aspen leaves on the splintered branches around us were already fading to brown. Gayle began to take photographs. She was so quiet, I almost found myself forgetting she was with me, except that I started to hand out orders as if she couldn't think for herself. "Get one with this carnage in the foreground and the doc's house in the background," I said. She knelt down and tried to do just that. I stared at her and realized I'd been barking commands like some jerk captain on a ship.

"Gayle, thanks," I said, when she stood up. She nodded. "The doc is a friend," I added. "An interesting lady. She doesn't deserve this."

"I wonder what they are going to put in here," said Gayle.

"Well, we need to find out." There was a moment's silence as we walked back to my car. I thought about it.

"Would you be interested?" I said.

"In what?"

"Pursuing this. Start with a few calls to the Borough, find out who owns this property, call the owners and go from there. Gather a little information. What do you think, do you have that kind of time?

"You mean, write a story?"

"We have to find out if there is a story here, first of all."

Maybe she felt I was bumping her up from ad sales to reporter a little too suddenly; I didn't even know how far along she was on the road toward her journalism degree. This tree-slashing was clearly a case of some aggressive developer with big plans. Why not let Gayle take a stab at it, flesh out the details, find a few answers, if she wanted the job? "What do you think? You have time for this?"

"I can try," she said, after a minute. "It's why I'm in school."

I noticed that she didn't respond to things right away in conversation, she had her own timing. I took a closer look when we were in the car. She might be close to forty—she had that trembling kind of skin along her jaw, and she looked kind of savvy, too, like she'd done a few things. While I drove she rewound her film and emptied the camera. We looked back at the clearcut from the bridge; I was glad I could drive away from it.

Treeless, the land looked so exposed, so pathetic, no longer able to do its job of shielding us from each other. But we'd get used to it, before too long—everyone but Doctor Leasure, I guess. You see a town changing so fast, you learn how short memory can be.

On the streets of Fairbanks, a few old birch and white spruce still grow here and there, prize shade plants or sentinels to be strung with Christmas lights. This far out of town, jungly forest can be found in patches along the river. A boat ride down the Chena has you drifting through ragged oases of wilderness, interspersed with gravel quarries, hotels, waterfront bars, suburban homes. The river water is dark brown, opaque even, lethally cold to humans but home to beavers, ducks, kingfishers, and plenty of fish: grayling, burbot and king salmon. Not long ago a moss-covered barge, long-abandoned, was sinking into the riverbank downriver from the doctor's house. The sudden peace of wild country surrounded you, removed you from the city, even just a few miles from town.

Until recently. Something's happened to this town in the past decade. Maybe it's inevitable. We've started pouring concrete again in a big way. This half-mile of trees across from Doctor Leasure's house was one of the few bits of forest left close to town, to show us where we started.

Gayle, I thought, might be a novice reporter, but maybe she'd have an interesting perspective on this land-development angle. Nice to think I was giving a student this chance, a leg up. Made me feel more upbeat as we drove back to the little house on College Road we called an office.

But then it was time to lay out this week's paper. Spread out on my desk like a fine hand of cards were half-finished editorials and notes on other story ideas: a local group forming to bring back the state income tax, which had been eliminated from the Alaska statutes by the legislature at the height of the oil boom; a proposal to offer timber concessions in the State Forest; a university scientist winning a big prize for discovering that squirrels could lower their body temperature below freezing during hibernation; a scandal out at the Hot Springs, where a local assemblyman shot out his neighbor's TV with a Luger. What was he doing with a Luger? And the closing of our Nordstrom's store, downtown. According to one woman I had talked to earlier in the week, Nordstrom's departure would leave us without a good woman's store for the first time in seventy or eighty years, and result in the razing of our last historic building.

"Nothing but junky boutiques out in the malls," she moaned. "I'll spend more, if they'll stay!"

Not thrilling stuff, but it was taking hold of people. It mattered. More changes coming to the character of Fairbanks.

I fanned out my stories and delighted in the range of them. Wednesday was the worst day of the week, for me, and the best: too much to choose from, unable to pursue everything, I wasn't blind to the wealth of it all or the privilege of my position. When I got going on bringing another issue to life, I didn't have to worry about finances or white space: I just built my picture of Fairbanks. As brave and fair as we could be. Sounds like a song, almost—what song?

Noreen had dug up a few more items. She handed me a brief article on a book that a group of conservative parents had just challenged at the public library and her interview with the visiting marine biologist, along with her proofed copy of my editorial in support of the income tax, and finally, an extra-long Police Blotter.

Several inches described a man who had died a couple of nights ago in the detox van, while the driver was trying to pluck a few more customers out of the alley behind the Homestead Bar on Second Avenue. Turns out the poor guy died of a bleeding ulcer, wasn't even intoxicated this time. Why, I wondered, didn't they send an ambulance for him in the first place? Could someone with a little more training have saved his life? It seemed worthy of note.

Noreen and I talked the issue through as Gayle made a few phone calls and gathered her material. She'd develop the film up at the university, and stop at the Borough Property office the next morning but right now, she said, "I need to pick up my son." Then she added, putting a finger on the Police Blotter copy. "I know him. I used to drive that van."

"The detox van?"

"Wally Stonington, the man who died," she said. "He's from home, from my village. You want some more information about him? You talk to the lady who runs the bead store on Third Avenue. She fed him lunch every day. I stopped driving the van a couple years ago, for that reason—made me nervous."

"I should think so," I said.

"Not for the reason you might think." She shuffled back into her light cloth parka. "Made me nervous because sometimes, people were really sick, and we didn't have any way to help them. I'm not a medic. But the city thought they couldn't afford the ambulance. So they'd send us."

Noreen and I looked at her for a minute. Gayle's timing was such that you still looked at her, even after she fell silent. Different than ours. I looked away.

"So, time to move on, I said to myself."

"How long ago was that?" Noreen asked.

"Oh, my. Five years ago? I was with the Native corporation. Did a lot of things."

"And you wrote a play," said Noreen.

"Oh, just the one," said Gayle.

A play? Should I express curiosity, thus indicating that I'd never heard of her play, or take this revelation in stride? But Gayle was already out the door.

"What play is that?" I asked Noreen as we turned back to the pages of the dummy.

"A sort of tragicomedy about being lost in the woods," said Noreen. "You were working in Juneau that year. You missed a few things."

"I've heard of that play. Did she write it?"

"She's done a lot of things, it turns out. And get this." Noreen warmed to the delivery of intimate details. "She's been married four times."

"No kidding."

"How would a person manage to get married four times, plus spend a few years as a single mom, before even reaching forty?"

"We wouldn't know, I guess." I was trying to be gentle.

"No," said Noreen, with regret. "We wouldn't." We didn't have much success in our love lives, Noreen and I, myself with fairly little activity and Noreen with, I thought, a bit too much. It seemed like I had stopped looking for love, and Noreen couldn't stop.

"Come on now, let's get to work," I said, attempting to steer us away from Noreen's heartache and Gayle's interesting private life. I noted it down, though, while Noreen went right ahead and filled me in on Gayle's work history, bits and pieces she had found out over the past few weeks of running this office while I made rounds here and there. Gayle had not only written a play which had been produced at the Civic Center. She had also organized cottage industries for the regional corporation, such as waxing spruce cones for export to Germany and organizing crews of homeless men to scavenge for morels in August. She ran the Head Start office for a year. She had worked at the jail. It seems Gayle took unusual part-time jobs until she tired of them (I understood that) or until they vanished beneath her feet. Her father or mother was Athabascan, the other parent part Swedish. Gayle moved through her various cultures with enviable ease. She grew up in the village of Allakaket, Noreen said, northwest of Fairbanks. Up toward the Brooks Range.

What Gayle had to say about the man from her village who died in the detox van intrigued me.

"Why don't you call this lady at the bead shop? Or should one of us go down there?" I wondered aloud.

"Any excuse to get out of the office," Noreen said. "I won't be kept inside of any building I don't want to be in."

She was quoting me: I couldn't live that remark down, and maybe I didn't want to. Years ago, when I was in the Borough Assembly, one of the members ordered a lockdown during a study session on her spending bill. I found a window in a hall outside of chambers and climbed out. When a reporter cornered me later, those were the first words out of my mouth.

"As I see it," I defended myself now, "a writer can get stuff first-hand you don't get on the phone. I feel called to be moving about. *As free and independent as the birds,*" I added, repeating the previous owner's masthead.

"Why don't you sell a few more ads while you're out there moving about," said Noreen. "We're getting pretty close to the edge these days."

She didn't even know the half of it. Finances were my department.

"Looks like we've got most of this issue sketched out," I said. "What are you going to do tonight?"

"Oh…"

I knew what she'd do at five: pour a tumbler of that red wine she kept in the refrigerator and turn on the news. Sometimes, if she didn't have a date, two tumblers. I didn't pry, but I wanted her to know I cared. It was important to extend myself a little bit in her direction, every day.

JOHNNY'S GIRL

A DAUGHTER'S MEMOIR OF GROWING UP
IN ALASKA'S UNDERWORLD

Kim Rich

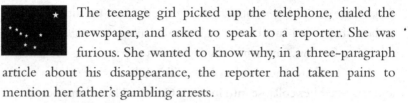 The teenage girl picked up the telephone, dialed the newspaper, and asked to speak to a reporter. She was furious. She wanted to know why, in a three-paragraph article about his disappearance, the reporter had taken pains to mention her father's gambling arrests.

Her father had been missing for almost a month. She thought the reporter had been unfair in writing about the arrests at a time when many believed he was not only missing but dead.

"Why do you guys always have to write about the gambling?" she asked. "Why do you always have to make him sound like a bad guy?"

The reporter said he believed her dad's gambling had something to do with his disappearance. The girl told the reporter he was wrong.

That call to the *Anchorage Daily News* took place September 20, 1973. I was that fifteen-year-old girl. My mother had died the year before. If my father was dead, I was an orphan.

Now resting on my desk is a copy of the newspaper clipping that prompted my call. In the three years I've spent researching and writing this book, I've wondered many times how I would have handled the story if I'd been the reporter. More important, how would I have handled a call from the daughter of a man who had been murdered?

It was a hot story. On an August night in 1973 my father, one of Anchorage's most notorious underworld figures, didn't return home from a visit to a local topless bar. Everyone knew my dad. Since the late 1950s, he had operated illegal gambling houses and run prostitutes all over Anchorage.

"State Troopers and city police have joined forces to hunt the whereabouts of John F. 'Johnny' Rich Jr.," began the newspaper story.

"Rich, who inexplicably disappeared Aug. 22, is the owner of Cindy's Massage Studio at 605 W. 29th Ave., the 736 Club, and Alaska Firearms Distributors.

"He was reportedly last seen in his brown 1971 Cadillac near the Pacific Auction on Old Seward Highway. A long-time Anchorage resident, Rich has had a number of convictions on misdemeanor gambling charges."

I was my father's only child, raised amid the denizens of Anchorage's nightlife—pimps, con men, gamblers, prostitutes, heroin addicts, strippers. I spent most nights home alone, staying close to the television for company while my father was out working the clubs.

I saw firsthand the ravages of "the life": It broke my mother's spirit and triggered her collapse into insanity. Cops and hoodlums beat down the door of our home in the middle of the night. My father taught me to be tough and fearless. He also taught me to speak my mind.

As I look back to that telephone call, which I made years before becoming a journalist myself, it's not surprising to me now that at only fifteen, I would tell a reporter how to do his job. If his mention of my father's arrest record hadn't bothered me so, I also might have pointed out that he was wrong to call my father's Cadillac "brown." The dealer had labeled it "bronzit," but it always looked gold to me.

I remember the car well. The last time I saw my father alive, he was driving it.

★

That Sunday morning was bright and sunny. I was working my summer job at one of the Twin Tesoro gas stations on Gambell Street near our house when my father drove up in his Cadillac.

In the summer of 1973, any street in Anchorage as busy as Gambell had a Tesoro station at nearly every major intersection. The Twin

Tesoros were in Fairview, the closest Anchorage comes to having a ghetto. In Italian, *tesoro* means treasure; the stations and their setting were assuredly not.

Like all the Tesoro stations in town, the Twins were simply strips of raised concrete, each topped by gas pumps bracketing a glassed-in cashier's booth at the center. The booths, about the size of walk-in closets, weren't comfortable, but the glass doors on either end let an attendent work all the pumps. A tall counter divided the booth in half and held a small cash register and a charge card machine. Narrow shelves, drooping under dozens of cans of oil, lined the walls below the banks of windows. Everything was painted white—the counter, the walls, even the wooden stool where I'd sit when business was slow. One of my assignments was to keep the booth clean. I was forever spraying industrial cleaner in a losing battle against the oil and dirt that collected on everything.

But I loved my job. I was popular with the customers, especially the men—they got a kick out of a girl working at a gas station. I didn't think anything of it.

There was no Tesoro uniform; the manager liked red and white, so I always wore a clean white shirt with my blue jeans and red baseball cap. I worked weekday afternoons and weekends—I usually signed up for the six A.M. to two P.M. shift. I liked Sunday morning, when business dragged and I could listen to the radio. Most other times, the place was a madhouse.

My father was alone in his Cadillac. He wanted a fill-up.

"You want to go to Big Lake?" he asked as he poked his head out the driver's side window, smiling broadly.

He was teasing me. He knew I was the only one working and it was hours before quitting time. It wasn't even nine A.M. yet. Even though he'd probably only had a couple of hours' sleep, there he was with the boat hooked up and ready for the fifty-mile drive north to his favorite lake.

When I was younger, I spent nearly every summer Sunday with him at Big Lake zipping around in his speedboat, the one with red and orange flames painted on the bow. We'd spend the day hitting all the lakefront bars. Since I'd entered my teens, however, there'd been fewer "family days," as my father used to call our Sunday outings. I was more interested in hanging around with my friends than with him.

He'd sold the speedboat several years back and moved on to a Chris-Craft. The new boat was more conservative-looking—green, with room for six—and was better equipped for sport fishing, my father's new hobby. Besides, it suited him at that point in his life. He had turned forty in the spring and he was slowing down.

He may have been going fishing, but as always, he could have been on his way to a night on the town dressed in dark trousers, open-collared shirt, and brown cotton waistcoat. The only clue that he was headed for a boat-loading ramp was what he called his "boat shoes"—the canvas tennies with the broad rubber sides.

I hadn't had a chance to go out in the new boat. He'd owned it only a few weeks, but I don't think there was anything he was more proud of, except perhaps for me. I knew that even then, despite everything that had gone on between us. For some time, relations between us had been strained.

"Why can't you be like other dads?" I'd yell at him. In a tired voice, he used to tell his friends, "You raise them just so they can grow up to hate you." That wasn't true; I loved my father, but for a long time, there just hadn't been much about him that I liked. We could hardly talk about anything without arguing and without my reminding him that I despised much of what he represented.

But that Sunday morning there was no argument. I was glad to see him. He was in a good mood and seemed happy.

I told him I couldn't join him.

"It's your loss," he said.

"Yeah, yeah, I know," I said.

After I finished gassing up his car and collecting his money, he leaned out the window a second time.

"You still my girl?" he asked.

"Sure," I answered, as I always did.

"You know I love you," he said, then leaning out even farther, he said, "Give your dad a kiss."

I leaned down and kissed him on the cheek.

He smiled again just before he rolled up the window and drove off, waving as he left the lot. How often I've wished I'd gone with him.

★

Five days later, sometime after five in the afternoon, I was visited at the same gas station by a man and a woman I'd never met before.

I was sitting in the station's booth listening to Led Zeppelin sing "Stairway to Heaven." I spotted the couple, walking side by side, the moment they rounded the corner of the station's asphalt lot. I remember thinking how they looked like real estate agents or bankers in their businesslike clothing, both carrying briefcases, faces dead serious.

He was wearing a tweed sportcoat, a tie, and brown slacks. She was matronly, with a tight coif of graying hair and clad in a skirt and jacket. I remember thinking how handsome he looked with his shaggy curly hair and mustache. There was something about her I didn't like; she reminded me of the brusque secretaries at the school office.

They walked up to the booth and I stepped outside to greet them. They smiled—his was wide and ingratiating; hers was strained. He spoke first, saying he was Duncan Webb, my father's new lawyer. He introduced the woman as his assistant, Caye Mason.

"Your father's in trouble," Webb said. "He's about to lose everything he owns."

Webb explained how somebody—he didn't give a name—had placed a lien against my father's assets. He then handed me a typewritten letter:

> Dear Miss Rich,
>
> Please be advised that I represent Mr. John Rich for purposes of managing his business interests and investments as described more fully in the attached copy of "Power of Attorney" dated August 22, 1973.
>
> This letter is to introduce Ms. Kay [sic] Mason who will instruct you in the procedure for payment of the lease on the property at 736 East 12th Avenue, Anchorage, Alaska. I will be in touch with you within

the next few days to answer any questions you may have.

Thank you for your cooperation in this matter.

Very truly yours,

Duncan C. Webb

Webb said my father had gone to Seattle to straighten out his business affairs and would be home in a few days and that he'd asked Webb to look after things in his absence. He took out a legal-size piece of paper, the top half of which contained a long, dense paragraph filled with jargon I didn't understand. At the bottom, however, I recognized one thing: my father's signature.

Webb said the paper was a "Power of Attorney" that gave him the ability to act legally on my father's behalf. He kept insisting he was protecting my father's interests and that he needed my cooperation. He said my father had sent him.

I felt confused. What was this stuff about lease payments? My cooperation? What exactly was a power of attorney? Webb kept talking, saying he needed me to let him into our house to inventory its contents to protect everything from being confiscated. I thought of my father's new boat, his Cadillac, some furniture we'd just bought—things Webb said we were about to lose.

My mind was racing. Who was trying to take my father's property? Why hadn't my father told me about this? Nothing added up. My father hadn't left town in nearly ten years. Why would he leave now? Why would he change lawyers? I knew his lawyer; my father liked him. I was frustrated that my father wasn't there to explain what was going on.

I hadn't seen my father since the Sunday before. But I was accustomed to having him disappear for days at a time, immersed in some poker game. I'd learned long before not to worry if I didn't see him every day. Yet, for all his casual attitudes about schedules and morality, my father lived a guarded life. He had many acquaintances, but few close friends. He was extremely secretive about his affairs. I was never, under any circumstances, to let anyone into our house unless I checked with him first. I was to trust no one, not even his best friends.

I didn't know what to make of Webb and Mason. They leaned toward me, body language demanding a decision. I asked why Al Bennett, my father's friend and roommate, wouldn't let them in.

"Al said to ask you," Webb said.

I didn't want to disappoint them. I've always tried to please, and maybe that's why my father was constantly repeating his warnings to me. He knew I was too trusting.

Webb pressed me for an answer. Nothing seemed right, but I relented. On the back of the envelope containing the letter addressed to me I wrote, "Al, let them in. Kim."

Webb and Mason left to return to our house, less than a half block away. Moments later, Al came running over.

"What the hell did you let them in for?" he yelled at me from across the gas station lot. "Wesley Ladd is with them!"

My heart froze. Webb hadn't mentioned Ladd. I didn't know much about Ladd except that he was my father's enemy. Before I could say anything, Al spun around and left.

I might have been more worried if I weren't accustomed to odd events and people coming and going from my father's life. I coped with my father's erratic life by separating it as much as possible from my own. At the end of my shift I wanted to buy tickets for an upcoming concert, the last big bash of the summer, featuring three bands—Spirit, the Chambers Brothers, and Stories. I called a taxi; it was only a short drive to the ticket outlet. I had the driver wait, then asked him to take me home.

As the cab neared our house, I saw my father's car pulling out of the driveway. I told the cabbie to catch him, but the Cadillac quickly disappeared into traffic. I was disappointed, but I was also elated and relieved. *He hadn't left town. He must have run into the lawyer at the house and everything would be all right.*

I paid the cabbie and walked across the gravel driveway toward our house. The exterior porch door was bolted. When Al opened it, he was carrying a rifle.

"What the heck is going on?" I asked.

"I'll explain in a minute, just hurry up and get in here," Al said as he grabbed me by the shoulder and hustled me into the house.

He told me what Webb and Mason had said—the same story I'd heard. It seemed plausible until Al mentioned that they were driving my father's Cadillac and they had his keys. My father had a large key ring, like the kind janitors carry, jammed with dozens of keys. I never realized how well I knew him until that moment. My father never let anyone drive his Cadillac; he would never have handed over all his keys. *Oh, God,* I thought. *Something is wrong. Something is really wrong.*

Later I learned that as Webb and Mason were talking to me, my father had been dead for two days. The gun that killed him sat in the glove compartment of his car. His murderer was behind the wheel.

PART II

Taking Risks, Confronting Consequences

★

★ ★
★ ★
★

★ ★

★

A MAN MADE COLD
BY THE UNIVERSE

Sherry Simpson

 Before we started our small journey to the place where Christopher McCandless died, I wondered whether we should travel on foot rather than by snowmachine. It was mid-April, probably the last weekend before the sketchy snow would melt and the river ice would sag and crack. If we waited a few weeks, we could hike the Stampede Trail to the abandoned bus where his body was found in 1992. Wouldn't it seem more real, more authentic somehow, if we retraced his journey step by step?

No, I thought. This is not a spiritual trek. I refuse to make this a pilgrimage. I will not make his journey my own.

And so we set off on the tundra near Healy, snowmachines screeling across a thin layer of hard snow. The five of us moved quickly, each following the other westward through the broad valley. To the south, clouds wisped across the white slopes that barricade Denali National Park and Preserve. Denali itself was a phantom presence on the horizon. I wore ear protectors to dull the grinding engines. When the sun burned through, we turned our faces toward it gratefully, unzipped our parkas, peeled away fleece masks. It had been a long winter—warmer than most in Interior Alaska, but even so each day was filled more with darkness than with light.

We kept on, the only motion against a landscape that seemed still and perfect in its beauty. It was the kind of day where you could think about Christopher McCandless and wonder about all the ways that death can find you in such a place, and you can find death. And then a few minutes later, you'd look out across the valley, admiring the way the hills swell against the horizon, and you might think, "Damn, I'm glad to be alive in Alaska."

★

A few summers ago I rode in a shuttle van from Fairbanks to the park with a group of vacationers and backpackers. As we left town, the driver began an impromptu tour of the final days of Christopher McCandless. In April 1992, he had hitchhiked to Alaska, looking for a place to enter the wilderness. The van driver pointed out a bluff near Gold Hill Road: the last place McCandlesss had camped in Fairbanks. He talked about the purity of McCandless's desire to test himself against nature. He slowed as we passed the Stampede Road, the place about a hundred miles south of Fairbanks where a man had dropped off McCandless so the young man could begin his journey, ignoring all offers of help except for a pair of rubber boots. He did not take a map. In the van, people whispered to each other and craned their necks to peer at the passing landmarks.

McCandless had hiked about 25 miles along the trail before stopping at a rusting Fairbanks city bus left there in the 1960s by roadbuilders creating a route from the highway to the Stampede Mine, near the park boundary. His only sources of food were a .22 rifle and a 10-pound bag of rice. In the back of a Native plant lore book, he scribbled brief and often cryptic entries. In July he tried to leave but apparently was turned back by the roiling Teklanika River. He did not know enough to search for a braided crossing. By August, he was in trouble. A note tacked to the bus pleaded for help from any passerby: "I am injured, near death, and too weak to hike out of here," it said in part. In early September, hunters found his body shrouded in a sleeping bag inside the bus. He had been dead for more than two weeks. Although he had tried to eat off the land, and had even succeeded in killing small animals and a moose, he had starved, an unpleasant and unusual way to die in America these days.

The strange manner of his death made the 24-year-old infamous in Alaska as authorities tried to puzzle out his story. The 1993 *Outside* magazine article by Jon Krakauer, followed by the 1996 bestselling book *Into the Wild*, made McCandless famous everywhere else.

The van driver was maybe in his early 30s, mild and balding. As he drove and talked, he held up a copy of Krakauer's book, a sympathetic and compelling portrait of McCandless. The driver confided that he kept the book with him always because he felt close to the dead man.

"I understand his wanting to come here and go into the wild," the driver said. He, too, had attended Emory University, and he and his wife had recently moved to Anchorage in search of whatever it is people want when they come to Alaska.

In a van full of out-of-state vacationers, the driver felt safe criticizing the response of Alaskans to the story of McCandless. "They called him a young fool who deserved what he got. There was not a positive letter to the editor written about Chris McCandless. It went on for days." He checked our reactions in the rearview mirror. "It was pretty chilling to read."

We do talk about Christopher McCandless in Alaska. We talk about him a lot. We can't help ourselves. Mostly the discussion is in response to the book, and mostly it is not favorable because of the way McCandless stars as a romantic hero. Krakauer described McCandless as searching for something beyond his privileged but disappointing middle-class existence. "It would be easy to stereotype Christopher McCandless as another boy who felt too much, a loopy young man who read too many books and lacked even a modicum of common sense," Krakauer wrote. "But the stereotype isn't a good fit. McCandless wasn't some feckless slacker, adrift and confused, racked by existential despair. To the contrary: His life hummed with meaning and purpose. But the meaning he wrested from existence lay beyond the comfortable path: McCandless distrusted the value of things that came easily. He demanded much of himself—more, in the end, than he could deliver."

Many Alaskans take a simpler view. They think the entire meaning of his death was this: he made some dumb-ass decisions, and he died. Others believe he secretly wanted to die, else why would he have made the puzzling choices he did? A few say he was mentally ill; one Anchorage columnist insists that McCandless was clearly schizophrenic. And still others say he died because he was arrogant and prideful, because he didn't honor the power of the land, because he didn't have the humility to observe and ask questions and think.

Nevertheless, because McCandless starved to death in the wilderness—or what many people conceive of as wilderness—by some strange transmogrification he has become a culture hero. Web sites preserve high school and college essays analyzing *Into the Wild*, which is popular on reading lists everywhere and frequently seen in the hands of people touring the state. *The Milepost*, the most detailed road guide in Alaska, now mentions the site: "If you've read *Into the Wild* and want to visit the memorial at the bus, locals advise it is a long hike in from the end of Stampede Road and you have to cross the Savage and Teklanika Rivers." A composer named Cindy Cox wrote a piece meant to convey musically the dying man's states of mind—fear, joy, acceptance, etc. A young outdoorsman I know, Joseph Chambers, says that among his friends a new phrase has emerged: "pulling a McCandless." A person who pulls a McCandless may be trying to test himself or to find himself, Chambers explained, or he may be on a fool's mission, risking his life and causing pain to others while recklessly searching for something that may have been meaningless or stupid all along.

And then there are the pilgrims, the scores and scores of believers who, stooped beneath the weight of their packs and lives, walk that long Stampede Trail to see the place where Christopher McCandless died, and never take a step beyond.

For two hours we rode along the rim of the shallow valley. Heat from the engines warmed our hands. We followed a trail used by dog mushers and snowmachiners; here and there other trails looped to the north or south. We had barely beaten spring. Russet scraps of tundra patched the snow, and the packed trail wound across the ground like a boardwalk. A Healy woman named Connie led most of the time because she knew the way. The others in the group were my friends Kris, Joe, and Charles. Kris and Joe live just outside the park; Kris, a freelance writer, covered the McCandless story when it first broke in Alaska, and she's the one who told me that people had been visiting the bus like it was Jim Morrison's grave in Paris. Joe had visited the site shortly after the body was discovered. Charles, a photographer, came along to document the bus and to make tasteless jokes. I suggested our journey should be titled "Into the Weird."

Now and then we rode by other trails looping across the snow, and an hour into our trip, two snowmachiners passed us before we reached the Teklanika River. They were friends of Joe's on their way northward to fix an off-road tracked vehicle that had broken a fuel line during a fall moose hunt. Their trail curved across a distant ridge, and I admired their ease and confidence roaming around out here, where machines can break down or dogs can run away and the walk home will be long and troublesome. You couldn't call it the middle of nowhere; the Stampede Trail has been mapped for decades. Still, you'd want to know what you're doing, so as not to make your next public appearance in a newspaper headline, or as another statistic.

The Teklanika River ice had not yet softened, and we crossed its smooth expanse without trouble, just below where it emerges from a gulch. We cruised through Moose Alley, dipped into the forest, wound across the beaver ponds, and rose along an alder-thick ridgeline. Occasionally moose tracks postholed the snow. I tried to imagine hiking here in the summer, calling out to bears and waving away mosquitoes.

We rounded a bend and suddenly there was the bus, hollow-eyed and beat up, the most absurd thing you could imagine encountering in this open, white space. Faded letters just below the side windows said, "Fairbanks City Transit System." The derelict bus seemed so familiar because we had seen its picture many times in newspapers and on the jacket of Krakauer's book. For decades it had served as a hunting camp and backcountry shelter, a corroding green-and-white hull of civilization transplanted to a knoll above the Sushana River. Now it was haunted real estate.

We turned off the snowmachines and stood stretching in the sunshine and the kind of quiet that vibrates. A trash barrel, a fire grill, plenty of footprints, and frozen dog shit provided evidence of passing dogsleds and snowmachines. A wire chair leaned against the bus, and I wondered how many people had posed there for photographs. The bus made me uneasy, and I was glad to be there with friends. It must have sheltered many people over the years who came to shoot and drink and close themselves up against the night.

Kris and I squeezed through a gap in the jammed bus door and climbed in. It was warm enough to remove hats and gloves while we looked around, though an occasional draft swept through the broken windows. A bullet hole had pierced the windshield on the driver's side. [...]

Three notebooks sat on the plywood table. They included a three-ring binder protecting a photocopy of Krakauer's original magazine article with its blaring headline: "Lost in the Wild." It was a Monty Python moment when someone pointed out an unrelated title on the cover. "Are you too thin? The case for fat." This kind of humor is one reason why Alaskans fear dying ridiculously: the living are so cruel to the foolish dead. It's a way of congratulating ourselves on remaining alive.

Kris and I began flipping through the steno notebooks, which had been filled with comments by visitors, the way people write in logbooks left in public cabins or guestbooks set out at art galleries. [...]

Among my friends and acquaintances, the story of Christopher McCandless makes great after-dinner conversation. Much of the time I agree with the "he had a death wish" camp because I don't know how else to reconcile what we know of his ordeal. Now and then I venture into the "what a dumbshit" territory, tempered by brief alliances with the "he was just another romantic boy on an all-American quest" partisans. Mostly I'm puzzled by the way he's emerged as a hero, a kind of privileged-yet-strangely-dissatisfied-with-his-existence hero.

But it's more complicated that that. I can almost understand why he rejected maps, common sense, conventional wisdom, and local knowledge before embarking on his venture. Occasionally when I hear others make fun of Christopher McCandless, I fall quiet. My favorite book growing up was Scott O'Dell's *Island of the Blue Dolphins*, based on a true story about a 19th-century Chumash Indian girl who survived for years alone on an island off the California coast. How often I had imagined myself living in that hut of whale bones, catching fish by hand and taming wild dogs for companionship. It's common, this primal longing to connect with a natural world that provides and cradles, that toughens and inspires.

This is the easiest thing to criticize, though—the notion that wilderness exists to dispense epiphanies and spiritual cures as part of the scenery. Live here long enough, and you'll learn that every moment spent admiring endless vistas or wandering the land is a privilege, accompanied by plenty of other moments evading mosquitoes by the millions, outlasting weather, avoiding Giardia, negotiating unruly terrain, and thinking uneasily about the occasional predator. Walking cross-country through alder thickets or muskeg may be the hardest thing you do all year, as you fight against the earth's tendency to grab hold of you for itself.

And of course it's hard to eat out there. A friend who trapped in his youth likens the Bush to a desert, nearly empty of wildlife. One winter he ate marten tendons for days because his food ran out. Read the journal of Fred Fickett, who accompanied Lt. Henry Allen on a 1,500-mile exploration of the Copper, Tanana, and Koyukuk river valleys; it is the story of hungry men. May 20, 1885: "One of our dogs found a dead goose. We took it from him and ate it." May 22: "Had rotten salmon straight for breakfast. It was so bad that even the Indian dogs wouldn't eat it." May 28: "Had a little paste for breakfast, rotten and wormy meat for dinner, rotten goose eggs and a little rice for supper, about $1/4$ what we needed." May 30: "Indian gave us a dinner of boiled meat from which he had scraped the maggots in handfulls before cutting it up. It tasted good, maggots and all."

There's a reason the Natives sometimes starved in the old days— and they knew what they were doing. There's a reason that many homesteaders and Bush rats collect welfare to supplement hunting and fishing. There's a reason we gather in cities and villages. So many people want to believe that it's possible to live a noble life alone in the wilderness, living entirely off the land—and yet the indigenous peoples of Alaska know that only by depending upon each other, only by forming a community, does survival become possible.

People have been dying in the wilderness for as long as people have been going into it. There are always lessons to be learned from such sad stories, even lessons as simple as: Don't forget matches, don't sweat in the cold, don't run away from bears. But sometimes there are no learning moments, no explanations. [...]

So many ways to die in the north, in manners grand and surprising and sad. A moment's inattention, the proverbial series of small miscalculations that add up to one giant screw-up, delusion about one's abilities, hubris, mental imbalance, plain bad luck—that's all it takes.

For a few weeks one spring, I kept track of news articles reporting outdoor deaths. Over the winter, more than 30 Alaskans died in snowmachine accidents, a record. They had lost their way in blizzards, fallen through ice and drowned, been buried in avalanches, collided into each other. An intoxicated man perched on a boat's gunwales fell into the Chena River in downtown Fairbanks when waves rocked the vessel; his body did not emerge for days. Two men suffocated from carbon monoxide poisoning after they brought a charcoal grill into their tent near Chena Hot Springs. Two young kayakers were missing and presumed dead in the Gulf of Alaska. Campers found the bones of an 18-year-old soldier who disappeared while ice fishing near the Knik Arm 15 years ago. And even as searchers looked for a man who had disappeared in the Chugach Mountains came the news that 70-year-old Dick Cook, an extraordinary woodsman described by John McPhee as the "acknowledged high swami of the river people," had drowned in the Tatonduk, a river he knew intimately. Some days it seemed surprising that people survive the outdoors at all.

And yet there we were, we crude Alaskans, scoffing and making jokes in Fairbanks 142, shaking our heads and posing with cans of Spam. We want it both ways, it seems. We want to impress people and ourselves with scary tales of death defied at every turn, to point out that Alaska is so unforgiving that a person could die just a few miles away from help. And still we scorn those drawn to that mystique, to those poor, foolish slobs who manage to die out of ignorance or stupidity or even bad luck. Perhaps that's because we know that one day—just like that, really—we could so easily become one of those poor, foolish slobs ourselves. [...]

Occasionally I paused while flipping through the notebooks and looked out a busted window to watch how the mid-afternoon sun glazed the snow. We needed to return before dark, so I started skimming the entries, my eyes catching only certain words: Peace. Solitude. Meaning.

It was hard work, resisting the longing that rose from the scribbled words. I spent some moments puzzling over this comment written by a man from Ontario: "[Chris] gave his life in exchange for knowledge and his story is his contribution to the world. I feel complete now to put this story behind me as it was on my mind for quite some time."

This may be our oldest, truest survival skill: the ability to tell and to learn from each other's stories, whether from Aesop's fables, quest narratives, Greek mythology, the Book of Genesis, office gossip, the wisdom of elders, or made-for-TV movies. In some ways, Alaska is nothing but stories. We have constructed many of our ideas about this place, and about ourselves, from creation stories, gold rush stories, hunting and fishing stories, pioneer stories, family stories, clan stories. Even the animals told tales in the old Story Time, which is long behind us now.

Pay attention to what people say in bars and across dinner tables and around campfires, and how often they are really telling survival stories of some sort or another. How I crossed the river, how I lost the trail, how I got my moose, how I fixed my boat, how I left home for the north, how I beat the storm, how I made it through another cold and lonely winter, how I became a true Alaskan. What all these stories mean, though—that's up to you, the listener.

We can't know exactly why Christopher McCandless died. What matters now is what people want to believe about his death. Krakauer hypothesized that toxic seeds of the wild potato plant weakened him, and early test results seemed to support that. But chemists at the University of Alaska Fairbanks further studied wild potato seeds, as well as seeds from the similar-looking wild sweetpea, and their work seemed to eliminate the poisoning theory.

"I would be willing to bet money that neither species had toxic metabolites that would account for the fate of McCandless," chemist Tom Clausen wrote to me in an e-mail. His conclusions appeared in the *Fairbanks Daily News-Miner* but never received wide coverage. Clausen added, "I believe McCandless died not from toxic foods but from foolishness. I hate to be so blunt about the dead but he clearly went 'into the wild' unprepared."

But the idea that McCandless was poisoned accidentally has become critical to his legend, because it means he wasn't stupid, wasn't seeking death. When I mentioned the research to the bus driver he gave me an obstinate look and said, "The question is still open." He could not surrender the "right" story.

McCandless's biggest mistake may have been his failure to listen to the right stories. He ignored advice about the scarcity of game, the practicalities of bear protection, the importance of maps, the truths of the land. He was too intent on creating the story of himself.

And yet, that story has such power, such meaning for so many people, that they feel drawn—called personally—to travel across the globe and hike the trail all that way to the bus to look for Christopher McCandless or Alexander Supertramp, or themselves. They endure mosquitoes and rain and tough walking and bad river crossings and the possibility of bears. The burden the pilgrims carry to the bus is so heavy, laden with their frailties and hopes and desires, and with their lives that don't quite satisfy. And when they arrive, they sit in that cold bus and think, and sometimes they cry from loss and longing and relief.

Well, so many of them are young, and they're lost, somehow, just as he was.

As he was dying, Christopher McCandless made a self-portrait of himself propped against the bus. He held up a good-bye note, a smile on his gaunt face, and from this photograph Krakauer concluded that "Chris McCandless was at peace, serene as a monk gone to God." But only Christopher McCandless could have known what truth was in his heart, there at the end. All we can say is that whoever he was, he's not that person anymore. Jon Krakauer made a story about him, by way of telling his own, and every pilgrim since his death has shaped him into something different as well. I'm doing it right now, too.

For many Alaskans, the problem is not necessarily that Christopher McCandless attempted what he did. Most of us came here in search of something, didn't we? Haven't we made our own embarrassing mistakes? But of all the stories in Alaska—stories about Raven and Koatlekanee and Oddarne Skaldebo and the two girls from Selawik—this is the one that people buy in airports and read on the way to their Alaskan adventure. This is the one that makes people walk out to the bus, cry a little, and think they've learned something about the north. This is the one that fools people into thinking they understand something about Christopher McCandless and themselves.

We can't afford to take his story seriously because it doesn't say much a careful person doesn't already know about desire and survival. The lessons are so obvious as to be laughable: Look at a map. Take some food. Know where you are. Listen to people who are smarter than you. Be humble. Go on out there—but it won't mean much unless you come back.

This is what bothers me—that Christopher McCandless failed so harshly, so sadly, and yet so *famously* that his death has come to symbolize something admirable. His unwillingness to see Alaska for what it really is has somehow become the story so many people associate with this place, a story so hollow you can almost hear the wind blowing through it. His death was not a brilliant fuck-up. It was not even a terribly original fuck-up. It was just one of the more recent and more pointless fuck-ups.

At 3 P.M., after we'd read through the notebooks, taken our silly and disrespectful photographs, and eaten our lunches, we climbed back on our snowmachines and left. We rode against the wind as the light softened and dimmed all around. It grew colder, but it was still a good day to be outside, with spring on its way. I could feel fond about winter, now that it was dwindling. What I really wanted was to keep going beyond the bus, across the Sushana River and maybe down into the park.

As we followed our tracks home, I thought about a story reported in newspapers the previous winter about a man who had disappeared during a snowmachine trip between two villages on the Yukon-Kuskokwim Delta. The chances of him surviving the frigid coastal winds seemed slight, but for weeks people reported seeing him on the tundra and in the village. The figure ran away when approached. Eventually his body was found, face down in the snow. He could not have survived more than two days, the coroner said. Yet people had seen him wandering around the delta, hiding among homes in the village, unable to move on. The Yu'pik elders explained that he was *cillemquellra*. Rough translation: "Made cold by the universe." He was mired in the thin place where two worlds rub together.

Poor Christopher McCandless, entombed by the tributes of his pilgrims, forever wandering between the world he wanted and the world that exists, still trapped by other people's desires to make him something he is not—which is why he came out here in the first place. People think they see him and feel him, there at the bus. Perhaps he is indeed within our vision, but he is not within our reach.

Too late he learned that the hard part isn't walking toward the wilderness to discover the meaning of life. The hard part is returning from the consolations of nature and finding meaning anyway, a meaning lodged within the faithfulness of our ordinary lives, in the plain and painful beauty of our ordinary days.

Some day, I told myself, I might return. I'd do what few people do anymore, which is to pass by that junky old bus with only a sidelong glance and see what else is out there.

THE QUITTER

Robert Service

When you're lost in the Wild, and you're scared as a child,
    And Death looks you bang in the eye,
And you're sore as a boil, it's according to Hoyle
    To cock your revolver and...die.
But the Code of a Man says: "Fight all you can,"
    And self-dissolution is barred.
In hunger and woe, oh, it's easy to blow...
    It's the hell-served-for-breakfast that's hard.

"You're sick of the game!" Well, now, that's a shame.
    You're young and you're brave and you're bright.
"You've had a raw deal!" I know—but don't squeal,
    Buck up, do your damnedest, and fight.
It's the plugging away that will win you the day,
    So don't be a piker, old pard!
Just draw on your grit; it's so easy to quit:
    It's the keeping-your-chin-up that's hard.

It's easy to cry that you're beaten—and die;
    It's easy to crawfish and crawl;
But to fight and to fight when hope's out of sight—
    Why, that's the best game of them all!
And though you come out of each gruelling bout,
    All broken and beaten and scarred,
Just have one more try—it's dead easy to die,
    It's the keeping-on-living that's hard.

FROM
COMING INTO THE COUNTRY

John McPhee

 The country is full of stories of unusual deaths—old Nimrod Robertson lying down on a creek in overflow and letting it build around him a sarcophagus of ice; the trapper on the Kandik who apparently knocked himself out when he tripped and fell on his own firewood and froze to death before he came to—and of stories also of deaths postponed. There are fewer of the second. I would like to add one back—an account that in essence remains in the country but in detail has largely disappeared.

On a high promontory in the montane ruggedness around the upper Charley River lies the wreckage of an aircraft that is readily identifiable as a B-24. This was the so-called Liberator, a medium-range bomber built for the Second World War. The wreckage is in the dead center of the country, and I happened over it in a Cessna early in the fall of 1975, during a long and extremely digressive flight that began in Eagle and ended many hours later in Circle. The pilot of the Cessna said he understood that the crew of the Liberator had bailed out, in winter, and that only one man had survived. I asked around to learn who might know more than that—querying, among others, the Air Force in Fairbanks, the Gelvins, various old-timers in Circle and Central, some of the river people, and Margaret Nelson, in Eagle, who had packed parachutes at Ladd Field, in Fairbanks, during the war. There had been one survivor—everyone agreed. No one knew his name. He had become a symbol in the country, though, and was not about to be forgotten. It was said that he alone had come out—long after all had been assumed dead—because he alone, of the widely scattered crew, was experienced in wilderness, knew how to live off the land, and was prepared to deal with the hostile cold. Above all, he had found a cabin, during his exodus, without which he would have died for sure.

"And the government bastards try to stop us from building them now."

"Guy jumped out of an airplane, and he would have died but he found a cabin."

If the survivor had gone on surviving for what was now approaching thirty-five years, he would in all likelihood be somewhere in the Lower Forty-eight. When I was home, I made a try to find him. Phone calls ricocheted around Washington for some days, yielding only additional phone numbers. The story was just too sketchy. Did I know how many bombers had been lost in that war? At length, I was given the name of Gerard Hasselwander, a historian at the Albert F. Simpson Historical Research Center, Maxwell Air Force Base, Alabama. I called him, and he said that if I did not even know the year of the crash he doubted he could help me. Scarcely two hours later, though, he called back to say that he had had a free moment or two at the end of his lunch hour and had browsed through some microfilm. To his own considerable surprise, he had found the survivor's name, which was Leon Crane. Crane's home when he entered the Army Air Forces had been in Philadelphia, but Hasselwander had looked in a Philadelphia directory and there was no Leon Crane in it now. However, he said, Leon Crane had had two brothers who were also in service—in the Army Medical Corps—during the Second World War. One of them was named Morris. In the Philadelphia directory, there was a Dr. Morris Crane.

When I called the number, someone answered and said Dr. Crane was not there.

I asked when he would return.

"I don't know" was the reply. "He went to Leon's."

The Liberator, making cold-weather propeller tests above twenty thousand feet, went into a spin, dived toward the earth, and, pulling out, snapped its elevator controls. It then went into another spin, and the pilot gave the order to abandon ship. There were five aboard. Leon Crane was the co-pilot. He was twenty-four and he had been in Alaska less than two months. Since the plane was falling like a swirling leaf, he had to drag himself against heavy centrifugal force toward the open bomb bay. He had never used a parachute. The outside air temperature was at least thirty degrees below zero. When he jumped, he forgot his mittens. The day was December 21st.

The plane fiercely burned, not far away from where he landed, and he stood watching it, up to his thighs in snow. He was wearing a hooded down jacket, a sweater, winter underwear, two pairs of trousers, two pairs of socks, and felt-lined military mukluks. He scanned the mountainsides but could see nothing of the others. He thought he had been the second one to go out of the plane, and as he fell he thought he saw a parachute open in the air above him. He shouted into the winter silence. Silence answered. Months later, he would learn that there had been two corpses in the aircraft. Of the two other fliers no track or trace was ever found. "Sergeant Pompeo, the crew chief, had a hell of a thick set of glasses. He must have lost them as soon as he hit the airstream. Without them, he really couldn't see. What was he going to do when he got down there?"

For that matter, what was Crane going to do? He had no food, no gun, no sleeping bag, no mittens. The plane had been meandering in search of suitable skies for the tests. Within two or three hundred miles, he had no idea where he was.

Two thousand feet below him, and a couple of miles east, was a river. He made his way down to it. Waiting for rescue, he stayed beside it. He had two books of matches, a Boy Scout knife. He started a fire with a letter from his father, and for the first eight days he did not sleep more than two hours at a time in his vigilance to keep the fire burning. The cold awakened him anyway. Water fountained from a gap in the river ice, and that is what he lived on. His hands, which he to some extent protected with parachute cloth or in the pockets of his jacket, became cut and abraded from tearing at spruce boughs. When he spread his fingers, the skin between them would split. Temperatures were probably ranging between a high of thirty below zero and a low around fifty. The parachute, as much as anything, kept him alive. It was twenty-eight feet in diameter, and he wound it around him so that he was at the center of a great cocoon. Still, he said, his back would grow cold while his face roasted, and sparks kept igniting the chute.

He was telling me some of this on a sidewalk in Philadelphia when I asked him how he had dealt with fear.

He stopped in surprise, and looked contemplatively up the street toward Independence Hall, his graying hair wisping out to the sides. He wore a business suit and a topcoat, and he had bright, penetrating eyes. He leaned forward when he walked. "Fear," he repeated. "I wouldn't have used that word. Think about it: there was not a hell of a lot I could do if I were to panic. Besides, I was sure that someone was going to come and get me."

All that the search-and-rescue missions had to go on was that the Liberator had last been heard from above Big Delta, so the search area could not be reduced much below forty thousand square miles. Needless to say, they would not come near finding him. He thought once that he heard the sound of an airplane, but eventually he realized that it was a chorus of wolves. In his hunger, he tried to kill squirrels. He made a spear, and threw it awkwardly as they jumped and chattered in the spruce boughs. He made a bow and arrow, using a shroud line from his parachute, but when he released the arrow it shot off at angles ridiculously oblique to the screeching, maddening squirrels. There was some rubber involved in the parachute assembly, and he used that to make a slingshot, which was worse than the bow and arrow. When he fell asleep by the fire, he dreamed of milkshakes, dripping beefsteaks, mashed potatoes, and lamb chops, with lamb fat running down his hands. Awake, he kicked aside the snow and found green moss. He put it in his mouth and chewed, and chewed some more, but scarcely swallowed any. Incidentally, he was camped almost exactly where, some twenty-five years later, Ed and Virginia Gelvin would build a cabin from which to trap and hunt.

Crane is a thoroughly urban man. He grew up in the neighborhood of Independence Hall, where he lives now, with an unlisted number. That part of the city has undergone extensive refurbishment in recent years, and Crane's sons, who are residential builders and construction engineers, have had a part in the process. Crane, more or less retired, works for them, and when I visited him I followed him from building to building as he checked on the needs and efforts of carpenters, bricklayers, plumbers. He professed to have no appetite for wild country, least of all for the expanses of the north. As a boy, he had joined a city Scout troop, and had become a First Class Scout, but that was not to suggest a particular knowledge of wilderness. When he flew out of Fairbanks that morning in 1943, his lifetime camping experience consisted of one night on the ground—with his troop, in Valley Forge.

He decided on the ninth day that no help was coming. Gathering up his parachute, he began to slog his way downriver, in snow sometimes up to his waist. It crossed his mind that the situation might be hopeless, but he put down the thought as he moved from bend to bend by telling himself to keep going because "right around that curve is what you're looking for." In fact, he was about sixty miles from the nearest human being, almost a hundred from the nearest group of buildings large enough to be called a settlement. Around the next bend, he saw more mountains, more bare jagged rock, more snow-covered sweeps of alpine tundra, contoured toward another river bend. "Right around that curve is what you're looking for," he told himself again. Suddenly, something was there. First, he saw a cache, high on legs in the air, and then a small cabin, with a door only three feet high. It was like the lamb chops, with the grease on his fingers, but when he pushed at the door it was wood and real. The room inside was nine by ten: earth floor, low ceiling, a bunk made of spruce. It was Alaskan custom always to leave a cabin open and stocked for anyone in need. Split firewood was there, and matches, and a pile of prepared shavings. On a table were sacks of dried raisins, sugar, cocoa, and powdered milk. There was a barrel stove, frying pans on the wall. He made some cocoa, and, after so long a time without food, seemed full after a couple of sips. Then he climbed a ladder and looked in the cache, lifting a tarp to discover hammers, saws, picks, drills, coiled rope, and two tents. No one, he reasoned, would leave such equipment far off in the wilderness. "I figured civilization was right around the corner. I was home free."

So he stayed just a night and went on down the river, anxious to get back to Ladd Field. The moon came up after the brief light of day, and he kept going. He grew weak in the deep cold of the night, and when the moon went below the mountains he began to wander off the stream course, hitting boulders. He had been around many corners, but no civilization was there. Now he was sinking into a dream-hazy sleepwalking numbed-out oblivion; but fear, fortunately, struck through and turned him, upriver. He had not retraced his way very far when he stopped and tried to build a fire. He scraped together some twigs, but his cut and bare hands were shaking so—at roughly fifty below zero—that he failed repeatedly to ignite a match. He abandoned the effort, and moved on through the snow. He kept hitting boulders. He had difficulty following his own tracks. He knew now that he would die if he did not get back to the cabin, and the detached observer within him decided he was finished. Left foot, right foot—there was no point in quitting, even so. About noon, he reached the cabin. With his entire body shaking, he worked at a fire until he had one going. Then he rolled up in his parachute and slept almost continuously for three full days.

In his excitement at being "right around the corner from civilization," he had scarcely looked in the cache, and now he found rice, flour, beans, powdered eggs, dried vegetables, and beef—enough for many weeks, possibly months. He found mittens. He found snowshoes. He found long johns, socks, mukluks. He found candles, tea, tobacco, and a corncob pipe. He found ammunition, a .22. In the cabin, he mixed flour, peas, beans, sugar, and snow, and set it on the stove. That would be his basic gruel—and he became enduringly fond of it. Sometimes he threw in eggs and vegetables. He covered his hands with melted candle wax, and the bandage was amazingly effective. He developed a routine, with meals twice a day, a time for hunting, a fresh well chopped daily through the four-foot river ice. He slept eighteen hours a day, like a wintering bear—not truly hibernating, just lying there in his den. He felt a need to hear a voice, so he talked to himself. The day's high moment was a pipeful of tobacco puffed while he looked through ten-year-old copies of *The Saturday Evening Post*. He ransacked the magazines for insights into the woods lore he did not know. He learned a thing or two. In a wind, it said somewhere in the *Post*, build your fire in a hole. He shot and ate a ptarmigan, and had the presence of mind to look in its stomach. He found some overwintering berries there, went to the sort of bushes they had come from, and shot more ptarmigan. Cardboard boxes, the magazines, and other items in the

cabin were addressed to "Phil Berail, Woodchopper, Alaska."
Contemplating these labels, Crane decided that Alaska was a fantastic
place—where someone's name and occupation were a sufficient
address. One day, an old calendar fell off the wall and flipped over on
its way to the floor. On the back was a map of Alaska. He stared at it
all day. He found Woodchopper, on the Yukon, and smiled at his foolishness. From the terrain around him, the northward flow of the
stream, the relative positions of Fairbanks and Big Delta, he decided—
just right—that he was far up the Charley River. The smile went back
where it came from.

He decided to wait for breakup, build a raft, and in late May float
on down to the Yukon. After five or six weeks, though, he realized
that his food was going to give out in March. There was little ammunition with which to get meat, and he had no confidence anyway in
his chances with the rifle. If he stayed, he would starve. He felt panic
now, but not enough to spill the care with which he was making his
plans. He had set off willy-nilly once before and did not want to
repeat the mistake. He patched his clothes with parachute cloth,
sewing them with shroud lines. He made a sled from some boards
and a galvanized tub. He figured closely what the maximum might
be that he could drag and carry. On February 12th, he left. The sled
would scarcely budge at first, and snow bunched up before it.
Wearing a harness he had made, he dragged the sled slowly downriver. Berail's snowshoes had Indian ties. Try as he would, he could
not understand how to secure them to his feet. The snowshoes were
useless. Up to his knees, and sometimes to his hips, he walked from
dawn until an hour before dark each day. He slept beside bonfires
that burned all night. Blizzards came up the river some days, and
driving williwaws—winds of a force that could literally stop him in
his tracks. He leaned against the wind. When he could, he stepped
forward. Once, at the end of a day's hard walking, he looked behind
him—on the twisting mountain river—and saw where he had started
at dawn. The Charley in summer—clear-flowing within its canyon
walls, with grizzlies fishing its riffles, Dall sheep on the bluffs, and
peregrines above it in the air—is an extremely beautiful Alaskan river
(it has been called the loveliest of all), but for Leon Crane it was little

more than brutal. He came to a lead one day, a patch of open water, and, trying to use some boulders as stepping stones, he fell in up to his armpits. Coming out, barging through snowdrifts, he was the center of a fast-forming block of ice. His matches were dry. Shaking as before, he managed this time to build a fire. All day, he sat steaming beside it, removing this or that item of clothing, drying it a piece at a time.

After a couple of weeks on the river, he found another cabin, with a modest but welcome food cache—cornmeal, canned vegetables, Vienna sausage. He sewed himself a backpack and abandoned his cumbersome sled. Some seven or eight days on down the river, he came around a bend at dusk and found cut spruce tops in parallel rows stuck in the river snow. His aloneness, he sensed, was all but over. It was the second week of March, and he was eighty days out of the sky. The arrangement of treetops, obviously, marked a place where a plane on skis might land supplies. He looked around in near darkness and found a toboggan trail. He camped, and next day followed the trail to a cabin—under smoke. He shouted toward it. Al Ames, a trapper, and his wife, Neena, and their children appeared in the doorway. "I am Lieutenant Leon Crane, of the United States Army Air Forces," he called out. "I've been in a little trouble." Ames took a picture, which hangs on a wall in Philadelphia.

Crane remembers thinking, Somebody must be saving me for something, but I don't know what it is. His six children, who owe themselves to that trip and to Phil Berail's fully stocked Charley River cabin, are—in addition to his three sons in the construction business— Mimi, who is studying engineering at Barnard; Rebecca, who is in the master's program in architecture at Columbia; and Ruth, a recent grad- uate of the Harvard Medical School. Crane himself went on to earn an advanced degree in aeronautical engineering at the Massachusetts Institute of Technology, and spent his career developing helicopters for Boeing Vertol.

"It's a little surprising to me that people exist who are interested in living on that ground up there," he told me. "Why would anyone want to take someone who wanted to *be* there and throw them out? Who the hell could *care*?"

Al Ames, who had built his cabin only two years before, harnessed his dogs and mushed Crane down the Yukon to Woodchopper, where a plane soon came along and flew him out.

Crane met Phil Berail at Woodchopper, and struggled shyly to express to him his inexpressible gratitude. Berail, sixty-five, was a temporary postmaster and worked for the gold miners there. He had trapped from his Charley River cabin. He was pleased that it had been useful, he said. For his part, he had no intention of ever going there again. He had abandoned the cabin four years before.

OLD YUKON

TALES—TRAILS—AND TRIALS

James Wickersham

 Soon after New Year's day we loaded our blankets and supplies on two light sleds, each drawn by three dogs, and set out for the Seventy Mile river. There was a well-used trail across the divide between Mission creek and the river. Prospectors' cabins were along the river, and we found a latch string hung on the outside of every prospector's door. It was the custom for any traveller to pull the string which raised the inside wooden bar, walk in, make a fire, and make himself at home. Every cabin on the Seventy Mile had a good bunk with a spruce bough bed, and a small sheet-iron Yukon stove as part of its furniture. Before leaving the cabin for the day's work, or a visit to a neighbor, or a trip to town, the occupant would invariably cut enough shavings from the dry wood always in the shelter of the door, and arrange the shavings and wood in the stove ready for a quick fire, and leave a square block of matches in sight, so that one coming in, sometimes almost perishing from cold, or wet from the treacherous overflow of water beneath the snow, might make a fire with the least possible waste of time. We visited all the cabins along the river, some occupied and others temporarily vacant, and observed evidences of this wise custom in every one.

SIGN ON A CABIN IN THE CARIBOU HILLS

Arlitia Jones

This cabin belongs to Eileen Black.
My husband Marvel and I built it
by hand in 1957. Friends
are welcome to use it: Perly and his
gang, Johnny Pete, Mike Klink, Bob Eber-
hard and Bob Jackovik, Diego Ron and
Steve Redmon. George & Maria, Margie
and Marty and the kids if they're along.
Donny Shelikov can come in and
Karl and Tony if he ever comes back.
Ed Greeley, keep out.
    If you're lost and need a place
to get in, you can spend the night. I left
Sanka and dry goods. Help yourself.
Please clean up. Don't attract bears.
Leave it the way you found it—woodpile
stocked and kindling dry. Remember, close
the door tight and leave it unlocked.

TRACKS OF THE UNSEEN

Nick Jans

I sit on a tundra hill, waiting for the evening light. It's fall in the Arctic, the most beautiful and ephemeral of seasons. A week ago, the willows along the creek were green. Now snow might come tomorrow. Gray sheets of cloud furrow the mountains to the north; shafts of sun fall golden on the ache of tundra between. At my feet, clusters of bearberry glow bright as blood, and wolf tracks mark the rain-bruised sand. No drops have fallen in the tracks.

Scattered bands of caribou flow past, cows and calves with a few smaller bulls. I follow them with my eyes, but don't stir. Before my low-set tripod lies a bleached skull, the antlers gnawed and lichen stained, brittle as chalk. I have the lens chosen, the picture composed, perfect in my mind as it will never be. What I need now is light.

It's been two years since Michio died. I've come back each fall since, because this is the place I remember him best. This is the same skull he knelt before, waiting for hours as sun-split clouds shouldered low against those same blue hills, impossibly clear in the distance. *Neek,* he said (transforming, as always, my name into music), *we must wait here. It is so beautiful.*

And so we waited, Michio, his new bride, Naoko, and I, for hours on that late August day, waiting for the light to fall. Caribou trotted past—not many, but enough so that the land was always moving. I sat, but after a while, I'd had enough. I wanted to shoulder my tripod and scurry left or right five hundred yards, make something happen. What about that bunch over there? Michio didn't try to stop me. Kneeling before the caribou skull, he occasionally shifted his camera higher or lower, took a few exposures, consulted his light meter. For minutes at a time he didn't move or speak, scarcely seemed to breathe. When I asked him what he was doing, he said, *Neek, to make beautiful picture, you must look very carefully. You must see everything.*

I can't claim to have known him very well, or for very long. But the first time he smiled, we were friends. That's the way it was with Michio. Everyone and everything—a stranger hitchhiking, a lone moose, a sow grizzly with cubs—seemed drawn to his relaxed, gentle presence. Lucky, some said. He just sits there, and animals walk up to him.

He never carried a gun; for that matter, never owned one. I think he truly believed in the world's good graces, that it would understand he meant no harm and offer the same in return. Friends sometimes shook their heads at his unwillingness to be more careful, at the risks he took without seeming to understand.

Someone who took such intimate, telling portraits of moose and grizzlies must have been, you'd suppose, a hell of an outdoorsman— able to navigate by compass, tie good knots, and build a campfire in the rain. But Michio had trouble with anything much beyond pitching a tent and unrolling a sleeping bag.

Neither was he a student of animal behavior, attuned to the nuances of posture and motion, the silent messages all creatures send and receive. I remember sitting by him as a handful of bull caribou milled, fifty yards away. They winded us and stood stiff-legged, alternately staring in our direction and glancing right and left. *Michio*, I hissed, *hurry up, they're going to bolt.* Which of course they did. *Neek,* Michio asked me, an astonished look on his face, *how did you know?*

He was absentminded, forever tripping over things, nonplussed by all manner of mechanical contraptions, including his own body. On that trip with me and Naoko, he beaned himself four times on the lantern that was hanging from our wall tent's ridgepole, all in the space of an evening. The fifth time he missed—because I took the lantern down. The next day, he brushed against my jet boat's throttle, jamming it wide open in the middle of a shallow, boulder-strewn run. The collision with the rock pile was hard enough to rip the outboard's cover off and slam it into my back. Stunned, in the bottom of the boat, Michio had no idea what had gone wrong, and I didn't have the heart to tell him.

You might think that all this lack of practical focus was a handicap Michio had to struggle against; in fact, it was his gift. Freed from the encumbrance of details, all energy and concentration funneled into his art, the often sophisticated, always beautiful images he created. Leaning into his Nikon's viewfinder, he'd become so absorbed in light and color that all else ceased to exist. The laws of physics and probability were distractions he either couldn't or wouldn't deal with; which it was doesn't matter. But on some level, he must have known there was a price. Maybe in part that's why he accepted whatever befell him with such Zenlike calm and unfailing humor.

That was the essential paradox of this man: photographer of powerful, sometimes dangerous animals in an equally harsh landscape, he moved at the heart of a purely physical world, capturing its essence with unerring vision, all the while naked as a child in a huge, cold wind.

The night my friend Michio Hoshino died, dragged from his tent, screaming in the dark, by a brown bear somewhere in the Russian Far East, I was camped up the Nuna River in Northwest Alaska, more than a thousand miles away. In the dream I awoke from, photographer Tom Walker and I were surrounded by man-eating Dall sheep, fending them off with our tripods, more surprised than frightened, telling each other this just doesn't happen. They don't eat people.

Next to me, Sherrie stirred from her own nightmare, whispering there was a bear out there, a bear. I poked my head out into the arctic twilight, looked around, and tried to reassure her. No bear.

I fell back into a dream-wracked sleep, and wandered the rest of the night through Russia, invisible to everyone, trying to find my way home. Two days later, when we returned to Ambler, Tom called to tell me Michio had died that same night.

I don't claim any prescience. All I know is that I had those dreams. Months before, Michio had asked me to go with him to Russia—we'd agreed to create a book about bears together—but I already had plans for sailing Prince William Sound. And so I wished him luck, not knowing how dark and hollow those words would turn.

It's been two years, and still he passes almost daily in my thoughts. Strange to sense the loss so deeply of one I knew for so little time; but I know there are others haunted as I am. All across Alaska, in the telling and retelling of stories among friends, he becomes almost alive again, stumbling over his tripod, telling bad jokes across a campfire, sitting in the rain, waiting. Late at night, we lean in, ask each other if somehow one of us might have been able to save him.

And now, on this tundra hill, the clouds part, and the light I've waited for comes at last, flowing across the tundra, the bearberry leaves, and the antlered skull—a golden, liquid glow cast against the coming night. I have minutes, maybe seconds to work. At my shoulder drifts a whispered voice: *Oh look, Neek, look, it is all so beautiful.*

ROWING TO LATITUDE

Jill Fredston

When Doug first started teaching people how to travel safely in the mountains, he focused on the physical parameters that make avalanches possible—the terrain, the snowpack, the weather. But without people, there is no hazard. When dealing with objective hazards, the subjective thinking our society values—*How do I feel? What do I want?*—can kill, because Nature doesn't care about the answers. Our assumptions, schedules, goals, and abilities make no difference to an unstable slope or a stormy ocean. Before long, Doug pioneered a new approach to avalanche education, emphasizing the importance of what he termed the "human factor" in allowing accidents to happen. In the outdoors, biased judgments are at the root of most trouble—maybe our ego is at stake, or we are aggressively eager, or we're suffering from tunnel vision. We might be bolstered by Kodak courage, or pressured by peers, or afraid of approaching darkness. Perhaps we're tired, or not communicating well, or in denial that something bad could happen, or complacent because nothing bad has ever happened before. Maybe we're worried about being back at work on Monday. So what? An analogy we use when teaching is that few of us would choose to cross a busy city street without first looking both ways and listening for the traffic. But if we attempt to negotiate any wild place on our own terms, without heeding Nature's clues, we might as well be donning blinders and earplugs. When in the mountains, we have to think like an avalanche.

The terms *hazard* and *risk*, though often used interchangeably, are not the same. Hazard takes into account the exposure to potential danger—the angle of the slope, the size of the waves, the intensity of the storm—as well as the probability of an event occurring. Risk is the hazard multiplied by the consequences—in other words, what might happen if something goes wrong. Given the same snow instability, skiing on a slope with a cliff below it involves potentially greater consequences and, thus, greater risk. The risk of paddling in Spitsbergen, where the water is frigid and help far away, is inherently higher than paddling in the same marginal conditions along a lifeguard-patrolled section of warm California coast.

At our wedding, embarrassed by toasts to our bravery, Doug stood up and declared, "You know, the most dangerous thing we've done for years is try to drive around here." Most of the guests thought he was joking, but I knew he was not. In the outdoors, our own decisions primarily determine our safety; on New York streets, we are at the mercy of other people. Doug and I have learned to make good decisions through experience, which has often been gained as a result of bad decisions. Close friends have died making the same mistakes in similar situations. The process of learning to make sound judgments is the most dramatic journey we have ever undertaken. Along the way, we have amassed an extensive "geography of fear."

One of us only need mention Smith Bay for the other to remember with dread a combat crossing along Alaska's north coast, where a wide scoop in the shoreline necessitated a jump of at least sixteen miles. Paddling from a leeward to a windward shore is a setup for trouble, because as the winds work a greater surface area, the waves increase in size and power. From the back side, these waves can look misleadingly benign. The brisk northeasterly tailwinds that had pushed us an exhilarating nine miles an hour the day before were blowing again. But we were restless from being tentbound for much of the week, and we thought we could make it.

Within a hundred feet of the shore, cat's paws—the diamond-shaped ripples that are the first step in the genesis of any wave—began to ruffle the surface of the water. In less than an hour, we were angling through the three-to-four-foot seas we had anticipated. But the ocean has a way of exceeding our expectations. As the fetch increased and the depth of the ocean bottom decreased, the waves grew disproportionately, some cresting at heights of ten, even twelve feet. Instead of making a beeline for land, we had to cut a wider angle to keep our sterns into the waves, which lengthened the crossing to twenty-two miles.

There were no good answers to the "what-if" questions. Water at 30°F is so cold it burns. We couldn't expect to swim more than a few minutes, assuming we survived the first gasp of immersion. With land far away in any direction, we were entirely dependent on our skills. It was no different from crossing a high wire without a net except that no one was watching. The effort took more than three stomach-clenched hours. We took each wave as it came, concentrating on climbing up and sashaying down without swinging broadside, a precursor to flipping or swamping. With an open cockpit, I faced greater danger of swamping than Doug, but at least I could see the waves coming; in his kayak, he was being assaulted from behind. When we were within reach of the far shore, my concentration wavered for a fraction of a second, enough for a wave to plunge down my neck, coursing all the way into my boots. Shivering, I lined up with the incoming waves and joined them in crashing onto the beach. They instantly began to seep back to sea, but I didn't plan to leave land until the ocean granted us clear permission. [...]

WAGER WITH THE WIND

THE DON SHELDON STORY

James Greiner

 No one, including Sheldon, had ever made a landing near the 14,000-foot level on McKinley. He knew that pilots who fly at these heights, unless properly equipped, suffer hypoxia, the insidious disease of oxygen starvation. In the anemic air at this altitude, the engine of any fixed-propeller aircraft would lose about 45 percent of its total power capabilities. In addition to the lower power capabilities of the airplane, the pilot must exercise extreme care in selecting a landing site that will allow for a reduced-power, gravity-assisted takeoff with the added load of a bulky passenger. The powerful, unpainted six-place Cessna would not meet this challenge due to its high empty weight, and the only choice he had left was the small two-place Piper Super Cub, upon which he had depended so often before.

"The Super Cub is powered by a 4-cylinder Lycoming engine, which develops 150 horsepower. Its greatest single advantage lies in the fact that it is an extremely light airplane. Fabric-covered, it only weighs a bit over a thousand pounds and is a frail bird of very high performance."

Finely tuned, the Super Cub would be the only tool that Sheldon could use to answer this plea for help. His next thought automatically shifted to the weather.

"After May 17, the weather began to go ape and was shifting into a tremendous storm cycle. The wind of the past 3½ days was still in the process of blowing itself out on McKinley."

Sheldon knew that he would have to stifle his natural desire to leave immediately. He would have to endure the terrible waiting, which is the bane of all pilots even when there is no emergency at hand.

Standing upon his dirt strip in Talkeetna, with the warm 70-degree breeze from the west carrying sounds of the children playing and birds singing among green leaves, he had to project his thinking to appraise a seemingly impossible rescue mission at 14,000 feet in gale-velocity winds, with the accompanying vortices of snow and multilayered clouds. On McKinley, a mere 60 land miles away, the air temperature could be near zero, with an accompanying chill factor that would plunge the temperature still lower.

In the almost 24-hour daylight of the Alaskan spring, Sheldon could look northwest at virtually any time of day and view the weather near McKinley. As he stared at the mountain on the evening of May 19, he could see that he would have to continue to control his impatience. The entire lower two-thirds of the peak was socked in, and the gray scud seemed to cling there without motion. Sheldon watched continuously until late that night, slept for a few hours, and was back keeping his vigil early the next morning.

On the morning of May 20, Sheldon was up at about 4:00 A.M. as usual, after a brief three-hour nap. He found that the weather had broken substantially, and the sky around the mountain was now relatively free of clouds. He made his move at midmorning.

"On the 19th, Jack Wilson of Gulkana, Jim Gibson of Kenai, and George Kitchen along with Ted Huntley, both of Anchorage, had flown in to lend a hand. The thought of landing at 14,000 feet didn't particularly bother me, though I knew I would have a weight problem with the Super Cub. I also knew that I had a power problem with it. I had flown over the top of McKinley in it on many occasions, so ceiling was no consideration, but performance at high altitude is mainly dependent upon the weight you're carrying. I had to haul my own oxygen gear and survival equipment in case I didn't get there in one piece. I asked George Kitchen to fly cover for me for the same reason."

After carefully stowing these bare essentials of equipment, along with a generous bundle of fresh spruce boughs and willow wands, in the rear of the Super Cub, Sheldon began to think about gassing the plane. This consideration would be most important. He knew that too much gas in his tanks might negate a high-altitude takeoff, especially with a passenger in the airplane. Too little fuel could leave him stranded with a dead engine somewhere between the mountain and Talkeetna.

"A landing above 14,000 feet was no sweat, providing I could find a decent piece of steep snow-covered ice to do it on. It was the takeoff that was the big problem. All of the basics of glacier landings would apply, but even with the loss of power I knew I'd get up there, I had to play the weight factor real close. I figured what would be the best fuel load and gassed her up. I filtered the gas carefully through the chamois because the last thing I could afford was ice particles on this deal."

All aviation gasoline has small quantities of water no matter how well it is filtered. If this water, which is liquid in air that is above 32 degrees, is present in great enough quantities, the ice crystals that form as the temperature drops can plug a fuel line or filter. This fact has been learned the hard way by scores of pilots the world over, especially in the Arctic. Sheldon is so meticulous that he filters each and every drop of fuel he uses, even when he gasses up at the Anchorage International Airport.

"As soon as everything was ready, Kitchen and I blasted off. On the way, I noticed that the weather up to 17,000 feet looked pretty good, and I kept thinking about what Washburn had told me over the phone."

Brad Washburn and his wife Barbara first heard about the situation on McKinley while listening to the radio news in their Boston home on the hot sultry evening of May 19. As Washburn remembers the situation:

"To our astonishment, they were reporting an accident on McKinley and telling of John Day having been injured. We knew that the Day party was up on the mountain, because he had been in Cambridge earlier, and I had shown him some pictures of the route he would take and discussed the climb with him. I remember remarking to Barbara that John was, indeed, in a hell of a bad situation. I knew the place well, and to be isolated there with a badly broken leg was an appalling thought. I telephoned Talkeetna direct. I was lucky. Don was there, and I asked him about John Day. Sheldon said, 'Right now, he's not our main concern. They're going to bring Helga Bading, an

Anchorage climber, down the mountain from 17,000 on a sled, and she's got a bad case of altitude sickness. Is there anyplace I can land at about 14,000?'

"I thought for a moment and then replied, 'There's a shelflike basin immediately south of the West Buttress, near where we camped in 1951. It's at about 14,000 feet, and I'm certain that you can get in there with no trouble, but I can't say about coming out. Get 15,000 feet of altitude as you fly up Kahiltna Pass and fly due north until you're over your strip at 10,000 feet. Now, turn your airplane exactly 90 degrees to the right, and directly in front of you will be a large triangular pyramid of granite rock. Fly directly toward it until you are really close, drop some power, pull on your flaps, and fly around the right-hand side of the pyramid. Right in front of you will be your landing spot.'"

These directions were repeating themselves in Sheldon's mind as he glanced ahead through the white haze that hung over Kahiltna Pass. He looked to his right and could see Kitchen flying slightly above and behind his position.

"The Cub was purring like a kitten, and as I made the sharp right turn over my strip at the 10,000-foot level, I began to look for the granite triangle. It wasn't hard to spot, and I put the nose of the airplane on it and flew. Washburn had said to get close, as close as possible, before making my last turn, and I could count the rocks, as I finally rolled into it. Just as I throttled down and began to pull on the flaps, I saw it. Jeez, I was sweating like a champ, and it was the Devil's Canyon bit all over again. The spot looked mighty small and had a brisk slope, but I figured I could make it."

Sheldon's landing site had every right to look small, for it was situated on a tiny, shelflike field of snow that tilted upward to the east. It ended abruptly at the foot of a steep slope leading to the top of McKinley, and its lower end deteriorated into a broken jumble of evil-looking crevasses, followed by a staggering cliff. The entire usable surface was only about 2,000 feet long—but it was steep and smooth, and it was where it was needed.

Reducing power slightly, Sheldon flew lower over the tiny area and dropped a line of spruce boughs along the surface upon which he would land. These dark branches would be critical in the actual landing during the next go-around, for he would not be able to gauge his height above the unblemished snow without them.

"The worst part was that this had to be a one-shot deal—no second chance, no nuthin'. Once I lined up on short final here, I would be committed to a landing, like it or not. I knew that I'd have to paint it on or slide backward into the crevasses."

Fortunately, there was little turbulence, and as Sheldon lined up the Super Cub, he had the spooky feeling that he was on a collision course with the mountain, which filled his entire field of vision and rose high above it. Then he reached the point of no return, and his eyes watered with intense concentration.

"I sucked in my breath and played the lower end of that little slope against the crevasses I could see. I knew I had to get every available inch out of the landing surface or risk spreading my airplane and myself all over the side of McKinley."

Sheldon also knew that after he was down, he must continue upslope under full power, for his turnaround must be made just scant feet short of the near-vertical buttress.

During the next few fleeting seconds, with the Super Cub under full power, time stood still. As the shadowy crevasses flickered beneath his skis, he pulled the nose up sharply to match the angle of the snow surface that leaped upward before him. The Super Cub screamed in protest in the thin air as he felt for the snow surface with his skis. Then they touched with a metallic hiss, and he was climbing upslope. The plane bounced gently, and with the steepening face of the buttress leaping toward him, Sheldon kicked hard on the left rudder. The Super Cub turned abruptly, and he pulled the throttle back to idle. Sheldon was now parked crosswise on the slope, his left wing pointing downward at a severe angle. His skis held the plane, and he reached up to flip off the master switch. Then, to the popping sounds of cooling metal, he began to consider other pressing matters, such as drawing a deep breath.

Don Sheldon thus became the first man to ever land at the unprecedented altitude of 14,300 feet on the western flank of McKinley. Within an hour after touchdown, and sweating profusely with the heavy exertion of snowshoe-packing the fluffy snow, he had the tiny airfield flattened and flagged with orange survey tape and willow wands that he had brought with him. He then got Kitchen, who still circled above him, on the HF radio and told him to "come on in."

"Kitchen was an old flight instructor, and I had told him he had to make the landing with full power on. This is tough to do, because in a normal landing, the power is reduced just before touchdown. In spite of my suggestions, his instincts made him drop some power, and he hit without enough thrust to climb the steep grade and began to slide backward. Luckily, he stopped just short of the crevasses."

It then took Sheldon and a crew of six mountain climbers who happened to be in the area three hours of punishing exertion to push the plane, at full power, upslope to the takeoff position. Just as Kitchen's Super Cub was finally placed on the high end of the short slope near Sheldon's, Paul Crews and Chuck Metzger, on the verge of total physical exhaustion, arrived on the scene pulling the sleeping-bag-swathed Helga Bading on a fiberglass sled that had been airdropped earlier by the Army. They had made the descent, over highly difficult and steep terrain, in $5^{1}/_{2}$ hours and arrived at Sheldon's landing site during midafternoon.

Though she had regained consciousness because of the increased oxygen in the air at 14,300 feet, one glance told Sheldon that Mrs. Bading was in a condition very close to death, in the grip of what the press would term "moaning hysteria." Her skin showed the typical shadings of blue and green that accompany the condition that would soon be recognized as cerebral edema by the medical profession. That she was still alive was a credit to the efforts of both Dr. Rodman Wilson and the two team members who had brought her down to the 14,300-foot level. Dr. Wilson had cared for the woman with limited supplies at the 16,400-foot level, and though still in desperate condition, she was improving at the lower altitude.

After Sheldon and the others had gently loaded the woman aboard the Super Cub, he turned the plane to point it downslope and firewalled the throttle. He knew that this would be another one-shot affair. If he failed to get enough airspeed on the downhill run to fly the airplane, he would plunge into the crevasses or over the edge of the cliff beyond.

The tiny plane grudgingly gained airspeed, hurtling him toward the crevasse field. After what seemed an eternity, the Super Cub's tail came up. Easing back on the stick, he raised the plane's nose just as the last orange marker strip flitted beneath his left wing tip. He was airborne.

With the most difficult part of his first operation at the 14,300-foot strip accomplished, Sheldon set his course for Talkeetna. And now a final figure emerged out of the place from which these momentary heroes come—the obscurity of everyday life in Alaska. His name was Link Luckett, an employee of Hughes Helicopter Service in Anchorage. After returning to Talkeetna with Helga Bading and watching the Air Force medics load her aboard a military aircraft for the trip to Anchorage, Sheldon found Luckett waiting. The balding chopper pilot, flying one of his boss's Hiller two-place copters, had come to render aid and was heading for McKinley.

"Will you fly cover for me?" asked Luckett, after explaining what he had in mind to Sheldon.

"Yowsah, let's put the burn on her."

Luckett's tiny rotor-powered craft was assumed to have an absolute operating ceiling of 16,000 feet, and to assure maximum performance, he had off-loaded his battery (after starting his engine) and all of his emergency gear and had gone light on gasoline, allowing just enough fuel to reach the Day party and attempt rescue operations. Sheldon would accompany Luckett to 17,500 feet, and as they ascended above 10,000, he knew that Luckett had the throttle of his tiny Hiller to the stops. The chopper reluctantly gained altitude, and after what seemed an impossible time period to the circling Sheldon, Luckett miraculously set his fragile craft down on the snow near Day's camp. With this landing, at 17,230 feet, he established an altitude record for this tiny chopper and was the first rescuer to speak personally with the members of the ill-fated team. It was 7:00 P.M. on May 20.

Luckett found that the four men were indeed "fortunate" to be alive. Day's left leg was immobilized by badly torn ligaments, and his hands and feet were badly frozen. The leg had been neatly splinted by Dr. Wilson. Schoening's fingers were puffy and black with frostbite, and he had suffered a severe concussion in the fall. As a result of this concussion, he would remember little of the incident and would suffer memory lapses for some time. One of the Whittaker twins had also received head and neck injuries, and the other suffered frostbite and contusions. All of the men's faces were blistered by exposure, and the injuries had rendered the party immobile. Until this moment, they had been at the mercy of the mountain they had "conquered."

Luckett then instructed the climbers on how to pack down and mark a landing pad, after which he took off empty. Later, at 9:30 P.M., he returned to the scene, and watched by Sheldon who circled overhead, loaded and removed John Day. The climber who had raced with Denali rode uncomplaining, though in excruciating agony, to Sheldon's 14,300-foot landing strip.

Early in the morning of May 21, Luckett made his third and final landing at the top of the world and plucked Pete Schoening from the snow for the relay to 14,300 feet. Meanwhile, the Whittaker twins climbed down to the 14,300-foot level under their own power. Sheldon then relayed the four members of the Day party down to 10,200 feet. Though both Sheldon and Luckett had slept briefly the night before, both were still in a state of near exhaustion, their faces burned by the rarefied sun that was now shining through the clouds.

Although fatigued and weakened by the long period of super-human effort, during which he had averaged only two or three hours of sleep per day, and the repeated exposure to the oxygen-weak air in which he had worked, Sheldon continued to remove 13 rescue climbers from the 14,300-foot strip and relay them to 10,200 feet. To accomplish the evacuation, he made a total of 18 landings between 3:00 A.M. on May 20 and noon of the next day. Prior to the marathon, he broke for one of his short naps between midnight and 2:00 A.M.

There followed a massive effort with both military and private aircraft to remove the remainder of the rescue teams from the mountain. Thus ended what the news media would herald as "one of the most daredevil and selfless feats in the long history of Alaskan aviation." Today, Sheldon returns only on certain occasions to his 14,300-foot airport on the desolate flank of McKinley's West Buttress. Because of regulations, he uses it only as an emergency landing site, for it is well within the park boundaries.

TO BUILD A FIRE

Jack London

 Day had broken cold and gray, exceedingly cold and gray, when the man turned aside from the main Yukon trail and climbed the high earth-bank, where a dim and little-travelled trail led eastward through the fat spruce timberland. It was a steep bank, and he paused for breath at the top, excusing the act to himself by looking at his watch. It was nine o'clock. There was no sun nor hint of sun, though there was not a cloud in the sky. It was a clear day, and yet there seemed an intangible pall over the face of things, a subtle gloom that made the day dark, and that was due to the absence of sun. This fact did not worry the man. He was used to the lack of sun. It had been days since he had seen the sun, and he knew that a few more days must pass before that cheerful orb, due south, would just peep above the sky line and dip immediately from view.

The man flung a look back along the way he had come. The Yukon lay a mile wide and hidden under three feet of ice. On top of this ice were as many feet of snow. It was all pure white, rolling in gentle undulations where the ice jams of the freeze-up had formed. North and south, as far as his eye could see, it was unbroken white, save for a dark hairline that curved and twisted from around the spruce-covered island to the south, and that curved and twisted away into the north, where it disappeared behind another spruce-covered island. This dark hairline was the trail—the main trail—that led south five hundred miles to the Chilcoot Pass, Dyea, and salt water; and that led north seventy miles to Dawson, and still on to the north a thousand miles to Nulato, and finally to St. Michael, on Bering Sea, a thousand miles and half a thousand more.

But all this—the mysterious, far-reaching hairline trail, the absence of sun from the sky, the tremendous cold, and the strangeness and weirdness of it all—made no impression on the man. It was not because he was long used to it. He was a newcomer in the land, a *chechaquo*, and this was his first winter. The trouble with him was that he was without imagination. He was quick and alert in the things of life, but only in the things, and not in the significances. Fifty degrees below zero meant eighty-odd degrees of frost. Such fact impressed him as being cold and uncomfortable, and that was all. It did not lead him to meditate upon his frailty as a creature of temperature, and upon man's frailty in general, able only to live within certain narrow limits of heat and cold; and from there on it did not lead him to the conjectural field of immortality and man's place in the universe. Fifty degrees below zero stood for a bite of frost that hurt and that must be guarded against by the use of mittens, ear flaps, warm moccasins, and thick socks. Fifty degrees below zero was to him just precisely fifty degrees below zero. That there should be anything more to it than that was a thought that never entered his head.

As he turned to go on, he spat speculatively. There was a sharp, explosive crackle that startled him. He spat again. And again, in the air, before it could fall to the snow, the spittle crackled. He knew that at fifty below spittle crackled on the snow, but this spittle had crackled in the air. Undoubtedly it was colder than fifty below—how much colder he did not know. But the temperature did not matter. He was bound for the old claim on the left fork of Henderson Creek, where the boys were already. They had come over across the divide from the Indian Creek country, while he had come the roundabout way to take a look at the possibilities of getting out logs in the spring from the islands in the Yukon. He would be in to camp by six o'clock; a bit after dark, it was true, but the boys would be there, a fire would be going, and a hot supper would be ready. As for lunch, he pressed his hand against the protruding bundle under his jacket. It was also under his shirt, wrapped up in a handkerchief and lying against the naked skin. It was the only way to keep the biscuits from freezing. He smiled agreeably to himself as he thought of those biscuits, each cut open and sopped in bacon grease, and each enclosing a generous slice of fried bacon.

He plunged in among the big spruce trees. The trail was faint. A foot of snow had fallen since the last sled had passed over, and he was glad he was without a sled, travelling light. In fact, he carried nothing but the lunch wrapped in the handkerchief. He was surprised, however, at the cold. It certainly was cold, he concluded, as he rubbed his numb nose and cheekbones with his mittened hand. He was a warm-whiskered man, but the hair on his face did not protect the high cheekbones and the eager nose that thrust itself aggressively into the frosty air.

At the man's heels trotted a dog, a big native husky, the proper wolf dog, gray-coated and without any visible or temperamental difference from its brother, the wild wolf. The animal was depressed by the tremendous cold. It knew that it was no time for travelling. Its instinct told it a truer tale than was told to the man by the man's judgment. In reality, it was not merely colder than fifty below zero; it was colder than sixty below, than seventy below. It was seventy-five below zero. Since the freezing point is thirty-two above zero, it meant that one hundred and seven degrees of frost obtained. The dog did not know anything about thermometers. Possibly in its brain there was no sharp consciousness of a condition of very cold such as was in the man's brain. But the brute had its instinct. It experienced a vague but menacing apprehension that subdued it and made it slink along at the man's heels, and that made it question eagerly every unwonted movement of the man as if expecting him to go into camp or to seek shelter somewhere and build a fire. The dog had learned fire, and it wanted fire, or else to burrow under the snow and cuddle its warmth away from the air.

The frozen moisture of its breathing had settled on its fur in a fine powder of frost, and especially were its jowls, muzzle, and eyelashes whitened by its crystalled breath. The man's red beard and mustache were likewise frosted, but more solidly, the deposit taking the form of ice and increasing with every warm, moist breath he exhaled. Also, the man was chewing tobacco, and the muzzle of ice held his lips so rigidly that he was unable to clear his chin when he expelled the juice. The result was that a crystal beard of the color and solidity of amber was increasing its length on his chin. If he fell down it would shatter itself, like glass, into brittle fragments. But he did not mind the appendage. It was the penalty all tobacco chewers paid in that country, and he had been out before in two cold snaps. They had not been so cold as this, he knew, but by the spirit thermometer at Sixty Mile he knew they had been registered at fifty below and at fifty-five.

He held on through the level stretch of woods for several miles, crossed a wide flat of nigger heads, and dropped down a bank to the frozen bed of a small stream. This was Henderson Creek, and he knew he was ten miles from the forks. He looked at his watch. It was ten o'clock. He was making four miles an hour, and he calculated that he would arrive at the forks at half-past twelve. He decided to celebrate that event by eating his lunch there.

The dog dropped in again at his heels, with a tail drooping discouragement, as the man swung along the creek bed. The furrow of the old sled trail was plainly visible, but a dozen inches of snow covered the marks of the last runners. In a month no man had come up or down that silent creek. The man held steadily on. He was not much given to thinking, and just then particularly he had nothing to think about save that he would eat lunch at the forks and that at six o'clock he would be in camp with the boys. There was nobody to talk to; and, had there been, speech would have been impossible because of the ice muzzle on his mouth. So he continued monotonously to chew tobacco and to increase the length of his amber beard.

Once in a while the thought reiterated itself that it was very cold and that he had never experienced such cold. As he walked along he rubbed his cheekbones and nose with the back of his mittened hand. He did this automatically, now and again changing hands. But, rub as he would, the instant he stopped his cheekbones went numb, and the following instant the end of his nose went numb. He was sure to frost his cheeks; he knew that, and experienced a pang of regret that he had not devised a nose strap of the sort Bud wore in cold snaps. Such a strap passed across the cheeks, as well, and saved them. But it didn't matter much, after all. What were frosted cheeks? A bit painful, that was all; they were never serious.

Empty as the man's mind was of thoughts, he was keenly observant, and he noticed the changes in the creek, the curves and bends and timber jams, and always he sharply noted where he placed his feet. Once, coming around a bend, he shied abruptly, like a startled horse, curved away from the place where he had been walking, and retreated several paces back along the trail. The creek he knew was frozen clear to the bottom—no creek could contain water in that arctic winter—but he knew also that there were springs that bubbled out from the hillsides and ran along under the snow and on top the ice of the creek. He knew that the coldest snaps never froze these springs, and he knew likewise their danger. They were traps. They hid pools of water under the snow that might be three inches deep, or three feet. Sometimes a skin of ice half an inch thick covered them, and in turn was covered by the snow. Sometimes there were alternate layers of water and ice skin, so that when one broke through he kept on breaking through for a while, sometimes wetting himself to the waist.

That was why he had shied in such panic. He had felt the give under his feet and heard the crackle of a snow-hidden ice skin. And to get his feet wet in such a temperature meant trouble and danger. At the very least it meant delay, for he would be forced to stop and build a fire, and under its protection to bare his feet while he dried his socks and moccasins. He stood and studied the creek bed and its banks, and decided that the flow of water came from the right. He reflected awhile, rubbing his nose and cheeks, then skirted to the left, stepping gingerly and testing the footing for each step. Once clear of the danger, he took a fresh chew of tobacco and swung along at his four-mile gait.

In the course of the next two hours he came upon several similar traps. Usually the snow above the hidden pools had a sunken, candied appearance that advertised the danger. Once again, however, he had a close call; and once, suspecting danger, he compelled the dog to go on in front. The dog did not want to go. It hung back until the man shoved it forward, and then it went quickly across the white, unbroken surface. Suddenly it broke through, floundered to one side, and got away to firmer footing. It had wet its forefeet and legs, and almost immediately the water that clung to it turned to ice. It made quick efforts to lick the ice off its legs, then dropped down in the snow and began to bite out the ice that had formed between the toes. This was a matter of instinct. To permit the ice to remain would mean sore feet. It did not know this. It merely obeyed the mysterious prompting that arose from the deep crypts of its being. But the man knew, having achieved a judgment on the subject, and he removed the mitten from his right hand and helped tear out the ice particles. He did not expose his fingers more than a minute, and was astonished at the swift numbness that smote them. It certainly was cold. He pulled on the mitten hastily, and beat the hand savagely across his chest.

At twelve o'clock the day was at its brightest. Yet the sun was too far south on its winter journey to clear the horizon. The bulge of the earth intervened between it and Henderson Creek, where the man walked under a clear sky at noon and cast no shadow. At half-past twelve, to the minute, he arrived at the forks of the creek. He was pleased at the speed he had made. If he kept it up, he would certainly be with the boys by six. He unbuttoned his jacket and shirt and drew forth his lunch. The action consumed no more than a quarter of a minute, yet in that brief moment the numbness laid hold of the exposed fingers. He did not put the mitten on, but, instead, struck the fingers a dozen sharp smashes against his leg. Then he sat down on a snow-covered log to eat. The sting that followed upon the striking of his fingers against his leg ceased so quickly that he was startled. He had had no chance to take a bite of biscuit. He struck the fingers repeatedly and returned them to the mitten, baring the other hand for the purpose of eating. He tried to take a mouthful, but the ice muzzle prevented. He had forgotten to build a fire and thaw out. He chuckled at his foolishness, and as he chuckled he noted the numbness creeping into the exposed fingers. Also, he noted that the stinging which had first come to his toes when he sat down was already passing away. He wondered whether the toes were warm or numb. He moved them inside the moccasins and decided that they were numb.

He pulled the mitten on hurriedly and stood up. He was a bit frightened. He stamped up and down until the stinging returned into the feet. It certainly was cold, was his thought. That man from Sulphur Creek had spoken the truth when telling how cold it sometimes got in the country. And he had laughed at him at the time! That showed one must not be too sure of things. There was no mistake about it, it *was* cold. He strode up and down, stamping his feet and threshing his arms, until reassured by the returning warmth. Then he got out matches and proceeded to make a fire. From the undergrowth, where high water of the previous spring had lodged a supply of seasoned twigs, he got his firewood. Working carefully from a small beginning, he soon had a roaring fire, over which he thawed the ice from his face and in the protection of which he ate his biscuits. For the moment the cold of space was outwitted. The dog took satisfaction in the fire, stretching out close enough for warmth and far enough away to escape being singed.

When the man had finished, he filled his pipe and took his comfortable time over a smoke. Then he pulled on his mittens, settled the ear flaps of his cap firmly about his ears, and took the creek trail up the left fork. The dog was disappointed and yearned back toward the fire. This man did not know cold. Possibly all the generations of his ancestry had been ignorant of cold, of real cold, of cold one hundred and seven degrees below freezing point. But the dog knew; all its ancestry knew, and it had inherited the knowledge. And it knew that it was not good to walk abroad in such fearful cold. It was the time to lie snug in a hole in the snow and wait for a curtain of cloud to be drawn across the face of outer space whence this cold came. On the other hand, there was no keen intimacy between the dog and the man. The one was the toil slave of the other, and the only caresses it had ever received were the caresses of the whip lash and of harsh and menacing throat sounds that threatened the whip lash. So the dog made no effort to communicate its apprehension to the man. It was not concerned in the welfare of the man; it was for its own sake that it yearned back toward the fire. But the man whistled, and spoke to it with the sound of whip lashes, and the dog swung in at the man's heels and followed after.

The man took a chew of tobacco and proceeded to start a new amber beard. Also, his moist breath quickly powdered with white his mustache, eyebrows, and lashes. There did not seem to be so many springs on the left fork of the Henderson, and for half an hour the man saw no signs of any. And then it happened. At a place where there were no signs, where the soft, unbroken snow seemed to advertise solidity beneath, the man broke through. It was not deep. He wet himself halfway to the knees before he floundered out to the firm crust.

He was angry, and cursed his luck aloud. He had hoped to get into camp with the boys at six o'clock, and this would delay him an hour, for he would have to build a fire and dry out his footgear. This was imperative at that low temperature—he knew that much; and he turned aside to the bank, which he climbed. On top, tangled in the underbrush about the trunks of several small spruce trees, was a high-water deposit of dry firewood—sticks and twigs, principally, but also larger portions of seasoned branches and fine, dry, last year's grasses. He threw down several large pieces on top of the snow. This served for a foundation and prevented the young flame from drowning itself in the snow it otherwise would melt. The flame he got by touching a match to a small shred of birch bark that he took from his pocket. This burned even more readily than paper. Placing it on the foundation, he fed the young flame with wisps of dry grass and with the tiniest dry twigs.

He worked slowly and carefully, keenly aware of his danger. Gradually, as the flame grew stronger, he increased the size of the twigs with which he fed it. He squatted in the snow, pulling the twigs out from their entanglement in the brush and feeding directly to the flame. He knew there must be no failure. When it is seventy-five below zero, a man must not fail in his first attempt to build a fire—that is, if his feet are wet. If his feet are dry, and he fails, he can run along the trail for half a mile and restore his circulation. But the circulation of wet and freezing feet cannot be restored by running when it is seventy-five below. No matter how fast he runs, the wet feet will freeze the harder.

All this the man knew. The old-timer on Sulphur Creek had told him about it the previous fall, and now he was appreciating the advice. Already all sensation had gone out of his feet. To build the fire he had been forced to remove his mittens, and the fingers had quickly gone numb. His pace of four miles an hour had kept his heart pumping blood to the surface of his body and to all the extremities. But the instant he stopped, the action of the pump eased down. The cold of space smote the unprotected tip of the planet, and he, being on that unprotected tip, received the full force of the blow. The blood of his body recoiled before it. The blood was alive, like the dog, and like the dog it wanted to hide away and cover itself up from the fearful cold. So long as he walked four miles an hour, he pumped that blood, willy-nilly, to the surface; but now it ebbed away and sank down into the recesses of his body. The extremities were the first to feel its absence. His wet feet froze the faster, and his exposed fingers numbed the faster, though they had not yet begun to freeze. Nose and cheeks were already freezing, while the skin of all his body chilled as it lost its blood.

But he was safe. Toes and nose and cheeks would be only touched by the frost, for the fire was beginning to burn with strength. He was feeding it with twigs the size of his finger. In another minute he would be able to feed it with branches the size of his wrist, and then he could remove his wet footgear, and, while it dried, he could keep his naked feet warm by the fire, rubbing them at first, of course, with snow. The fire was a success. He was safe. He remembered the advice of the old-timer on Sulphur Creek, and smiled. The old-timer had been very serious in laying down the law that no man must travel alone in the Klondike after fifty below. Well, here he was; he had had the accident; he was alone; and he had saved himself. Those old-timers were rather womanish, some of them, he thought. All a man had to do was to keep his head, and he was all right. Any man who was a man could travel alone. But it was surprising, the rapidity with which his cheeks and nose were freezing. And he had not thought his fingers could go lifeless in so short a time. Lifeless they were, for he could scarcely make them move together to grip a twig, and they seemed remote from his body and from him. When he touched a twig, he had to look and see whether or not he had hold of it. The wires were pretty well down between him and his finger ends.

All of which counted for little. There was the fire, snapping and crackling and promising life with every dancing flame. He started to untie his moccasins. They were coated with ice; the thick German socks were like sheaths of iron halfway to the knees; and the moccasin strings were like rods of steel all twisted and knotted as by some conflagration. For a moment he tugged with his numb fingers, then, realizing the folly of it, he drew his sheath knife.

But before he could cut the strings, it happened. It was his own fault or, rather, his mistake. He should not have built the fire under the spruce tree. He should have built it in the open. But it had been easier to pull the twigs from the brush and drop them directly on the fire. Now the tree under which he had done this carried a weight of snow on its boughs. No wind had blown for weeks, and each bough was fully freighted. Each time he had pulled a twig he had communicated a slight agitation to the tree—an imperceptible agitation, so far as he was concerned, but an agitation sufficient to bring about the disaster. High up in the tree one bough capsized its load of snow. This fell on the boughs beneath, capsizing them. This process continued, spreading out and involved the whole tree. It grew like an avalanche, and it descended without warning upon the man and the fire, and the fire was blotted out! Where it had burned was a mantle of fresh and disordered snow.

The man was shocked. It was as though he had just heard his own sentence of death. For a moment he sat and stared at the spot where the fire had been. Then he grew very calm. Perhaps the old-timer on Sulphur Creek was right. If he had only had a trail mate he would have been in no danger now. The trail mate could have built the fire. Well, it was up to him to build the fire over again, and this second time there must be no failure. Even if he succeeded, he would most likely lose some toes. His feet must be badly frozen by now, and there would be some time before the second fire was ready.

Such were his thoughts, but he did not sit and think them. He was busy all the time they were passing through his mind. He made a new foundation for a fire, this time in the open, where no treacherous tree could blot it out. Next he gathered dry grasses and tiny twigs from the high-water flotsam. He could not bring his fingers together to pull them out, but he was able to gather them by the handful. In this way he got many rotten twigs and bits of green moss that were undesirable, but it was the best he could do. He worked methodically, even collecting an armful of the larger branches to be used later when the fire gathered strength. And all the while the dog sat and watched him, a certain yearning wistfulness in its eyes, for it looked upon him as the fire provider, and the fire was slow in coming.

When all was ready, the man reached in his pocket for a second piece of birch bark. He knew the bark was there, and, though he could not feel it with his fingers, he could hear its crisp rustling as he fumbled for it. Try as he would, he could not clutch hold of it. And all the time, in his consciousness, was the knowledge that each instant his feet were freezing. This thought tended to put him in a panic, but he fought against it and kept calm. He pulled on his mittens with his teeth, and threshed his arms back and forth, beating his hands with all his might against his sides. He did this sitting down, and he stood up to do it; and all the while the dog sat in the snow, its wolf brush of a tail curled around warmly over its forefeet, its sharp wolf ears pricked forward intently as it watched the man. And the man, as he beat and threshed with his arms and hands, felt a great surge of envy as he regarded the creature that was warm and secure in its natural covering.

After a time he was aware of the first faraway signals of sensation in his beaten fingers. The faint tingling grew stronger till it evolved into a stinging ache that was excruciating, but which the man hailed with satisfaction. He stripped the mitten from his right hand and fetched forth the birch bark. The exposed fingers were quickly going numb again. Next he brought out his bunch of sulphur matches. But the tremendous cold had already driven the life out of his fingers. In his effort to separate one match from the others, the whole bunch fell in the snow. He tried to pick it out of the snow, but failed. The dead fingers could neither touch nor clutch. He was very careful. He drove the thought of his freezing feet, and nose, and cheeks, out of his mind, devoting his whole soul to the matches. He watched, using the sense of vision in place of that of touch, and when he saw his fingers on each side the bunch, he closed them—that is, he willed to close them, for the wires were down, and the fingers did not obey. He pulled the mitten on the right hand, and beat it fiercely against his knee. Then, with both mittened hands, he scooped the bunch of matches, along with much snow, into his lap. Yet he was no better off.

After some manipulation he managed to get the bunch between the heels of his mittened hands. In this fashion he carried it to his mouth. The ice crackled and snapped when by a violent effort he opened his mouth. He drew the lower jaw in, curled the upper lip out of the way, and scraped the bunch with his upper teeth in order to separate a match. He succeeded in getting one, which he dropped on his lap. He was no better off. He could not pick it up. Then he devised a way. He picked it up in his teeth and scratched it on his leg. Twenty times he scratched before he succeeded in lighting it. As it flamed he held it with his teeth to the birch bark. But the burning brimstone went up his nostrils and into his lungs, causing him to cough spasmodically. The match fell into the snow and went out.

The old-timer on Sulphur Creek was right, he thought in the moment of controlled despair that ensued: after fifty below, a man should travel with a partner. He beat his hands, but failed in exciting any sensation. Suddenly he bared both hands, removing the mittens with his teeth. He caught the whole bunch between the heels of his hands. His arm muscles not being frozen enabled him to press the hand heels tightly against the matches. Then he scratched the bunch along his leg. It flared into flame, seventy sulphur matches at once! There was no wind to blow them out. He kept his head to one side to escape the strangling fumes, and held the blazing bunch to the birch bark. As he so held it, he became aware of sensation in his hand. His flesh was burning. He could smell it. Deep down below the surface he could feel it. The sensation developed into pain that grew acute. And still he endured it, holding the flame of the matches clumsily to the bark that would not light readily because his own burning hands were in the way, absorbing most of the flame.

At last, when he could endure no more, he jerked his hands apart. The blazing matches fell sizzling into the snow, but the birch bark was alight. He began laying dry grasses and the tiniest twigs on the flame. He could not pick and choose, for he had to lift the fuel between the heels of his hands. Small pieces of rotten wood and green moss clung to the twigs, and he bit them off as well as he could with his teeth. He cherished the flame carefully and awkwardly. It meant life, and it must not perish. The withdrawal of blood from the surface of his body now made him begin to shiver, and he grew more awkward. A large piece of green moss fell squarely on the little fire. He tried to poke it out with his fingers, but his shivering frame made him poke too far, and he disrupted the nucleus of the little fire, the burning grasses and tiny twigs separating and scattering. He tried to poke them together again, but in spite of the tenseness of the effort, his shivering got away with him, and the twigs were hopelessly scattered. Each twig gushed a puff of smoke and went out. The fire provider had failed. As he looked apathetically about him, his eyes chanced on the dog, sitting across the ruins of the fire from him, in the snow, making restless, hunching movements, slightly lifting one forefoot and then the other, shifting its weight back and forth on them with wistful eagerness.

The sight of the dog put a wild idea into his head. He remembered the tale of the man, caught in a blizzard, who killed a steer and crawled inside the carcass, and so was saved. He would kill the dog and bury his hands in the warm body until the numbness went out of them. Then he could build another fire. He spoke to the dog, calling it to him; but in his voice was a strange note of fear that frightened the animal, who had never known the man to speak in such way before. Something was the matter, and its suspicious nature sensed danger—it knew not what danger, but somewhere, somehow, in its brain arose an apprehension of the man. It flattened its ears down at the sound of the man's voice, and its restless, hunching movements and the liftings and shiftings of its forefeet became more pronounced; but it would not come to the man. He got on his hands and knees and crawled toward the dog. This unusual posture again excited suspicion, and the animal sidled mincingly away.

The man sat up in the snow for a moment and struggled for calmness. Then he pulled on his mittens, by means of his teeth, and got upon his feet. He glanced down at first in order to assure himself that he was really standing up, for the absence of sensation in his feet left him unrelated to the earth. His erect position in itself started to drive the webs of suspicion from the dog's mind; and when he spoke peremptorily, with the sound of whip lashes in his voice, the dog rendered its customary allegiance and came to him. As it came within reaching distance, the man lost his control. His arms flashed out to the dog, and he experienced genuine surprise when he discovered that his hands could not clutch, that there was neither bend nor feeling in the fingers. He had forgotten for the moment that they were frozen and that they were freezing more and more. All this happened quickly, and before the animal could get away, he encircled its body with his arms. He sat down in the snow, and in this fashion held the dog, while it snarled and whined and struggled.

But it was all he could do, hold its body encircled in his arms and sit there. He realized that he could not kill the dog. There was no way to do it. With his helpless hands he could neither draw nor hold his sheath knife nor throttle the animal. He released it, and it plunged wildly away, with tail between its legs, and still snarling. It halted forty feet away and surveyed him curiously, with ears sharply pricked forward.

The man looked down at his hands in order to locate them, and found them hanging on the ends of his arms. It struck him as curious that one should have to use his eyes in order to find out where his hands were. He began threshing his arms back and forth, beating the mittened hands against his sides. He did this for five minutes, violently, and his heart pumped enough blood up to the surface to put a stop to his shivering. But no sensation was aroused in the hands. He had an impression that they hung like weights on the ends of his arms, but when he tried to run the impression down, he could not find it.

A certain fear of death, dull and oppressive, came to him. This fear quickly became poignant as he realized that it was no longer a mere matter of freezing his fingers and toes, or of losing his hands and feet, but that it was a matter of life and death with the chances against him. This threw him into a panic, and he turned and ran up the creek bed along the old, dim trail. The dog joined in behind and kept up with him. He ran blindly, without intention, in fear such as he had never known in his life. Slowly, as he plowed and floundered through the snow, he began to see things again—the banks of the creek, the old timber jams, the leafless aspens, and the sky. The running made him feel better. He did not shiver. Maybe, if he ran on, his feet would thaw out; and, anyway, if he ran far enough, he would reach camp and the boys. Without doubt he would lose some fingers and toes and some of his face; but the boys would take care of him, and save the rest of him when he got there. And at the same time there was another thought in his mind that said he would never get to the camp and the boys; that it was too many miles away, that the freezing had too great a start on him, and that he would soon be stiff and dead. This thought he kept in the background and refused to consider. Sometimes it pushed itself forward and demanded to be heard, but he thrust it back and strove to think of other things.

It struck him as curious that he could run at all on feet so frozen that he could not feel them when they struck the earth and took the weight of his body. He seemed to himself to skim along above the surface, and to have no connection with the earth. Somewhere he had once seen a winged Mercury, and he wondered if Mercury felt as he felt when skimming over the earth.

His theory of running until he reached camp and the boys had one flaw in it: he lacked the endurance. Several times he stumbled, and finally he tottered, crumpled up, and fell. When he tried to rise, he failed. He must sit and rest, he decided, and next time he would merely walk and keep on going. As he sat and regained his breath, he noted that he was feeling quite warm and comfortable. He was not shivering, and it even seemed that a warm glow had come to his chest and trunk. And yet, when he touched his nose or cheeks, there was no sensation. Running would not thaw them out. Nor would it thaw out his hands and feet. Then the thought came to him that the frozen portions of his body must be extending. He tried to keep this thought down, to forget it, to think of something else; he was aware of the panicky feeling that it caused, and he was afraid of the panic. But the thought asserted itself, and persisted, until it produced a vision of his body totally frozen. This was too much, and he made another wild run along the trail. Once he slowed down to a walk, but the thought of the freezing extending itself made him run again.

And all the time the dog ran with him, at his heels. When he fell down a second time, it curled its tail over its forefeet and sat in front of him, facing him, curiously eager and intent. The warmth and security of the animal angered him, and he cursed it till it flattened down its ears appeasingly. This time the shivering came more quickly upon the man. He was losing in his battle with the frost. It was creeping into his body from all sides. The thought of it drove him on, but he ran no more than a hundred feet, when he staggered and pitched headlong. It was his last panic. When he had recovered his breath and control, he sat up and entertained in his mind the conception of meeting death with dignity. However, the conception did not come to him in such terms. His idea of it was that he had been making a fool of himself, running around like a chicken with its head cut off—such was the simile that occurred to him. Well, he was bound to freeze anyway, and he might as well take it decently. With this new-found peace of mind came the first glimmerings of drowsiness. A good idea, he thought, to sleep off to death. It was like taking an anesthetic. Freezing was not so bad as people thought. There were lots worse ways to die.

He pictured the boys finding his body next day. Suddenly he found himself with them, coming along the trail and looking for himself. And, still with them, he came around a turn in the trail and found himself lying in the snow. He did not belong with himself any more, for even then he was out of himself, standing with the boys and looking at himself in the snow. It certainly was cold, was his thought. When he got back to the States he could tell the folks what real cold was. He drifted on from this to a vision of the old-timer on Sulphur Creek. He could see him quite clearly, warm and comfortable, and smoking a pipe.

"You were right, old hoss; you were right," the man mumbled to the old-timer of Sulphur Creek.

Then the man drowsed off into what seemed to him the most comfortable and satisfying sleep he had ever known. The dog sat facing him and waiting. The brief day drew to a close in a long, slow twilight. There were no signs of a fire to be made, and, besides, never in the dog's experience had it known a man to sit like that in the snow and make no fire. As the twilight drew on, its eager yearning for the fire mastered it, and with a great lifting and shifting of forefeet, it whined softly, then flattened its ears down in anticipation of being chidden by the man. But the man remained silent. Later the dog whined loudly. And still later it crept close to the man and caught the scent of death. This made the animal bristle and back away. A little longer it delayed, howling under the stars that leaped and danced and shone brightly in the cold sky. Then it turned and trotted up the trail in the direction of the camp it knew, where were the other food providers and fire providers.

PART III

Transformations

THE MAN WHO SWAM
WITH BEAVERS

Nancy Lord

He went as far as his two rented tanks of gas took him, and then the outboard quit and the world was wonderfully quiet, just the very small hollow-sounding slap of water against the drifting metal skiff. Once a line of dark birds flew past, so low and fast and near he heard their delirious wingbeats like a whir of something celestial, not music but less organized, fiber and air, there and gone.

The man sat in the bottom of the boat and let himself rock with the sea, and he looked up at the sun circling the sky and felt it warm on the top of his bare, balding head. After a while he stood up and could see an edge of land in the distance. After a longer time he raised himself again and the shoreline was closer. He could just make out a bouldery coast, v-shaped brown gullies folded into the pleats of high bluffs, dark spruce running uninterrupted along the top. In every other direction there was only open ocean and sky, gray and ceramic blue.

The skiff began to seem wrong to him: too even in its design, the welds like clay fingerprints, a railing and seats, too much domestication, the ridiculous large motor. He took up an oar, paddled with it first on one side of the bow, then on the other. The boat turned in circles, drifted, and came at last to land on the rocky, far-away, springtime shore. The man did not lift the motor; its skeg bumped in the gravel and among the rocks.

He left the boat there, grinding against the shore, and he walked on the beach until the boat was out of sight and he could no longer hear anything that sounded the least bit unnatural. He came to a break in the bluff, a gorge filled with budding greenery and a rattling creek that ran to the sea. The man stopped at the creek edge and sat on a smooth rock.

He did not think. He sat. For forty-five years he had done nothing but think and plan and account for, and he was tired. This city man, a little fat, soft in the gut, divorced (twice), with children who did not seem to care for him; this indoor, unathletic man who had gotten constipated rather than go on summer-camp overnights and who, with multiple academic degrees, had needed lessons from the boat-rental person on how to start an outboard; this man who had rarely spent a moment by himself except in his car (in which, to be sure, he was always accompanied by radio or tapes), in sleep, and one time when as a boy he'd run away from home and hidden in a neighbor's garage for a small part of one afternoon; this man sat on a rock, hunch-shouldered in layers of sporty new clothes, feet spread before him in high, calf-tight rubber boots. He looked at the wide, arcing, endless ocean. He breathed slowly—the sharp air, the hint of salt—and he listened to water—liquid and light running past on one side, the solider silty mass making a slow shore-lap in front. He did not think about what he was doing in the farthest and emptiest place he could find on a map, a continent away from what he had called home. He did not think about what he'd left, or what he was hoping to find. He lifted his head and looked at sky. He lowered it and looked at stones that were round and flat and circled with rings, at pebbles that were gray and black and red and speckled, and at clear, clear water cutting through the beach sand, leaving a honed edge, washing golden grains to the sea. He looked at where the creek met the ocean and saw how the waters mixed, the lens of flawless liquid spreading over gray, the clouding around the edges, swirling, joining.

After a time he noticed something swimming in the water, not far out, parallel to the beach. It had a black nose and dark, marble eyes, a head covered with chestnut-colored fur. It swam effortlessly, like a snake slithering through grass, its motor mechanisms hidden below the gray surface. When it came to the creek, it turned its head landward and floated ashore on the next lump of swell.

The man looked at the dripping animal, a yard from his boot, but it did not seem to be concerned with him. Without pause, it began to walk directly up the center of the creek. In its emergent form, it was no longer a sleek and slithery sea animal but a creature stout and waddling, wet fur stuck to its sides in sun-filled slicks. It dragged behind it a thick, black paddle-tail.

Beavers do not live in the ocean. The man had this single thought, pure reason, absolute knowledge gleaned from a lifetime of school-books, televised nature programs, and colored magazine photos. He had never seen an actual beaver, as far as he knew, but he knew the creature before him was one even as he knew that beavers did not live in salt water. Always, he'd had this keen sense of what was *not* possible. He closed his eyes and opened them, and he was angry with himself for not believing. What was worth believing, if not this beaver tail, beaver fur, entire beaver walking out of an ocean and away from him now, not looking back, climbing over a drift log at the top of the beach, going up the creek?

What was real? Not the life he'd had yesterday, last week, a year and twenty years ago. Had he sat at a desk in an air-conditioned office, picking up telephones, talking about something called insurance? He could no longer see himself there. He could not picture himself in a suit, or a car, or wearing a fluorescent vest in a vain attempt at jogging. He could not hear the sound of high heels on a tile floor or bracelets clacking on a woman's arm, and he could not see a face on the pillow beside him, or the pillow. What was real was the ocean and the sand, the rounded rock beneath him, the beaver walking way, leaving him. Or leading him.

He caught up to the beaver in the trembling willows above the beach. It had stopped at the first green leaves and was eating, plucking and stripping, nibbling down a thin branch like celery. The man watched its graceful hands fold around another branch. It ate from tip to tip with a tiny clicking noise. He became aware of how finely shaped the animal's head was, the brightness of its steady eye. Tufts of wet hair parted back from its face in a manner he could only think of as beguiling, and its whiskers quivered. But what he found most attrac-tive was the fullness over the upper lip, an aspect of overbite that reminded him of some other face long in his past, beyond remem-bering—a face that might have belonged to a teddy bear, a boyhood puppy, some downy girl-child in a smocked dress. It was not the memory that was important but the feeling that came to him now, of absolute acceptance, comfort, something as strong as love.

The beaver took a final chew and began to walk again up the creek, knocking rocks loose to clatter back behind. It glided through a pool, scrambled up a falls that broke over the top of a rock, waddled through ripples. It kept to the most-watered portion of the creek, as though water were its sole element, the centerline by which it steered.

The man followed.

Through willows and leafing alders, around boulders and tree trunks that had slid down the steep, sandy banks on either side, the beaver followed the creek and the man followed the beaver. The water rushed down cascading steps, flowed evenly over shallows. It foamed white and parted around rocks. It roared, deafening, and it tinkled like crystal bells. At the top of the bluff it spilled over one last lip. In the forest beyond, it lay flat and shaded, slowly moving, quiet. The beaver, immersed to its nose, swam again. The man crashed through alders and bushes alongside, pricking himself on devil's club thorns, ducking jagged dead branches. Ancient evergreens, splintered with age and draped with skeins of hairy moss, towered overhead. A spruce hen, unnoticed by the man, perched in a lower branch and merely turned its ruffled head to follow his clumsy passing.

After a time the man became aware of the sound of more running water, a higher-pitched and faster flow. The trees opened up, there was more sky, more light, and then the man stood below a log and stick dam and looked out across a cobalt, satin-finished lake. On the far side, meadows led to more forest and then to snow-covered mountains that pierced billowy clouds. He took the scene in very quickly, felt it strike him in the heart; it was unimaginably beautiful, beyond anything he could have dreamed. In the next instant, he missed the beaver. He climbed to the top of the dam, surprised at how solid it was, and he could see the beaver's reddish round head and rump, heading down the center of the lake, away from him, leaving a v-shaped wake that widened all the way to shore. For several long moments the man stumbled back and forth along the top of the dam, but, short of diving into the water, there seemed no way to stay with the beaver. The brush on both sides of the lake was dense and overhanging, a near-impenetrable jungle. The beaver never looked back.

The man fought off the feeling of abandonment. Beaver or no beaver, he understood that he had arrived at a place of significance. He sat and then lay on top of the dam, spreading his weight over a thousand stick points. He waited. Water trickled with a soothing, clean sound. Offshore, among the early spears of lily pads, fish jumped, plocking in a rhythm the man at first associated with perking coffee and then came to recognize as something far more sublime. The sun stalled just where the trees scraped the sky, lighting one whole side of the lake with a warm yellow glow. From far off came a sudden report. The man recognized the sound, though he'd never, not in his life, heard the slap of a beaver's tail on water. He heard the slap with that part of his being—down at whatever cellular level recorded genetic history—that shot the impulse like echo back to raised hair and quickened heartbeat. He was warned.

Birds sang out from the woods, trills and melodies that crossed over each other, blended, repeated in what the man could only decipher as joyous exaltation. He let the water music and the birdsong wash around him, and he breathed the scent of spruce needles and softened pitch. After a while he sat up and studied the dam: the interweaving of uncountable logs and sticks, all of them tooth sharpened, bare of bark. This was real work, work that held a lake together, a lake that held a world. He looked back across the water. The sun had fallen below the trees, and the surface had darkened. The fish were no longer jumping.

The man had known there were places like this. You found them through the backs of wardrobes or mirrors, or over the walls of secret gardens. He knew the stories from childhood, but he'd not been adventurous enough, then, to want to look in those places, to follow the storybook children. He'd wanted limits; always, he'd been the child who colored within the lines. Though he remembered this now: a print on the wall of the room in which he stayed when he visited his grandmother, a glassy river running through a glen framed by rock walls and fabulous weeping trees, and ladies dancing—fat ladies in bare feet and flimsy gowns. As a boy, the thought had come and stood at the edge of his imagination, like something glimpsed with peripheral vision—the idea of entering the picture, another time, when the fat ladies had gone home, when the glen and the cliffs could have been his own—but he was never brave enough, in his grandmother's house, to try. And then he had gotten too old to imagine such a thing and had forgotten, until this moment, that other moment of invitation.

He lay down again on the dam. It was night, but darkness didn't come. He sought the dark behind closed eyelids and listened to the water as it seeped and dripped and trickled and flowed beneath him. He could feel its movement as though it were passing through his own body, finding its way into crannies of bone and through the loose spots around his heart. Water filled him to the brim. It spoke a language that began with *yes* and *do* and continued in liquid clear syllables an entire vocabulary of possibility.

After a time he became aware of other sounds—soft snorts of breath and a whisper like leaves being swept across water. When he sat up, the lake was patterned with the tracks of two approaching beavers, the nearer one with the butt end of a branch fastened in its teeth. They came to the dam, climbed up over one end of it, and went to work, the one fixing the branch into place, the other scooping mud and a mash of reedy grasses and pressing the mixture, with probing hands and an occasional push of nose, into chinks in the structure. Both beavers were larger and darker than the one he'd followed up the creek. The first one disappeared into the brush; seconds later, alders began to shake. The man heard the grate of incisors on wood and felt his own teeth ache. A third beaver floated down the still lake and shuffled around the dam, gnawing a green stick in half and then turning it in its hands, like a corncob, to strip it of bark. It watched the man as it did this, and he watched the stick turn. This beaver was small, like the one he'd followed up the creek, but had a longer face and an angular, masculine chin.

There were many things that the man could not do, but he forgot what they were. He took mud in his hands and let the sound of water tell him where it should go, and he gathered weeds and rocks to fit among the sticks. In the woods, he circled among trails flattened by beaver tails and witnessed the many rounded stumps and clipped branches, and he dragged back to the dam a fresh branch of alder and tried to fit it along one side. He watched what the beavers ate—not just green bark, but the reedy underwater grasses, and he ate them too and found them sap-sweet and good.

He rested on the top of the dam. One of the large beavers sat very close to him, turned so that its thick, gorgeous, wet-fur back was facing him. The blunt edge of its tail touched his thigh, and he saw the perfect design of it, the overlapping scales and the stiff dark single hairs that grew from between the scales. While the beaver nipped at alder twigs, the man leaned closer. He held his hand out and, ever so carefully, let his fingertips touch fur. The beaver shifted its haunches away and turned a cool eye.

For a moment, a split second only, the man thought he heard the familiar first ring of a fax machine, but then it was gone and he was again in perfect wilderness.

They worked through the night, all of them together, and the man did what he could. In the forest, he used his weight to wrestle down a cut tree that had caught in the branches of another, and the bounce of it against the earth filled him with immense pleasure. The beavers, though, stayed away, and he realized that the tree was too old, had been hung up too long and become too dry to be of use. He tried to understand what the three beavers were to each other and how they felt about him coming into their midst, but each one seemed to work privately within established routines. Sometimes, though, he felt them trading looks behind his back; when he turned and caught their eyes himself, he saw neither wariness nor aggression but only watchfulness.

One beaver left and swam back down the lake, and then another, and then the last, and the man was left alone on top of the dam. He listened to the water trickle through, and it sounded different to him now, less urgent. He knew where the leaks were and he could visualize the exact sticks, the perfect dabs of mud and weed, that would block or seal them, and how each change would alter the sound. He heard the water carry away a particle of chipped wood and a grain of dirt and felt the whole dam settle minutely. The man slept with running water, grinding his teeth.

The next day the large beaver that had not sat beside him returned with two smaller beavers, and they all worked together, the man doing what he could. He moved more adroitly around the dam and was quicker to recognize the suitability of materials and what needed to be done. He began to recognize patterns of birdsong and the creaks of specific trees, and he watched two white-collared loons dive as though they were following the tips of their bills through invisible rends in the lake's surface.

The beavers swam off in the middle of the day, and he could only stand in shin-deep water and watch them go, ruddering with their tails. He walked in the woods and looked at the bell-shaped pink flowers on the berry bushes, but he did not like to go too far from the sound of water. When he returned to the dam, he watched the far end of the lake for any ripple and listened for the slap of tails, but the lake was smooth and still. He looked into the water below his dam-perch and saw the tiny fish there, old leaves, soft green algae, shrimplike bugs. When he looked down the lake again, he thought he saw, amid trees, a traffic light change from green to yellow. His right foot pressed firmly against the dam, speeding up. But no, it was all green, only green, the sun casting meadow and trees in golden light.

He drank cold water, cupped into his hands, from the lake, and his mind filled with a desire for logs of a certain length and circumference, and then he saw those logs interwoven in layers, and that it was possible to build himself a floating structure that would both hold him above the lake and maneuver across it. He went to work, selecting materials from on and around the dam, careful not to disassemble any essential underpinnings. When the beavers returned later, they seemed unconcerned, and when they were gone again, the man found they'd left a stack of new-cut branches, exactly what he needed.

In two days he built his raft, and then he poled and paddled it away from shore and was on the water, floating and dry. A breeze helped push him down the lake, past ghost-gray trunks of flooded trees, slick trails that led up banks and into underbrush, bare drifting sticks. He floated with his face extended over the water, gaze fixed on lily stems and soft bending reeds and, over deeper water, straight down through a sunlit haze of plankton into absolute black. Once, a trout rose from nowhere, flashing its rose-colored, sequined side as it turned, and the man was so stunned by the sight he cried out. Halfway down the lake he came to a beaver lodge, tight against the shore and overgrown with a crown of new alders, and he knew from the age of its sticks and its smell that it was an old house, abandoned. One of the smaller beavers appeared beside the raft, circled, dived with a quick, playful slap of tail, and came up facing him.

The meadow drew closer, pale with old yellow stalks bent over new growth, and the lake stretched off to one side. When he rounded the corner, the man saw another beaver lodge, larger and fresher, like a haystack at the watery corner of the meadow. He paddled to the house, as close as his raft would take him, and he looked at the moat-like canal that circled it, the deep clear place that led inside. Other beavers swam around him, and he saw one beside the house and then gone. He heard noises, the mewing of babies.

For a second his mind filled with a spectral line of cold metal and glass photographs—his children, as bald babies and as toddlers, school-children, high school grads. But they had not mewed. They had screeched and thrown temper tantrums, had been sullen and played obnoxious loud music. It surprised him that instead of actual faces he could only see their images fixed in frames, but then he could only see the frames themselves and a bare wooden desk, and it was as though that distant life was escaping his imagination as much as any other possibilities once had.

This is how he came to live, then, on a pile of logs and sticks in a lake, with beavers. He traveled from end to end to work on the dam, but mostly he stayed near the beaver lodge. When he left his raft, he wandered the shoreline and along paths into the woods, and he learned where the tender branches grew and that it was safest to leave a tree incompletely gnawed for a later wind to blow down. He watched spring grow into summer, the forest thicken and erupt into flowers and then green berries. He saw where the loons nested with their one fuzzy chick and got to know the vocabulary of their cries.

He observed the beavers singly and together, and he came to understand that the large beavers were the parents of the others, except that the young one he'd followed the first day had come down the coast from another, overcrowded pond—was, in fact, an immigrant to the lake, the same as he. As with any first love, the man felt a particular and ineffable attachment to that beaver, but he understood that his place was with the parent beavers, that he had much to learn at (as he thought of it) their knees. Besides, his beaver-love had already paired with an older son recently turned out of the family home, and together they were building a new lodge in the lake's farthest corner. The man helped, in his worshipful, awkward way, by moving logs and clearing pathways.

Most of the time, though, the man stayed close to the one-year-olds and the fearless new kits. When they were tired of wrestling and playing tag, the young ones climbed onto the raft and preened, combing their glossy fur with the nails of their hind feet. They walked over him without the least shyness.

The parents, too, glided around the raft and sometimes brought him a new branch to be worked into its structure. He watched what they did, and how and when, and eventually he began to hear not only their snorts and silences and the clicking of their teeth but also their language, as though it were coming to him in words he could comprehend. They told him things he would not otherwise have known, serious lessons about eagles stealing kits and stories about brother hare and cousin moose. Mostly he listened, but sometimes he tried to respond with stories of his own. He could not remember much, but he sang themes from television shows he'd seen as a boy, Mister Ed the talking horse and M-I-C-K-E-Y-M-O-U-S-E. He remembered Rocky and Bullwinkle but couldn't recall any of their adventures, and so he could only report that such characters existed in cartoons, a fact that was not noted with much interest by anyone, including himself.

He lived in the world he knew now, a world of water and sky and growing things, and if he dreamed, it was only of forests full of young trees, of softest fur and a certain full and whiskered beaver lip. Every now and then some aspect of his earlier life would break through, and for a second he'd think he'd heard the beep of an alarm clock or smelled a turkey roasting, or he'd spot, behind a tree, the square corners of a chest of drawers or a flapping page of newsprint. These were always sudden—a beat or a glimpse or a quick inhalation—and then gone, a single synapse misfired deep in the memory vault of his brain. Their passing left him, always, with a sweaty sense of relief, as though the shadow of an eagle had crossed him and he was once again safe.

A day came in midsummer when the water lilies were open wide and gleaming under the sun and the man, sitting on his raft with his bare legs dangling in the water, realized that the water was no longer cold. He shed his clothes and dove in, and the water washed cool and clean all over him, and he heard, for a long second, what seemed to be music, oboes and clarinets, joyous measures of Beethoven's *Ninth Symphony* that rose and then faded and left him not relieved but elated, with a feeling he could only think of as *connected*. He opened his eyes to green, underwater light, and to beavers—long and sleek and perfectly graceful in their tucks and turns, fur pressed flat to their sides, hands fisted tightly against their chests.

The man swam with beavers. Although he had never been a good swimmer and tended to splash and flail in the water and could not stay under for long, his life now unfolded dimensionally, as though before he'd been stuck on a single flat plane. Below the surface, he saw lily stems sway with his passing and looked up at the dark undersides of pads. He watched fish skit by with vibrating tails and witnessed the wealth of stored food-branches anchored by the beavers in bottom mud. He gasped for breath and dove repeatedly, and the beavers teased him, good-naturedly, charging and veering away, brushing his legs and his shoulders ever so gently.

He swam again the next day, and this time the mother beaver turned toward the house and he knew he should follow. He filled his lungs with air and dove down and under and up through a narrow passageway, into a hollowed chamber. He pulled himself from the water onto a ledge blanketed with dry leaves and wood chips, and he lay on his side with knees tucked to his chest. The chamber was clean and close and smelled of warm wet fur, wood, and moldering earth. Soft light seeped through the crisscross of overhead branches, and beavers snuggled against his back. Never, never, until this moment, had the man felt such absolute bliss, such a sense of finally having made his way home.

From that day on, the man lived in the lodge, coming and going with the beavers. He continued to help with construction and repair, he peeled bark from branches, and he swam. He slept at the center of the beaver family, cushioned in a circle of shifting fur, and was lulled by beaver murmurs. He began to dream beaver dreams of perfect sticks and higher water, of touching his tongue to his own long, chisel-edged teeth. He almost never had those odd, old slips of perception to some other time and place, and when he did, he could make little sense of them. Once he thought he saw a glass punch bowl in water close to shore, and it took him an entire day to puzzle out the name for it and to recall the dim concepts of *flavored drinks in ice* and *party*, utterly foreign people in incomprehensible activity. Ice, though, was a thought that stayed with him; the idea of frozen water was something he could feel, like a chill in his bones.

In time, the lilies shed their ocher petals, the trees bent to a north wind, and the lake grew cold again. The man, finally, could not immerse himself in the water without a gasp of breath, and his shivering and need for burrowing deeper into the heap of beavers became more acute. The weather change troubled him, but he could not give up the interior life of the lodge for a return to an entirely outside existence. Then one day he emerged from the woods with an armload of green sticks, and the entire beaver family was busy on the roof of the lodge, cutting and adjusting. In no time at all they'd fashioned a door he could open from either side. To secure it against the entrance of wolves or bears, the man rigged a sort of latch system that required his dexterous, uniquely sapient abilities to hitch and release. With this door, he was freed from the water passage and could come and go as he liked, in comfort.

In this way they all learned to live with the man's limitations. For each allowance given him by the beavers, he tried in some other way to make up for his deficiencies. His greater size and strength proved a frequent asset, since he could both move heavy logs and topple trees. Together they developed a system in which the beavers gnawed trees to their creaking points and then moved out of the way while the man made the final felling push; as a result, the beavers avoided the danger of falling trees without needing to wait for a windstorm. The beavers and the man, every day, added to their underwater stores of food.

Ice came, crinkling around the edge of the lake in lacy layers and then spreading and hardening across the water. Snow came and lay on the ice and in the woods. All of them slept a great deal—restful, deep, slow-hearted sleep. Periodically, the beavers dragged a new selection of water-softened branches into the chamber, and they ate and then slept again. Sometimes the man went out his door to stand in awe before the drifts of undisturbed snow, the silence broken only by the cracking of lake ice and cold-hardened trees. He loved to listen to the shattering pops of birchwoods and spruce, woods he knew so well now, in their barks, their grains, the itching of his teeth. Nights, he walked the frozen, windblown lake, and stars illumined the world.

Spring followed winter with higher sun and longer days, and sap ran in the trees. The ice softened on the lake. Little by little open water extended around the lodge, and the woods began to empty of snow. Smells returned, and the sounds of running water, and birds. The mother beaver grew fat with new kits; when she rested against the man, he could feel the rumble of many heartbeats.

One morning very early, the beavers and the man woke with a start, as if from the shake of an earthquake. Three bears of enormous size, fresh from their den and very hungry, were attacking the roof of the lodge. Logs creaked and branches splintered, the entire structure rocked. The man reached for his door to check that it was tightly latched, but the bears, grunting and tearing, were digging straight down from the top.

The beavers huddled together, close, bodies flattened to the floor, and the man could feel them tremble with terror. Their eyes in the gloom were bead-bright. A roof log snapped and was jerked aside, and a shower of wood flakes and dust fell onto their backs.

The man, huddled and dusted with the rest, wanted to be heroic. He was large, after all; he had man-sized abilities. A sharp stick, if he had one, he could stab at the bears, fend them off, chase them away. But there were no sharp sticks in the lodge, nothing except ticklish twigs left from a meal, and nothing he could pull loose. The bears ripped apart more roof, and he could see daylight and then glimpses of huge, bobbing, yellow heads. He smelled bear smell, fetid and stifling.

A hole ripped wider and a paw stuck through, a paw bigger than the man's face, with long, straight, amber-colored nails.

The beavers moved, one following another as smooth and continuous as running water, slipping soundlessly into the pool and out the passageway. From outside came the warning slap of the mother beaver's tail, and then others, every tail slapping water.

The bears were ripping at his door.

The man dove, into clear, free, ice-cold water. He felt the cold go through him and stop at his heart, and then he heard again the slapping of tails on water, and they sounded as if they were in his own chest, the pounding of his heart, again and again, exploding outward into light. He kicked his legs and felt himself shoot forward, rapturously sleek and powerful, the pleasure of webbed feet, the ruddering by great black tail. He was warm now, and he was safe, swimming away with beavers.

THE MAN WHO SPENT THE WINTER WITH BEARS

Jennie Masruana Jackson

 Several families from Qallivik traveled to Squirrel River. Qutliuraq's husband, Ikaaq, used to talk about camping there.[1] The way Ikaaq put it, there was "good water" at Squirrel River. He was referring to the abundance of fish, bears, and other good things there.

When people heard all these good things described about the place, they must have decided to go there. Traveling from their homes in Qallivik, people spent their summers and autumns at Squirrel River.

One autumn, one of the men who had been out hiking did not return to camp. It so happened that bears had invited him to their den. The man spent the winter there and hibernated with them.

He found out that the bears slept all winter long, but they knew when spring was approaching. Around that time the bears held a meeting to decide what they would do during the summer.

The bear which the man stayed with told him, "I am not going to the meeting. The others will be here soon to pick me up for the meeting, but you go instead and listen in for me. In the spring, I will go out when everyone else does."

It was beginning to thaw outside, so the meeting would take place soon.

When the other bears came to fetch the man's host, the bear sent the man in his place to attend the meeting. The bears assembled in one of the caves.

The bears discussed what each would do during the summer. One of them said, "When I go out, I will be heading for Ulgunaviaq."

One of the bears commented, "The food that the people of Ulgunaviaq will give you will make you drowsy."

The bear who made that observation was right because he was referring to an arrow. What he meant was that the arrow would make the bear drowsy.

After the meeting was adjourned and the bears were ready to leave their dens, they let the man go home.

When he arrived at the place where his relatives had camped the previous fall, the man told everyone what had happened to him.

[1] As a young girl in the early 1900s, Jennie Jackson saw the remnants of the fish racks at Squirrel River. This would place the timing of the story in the mid-1800s.

AŊUN UKIIRUAQ PISRUKTUANI*

Masruan

 Siksriktuumunguuq Qalliviŋmiut ukua nuliaġiich qapsich imña taakmakŋaqhutiŋli tatkiuŋa Siksriktuumun aurityaġniqsut. Ikaaq Siksriktuumigguuq uqaġuuruq taatnasriuruamik,[1] naaggaqaagguuq qaluuruamik, imiġikmiugguuq naagga.

Itnaġuuruanik imma taatnatchimik tusraa'amiŋ taakmakŋa aurityaġataġniqsut, ukiaksrityaġniqsut, Qalliviŋmiut.

Ukiaġmigguuq ukiaksrisaġataqmata, tarani pisrukataqtuat iḷaŋat aŋiḷaanġitchuq. Sunauvva taatnatchich[1] isiqtitaŋat iŋmiknun. Ukiipchaqługuasrii tarani inimikni. Taragguuq ukiirut taatna.

Ukiikmiuq siñikhuni. Siñigaqniqsurguuq iñuich. Aglaagguuq uvva upinġaksraaq nalunġiññiġaat. Katimapmiraqniqsurguuq, sivunni-uqhutiŋ aniyumiŋ.

Tara taavrumagguuq tukkuan uqautigaa, "Uvaŋauvva kattityiaġni-anġitchuŋa. Aiyasrigaatŋa imma katimaniaqtuat. Ilvich uvva naalaktuaġiaġisirutin. Upinġaksraqpan anigisiruŋa apkua anikpata."

Uvva upinġaksratmun aullaqtuq. Taragguuq taatnatunpiuq.

Aikmatnigguuq tara taamna naalaktuaġiaqtitkaa tuyuġmiani. Tara katiplutiŋ, taatnatchim inaatniptuuq isiqhutiŋ.

Taragguuq uqaġaqniqsut, auraġmi uvani anilġataġutiŋ auravak sułiksraġmiknik taatna. Iḷaŋatgguuq nipliqsuq, "Uvaŋali tara aniyuma Ulġunaviaqsiuġisiruŋa."

Iḷaŋatagguuq tamaakŋa kiugaa, "Ulġunaviat makua niqiksrirrutaat siñiŋniaġnaqtuq."

---

*The Man Who Spent the Winter with Bears, told by Jennie Masruana Jackson, in Inupiaq.

Sunauvva, taragguuq taavruma kiusriruam qaġruq niqqiksrirrutaatnik piñiġaa. "Siñiŋniaġnaqtugguuq," itnaġniġaa.

Tara katimalġaaqhutiŋ taatna piraqniqsulli. Uvva aasrii anniviksraqtiŋ pipman, taamnali anipchaqługu.

Aŋiḷaaqhuni takanuŋa iḷamiñun, ukiaq imma unisaġmiñun. Taatnagguuq tara uqaaqtuaġutigigai tamatkua pisruktit, taavruma Qallivi ŋmiut iḷaŋata aŋiḷaaqami iḷamiñun.

---

[1]Pisruktuanik uvva ukua uqaaqtuqtuat piut.

FAIRY TALE

Sheila Nickerson

You wake one morning
with a swan's wing for an arm.
Lopsided you move to the window;
there is wind and rain over the marsh.
Autumn flocks are flying.
You stretch, unevenly.
Your children, your mate recoil,
their words a gabble around you.
You have no taste for food,
nor can you hold a fork.
Plates, newspapers slip to the floor.
You open the door, reading weather,
trying to remember: just how you reach,
how you find your way into the sky.

QADANALCHEN'S SONG[1]

Peter Kalifornsky

QADANALCHEN'S SONG
Another dark night has come over me.
We may never be able to return home.
But do your best in life.
That is what I do.

QADANALCHEN K'ELIK'A
Ki q'u ke sha nuntalghatl'.
Qint'a hk'u, q'iłdu ki.
Shesh t'qełani.
Shi k'u ki.

---

[1]Peter Kalifornsky's great-great-grandfather, *Qadanalchen*, composed this song while he was at Fort Ross, California sometime between 1811 and 1821. It is said that he was not sure he would ever get back to Cook Inlet, and to ease his loneliness he would sing this song. As he sang, he would take from a small bag a bit of soil he had brought from his home village, and he would rub the soil on the soles of his feet. This was a customary Dena'ina practice to ease the pain of homesickness.

FROM

PETER KALIFORNSKY'S DREAM

Alan S. Boraas

 One day about fifteen years ago, I was sitting with Peter Kalifornsky at his kitchen table. It was a brilliant late-winter day, and the sun streamed in through the windows as we talked for the better part of the afternoon. Gradually, the sun went down and the fading twilight cast a pale, yellow glow around the room. Ordinarily we would have had a light on, but in March the sun sets slowly on the Kenai Peninsula, and dusk had crept up on us.

As the light dwindled there was a lull in the conversation, and we sipped our tea as our minds went their separate ways. After a long pause, Peter looked out the window at the evening shadows and with a distant gaze asked, "How come we are the last?"

Peter was talking about the end of the Outer Inlet dialect of the Dena'ina language. For centuries this dialect was the language of the Kenai Peninsula; then Russians came and later Americans. Little by little the language fell into disuse until finally there were only three speakers left: Peter and his sisters, Mary Nissen and Fedosia Sacaloff.

He didn't expect an answer, and I had none to give him.

ENTERING THE SURROUNDINGS

Ann Fox Chandonnet

Entering the surroundings
one does not speak.
One enters into the chickadee
eating alder seeds
upside down,
and into the dry crunch of snow underfoot.
Enters into the pale moon above the mountains.
Enters into the cold,
the dogs' howls echoing from the ravine
where water dreams and thrashes its legs
under the ice.
Loses one's self entering.
Enters one's self.

GRANDPA JAKWTEEN
IN ECLIPSE

Nora Marks Dauenhauer

He told his family
of when,
as a young man
hunting along a beach,
he was caught in a midday
eclipse of the sun.
According to Tlingit folk belief,
this could turn you
into a stone.
So he climbed up
on a high rock
where he could easily be seen.
(If he had to be a stone,
he wanted to be seen.)
Lucky for us,
he lived to tell the story.
No stone,
and his descendants
are like sand.

WHAT WHALES
AND INFANTS KNOW
(Beluga Point, Turnagain Arm, Alaska)

Kimberley Cornwall

A beluga rising
from the ocean's muddy depths
reshapes its head to make a sound
or take a breath.

I want to come

at air and light like this.
To make my heart
a white arc above the muck of certain days,
and from silence and strange air

send a song

to breach the surface
where what we most need
lives.

ROWING TOWARD THE SPIRIT WORLD

Tom Sexton

After a long day of splitting windfalls
his neighbour had culled from the woods,
his back ached and his hands were covered
with pitch. The ground was still frozen
but spring's red haze was everywhere.
His thoughts turned to the Yup'ik who live
on the vast delta beyond the mountains.
What brought them to believe that everything
embodies spirit, even lice, even stone?
When the axe once again found the block,
he imagined a spirit emerging
from a light-struck chrysalis of heartwood.
When he looked up at last, a boat-shaped cloud
was rowing slowly toward the spirit world.

PART IV

Naming and Unnaming

ALASKA WILDERNESS

EXPLORING THE CENTRAL BROOKS RANGE

Robert Marshall

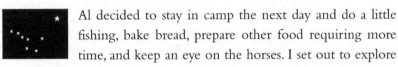 Al decided to stay in camp the next day and do a little fishing, bake bread, prepare other food requiring more time, and keep an eye on the horses. I set out to explore the upper North Fork. Despite the high water, I was able to go most of the way along bars or at the edge of the river. At a few places I had to climb over high banks, and now and then fight short, severe battles with dense alder and willow brush.

The flooded upper North Fork was turbulent and seemed to be unfordable. Leaning trees from cut banks extended over the water and framed shifting vistas of gray mountains, which looked exceptionally wild as a strong wind blew low-flying black scuds across their summits. On either side of the broad U-shaped glacial valley, tremendous rock masses rose into cloud-capped peaks. The highest and most rugged were to the south, forming the two easterly of the "ragged giants" which I had observed from Slatepile Mountain. These great mountains rose probably 5,000–6,000 feet above the valley floor. They were topped by hanging glaciers and sheer precipices. The most westerly of these two mountain masses I called Hanging Glacier. The easterly one was a towering, black, unscalable-looking giant, the highest peak in this section of the Brooks Range. For the moment I called it Matterhorn of the Koyukuk, although it looked less ascendable than its celebrated Swiss namesake. Two years later I renamed it Mount Doonerak and calculated its height at 10,100 feet,[1] based on observations I made with barometer and hypsometer; the name Doonerak I took from an Eskimo word which means a spirit or, as they would translate it, a devil. The Eskimos believe that there are thousands of dooneraks in the world, some beneficent, but generally delighting in making trouble. On my trip up the Alatna River two summers later, I heard more about these dooneraks and their importance to the power of medicine men.

As I walked for hours beneath the stupendous grandeur of these colossal mountains, I felt humble and insignificant.

---

[1]Mount Doonerak was shown with an elevation of 10,000 feet on government maps as late as 1945. Soon thereafter, the U.S. Geological Survey reestimated its height as 8,800 feet and on its 1956 Wiseman quadrangle as 7,610 feet.

GRANDMAMA'S VISIT

June McGlashan Dirks

You show me where
the ice water flows
from the stream.
This is the cold summer
water for the village.

You let me pick forbidden
rain flowers and now I
know it will rain tomorrow.
Just superstition, you say.
And lay them on the table.

And in Aleut, you have a name
for every person.
I know enough to understand
who you speak of in whispers
to the elderly.

Everyone in Akutan,
is allowed to call you
Grandma; and every hunter
knows to bring his catch
to you.

Mothers bring their babies
to you, each day.
You have the time to hold
each one.

I ask you if it is good
to be a grandmama.
You nod and smile.

PLACE OF THE PRETEND PEOPLE: GIFTS FROM A YUP'IK ESKIMO VILLAGE

NATIVE STORE

Carolyn Kremers

 One afternoon in February, I watched my first musk ox butchering. Teddy John had gotten a bull out on the tundra "with only one shot," he said. He and a brother had hauled it home on a big wooden sled behind their snowmachine.

When I walked by their house after school, Teddy and his parents, Nicolas and Athena, were butchering the musk ox on the snow. Teddy's brother was helping. The brother seemed young—maybe twenty?—and very quiet. I had not seen him before. His face was covered with scars.

I stopped to watch. Nicolas nodded and Teddy smiled.

The musk ox had been skinned, and now everyone was working to cut off the legs. In the cold air, the carcass steamed. Athena did most of the cutting with an ulu, getting dark red blood all over her mukluks and her flowered parka, especially the fur-trimmed cuffs. Everybody's bare hands were covered with blood. Besides two ulus, they used two big butcher knives and an axe.

Everyone butchered and piled meat on the sled: four legs and then the carcass, hacked into pieces. Teddy and his father reached inside the abdomen up to their elbows and dragged out a sack of innards and organs, including the heart. The sack was as big as a brown paper grocery bag, only greenish-white. They set it on the snow and three dogs pounced on it, licking and tugging.

Teddy peeled the spinal column from the carcass and fed it to the biggest dog, which gobbled it almost whole. Then he scooped something dark and slimy into a bucket. The liver?

Every few minutes, the family wiped their hands with snow to clean off the blood. Nicolas sent Teddy indoors for a bow saw and Athena asked him to fetch a small saucepan for scooping. Blood and bile.

When Athena lifted one of the musk ox legs onto the sled, the hoof caught in the front pocket of her parka and ripped the pocket half off. She laughed toothlessly. She joked in Yup'ik and chuckled almost the whole time I watched. I think she was delighted with the meat. She didn't seem to mind at all that her clothes were drenched with blood.

The musk ox head lay on the snow, a metal ring in its nose. The lower jaw had been broken off to send to the Department of Fish and Game in Bethel, as required by law. Half-closed wet brown eyes looked at me.

After almost an hour, the family finished piling all the meat on the sled. I stamped my feet, stiff and cold from standing still, and whirled my arms in windmills to thaw my hands. Athena smiled.

Teddy pulled the sled a few yards over to the food cache—gray boards—and unlocked the padlock. Then he and his father and brother (with the scalded face) piled the meat inside. It would freeze quickly there.

The parents gathered the tools from the blood-spattered snow and walked into the house without talking and without nodding goodbye. Nicolas, then Athena. At first I thought they were tired. Or was it a moment of humility and respect that I saw in their hunched shoulders and downcast eyes? How many, many times they must have butchered animals.

The two brothers carried the shaggy brown hide to the family's steambath and hoisted it up on the roof to dry, and I walked on.

★

Nicolas John died of heart failure in the summer of 1989. He was seventy-six.

I have a few photographs of him Yup'ik dancing, crouched on his knees in front of three women dancers, his eyes closed, white ptarmigan tail feathers waving in his hands.

I used to see Nicolas in the Native Store, when I stopped there after school. He would be buying something small like a can of Coca-Cola or a tin of snuff. He wore comfortable wool shirts and red suspenders, and his large ears covered half the side of his head. Sometimes a stubble of whiskers bristled his weathered chin, but he had such a compact body and a wide-eyed look that he always reminded me of a boy.

In spring, when the wind let up and my favorite clerk, Natalia, propped the door open to let the sun stream in, Nicolas sat on a box across from the cash register counter, hands propped on his cane. He greeted all the people who came in: giggling children, hungry teenagers, busy mothers, men back from seal hunting, creaky elders. Everybody knew everybody and they all said hello.

Whenever Nicolas saw me—at the store or church or post office— he nodded, and sometimes he shook my hand. But during my first three months in Tununak, we never said more than hello, probably because I felt intimidated by him. Several people had told me that Nicolas was a spokesperson for the village and for Nelson Island. He was president of Tununak's IRA Council, the organization that governed the village. The council had been established by the Indian Reorganization Act, amended by Congress in 1936 to include Alaska Native villages. Sometimes Nicolas traveled to speak at meetings and to appear on radio and television in Bethel, Nome, Anchorage, even Seattle.

I had never lived in a place where elders were so respected, and I could not speak with most of them because I did not know Yup'ik. I had never been good at small talk, anyway, in English or otherwise. Besides, Nicolas seemed different from my other male elder friends. Nicolas was more reserved, more intense. He wore a serious look instead of a smile. I knew I was that way, too, sometimes. Perhaps he thought the same of me.

One stormy afternoon in January, Nicolas surprised me. Maybe he had enjoyed the school Christmas program, when the elementary students sang songs and the junior high played guitars. Or maybe he just felt talkative that day. Not many people were in the store. Anyway,

I was peering down inside the freezer, looking for some ice cream and reindeer meat, when Nicolas came over and shook my hand. Then he reached behind his big left ear, turned up his hearing aid, and started talking. I had to listen carefully, since he was much shorter than I—at least a foot and a half—and he talked quietly.

"Too much to think about these days," Nicolas said, putting his small hand over his hearing aid and shaking his head. "I go to meetings Outside and I don't know anybody there. I get lonely in those places. Do you know how old Anchorage is? Anchorage is very young. Anchorage begun in 1914, only one acre large then, one acre. Now it is very big, very big. But some Native villages is very old. But very small, not big like Anchorage.

"I use to love to read at the school about Pilgrims. I read and read that story of that first Thanksgiving. I loved that story. How the Indians shared with Pilgrims and Pilgrims were good, religious people. But then look what happen to the Indians later."

I nodded and tried to say something like "I know what you mean," but Nicolas was coughing loudly. He cleared his throat and went on.

"I want to write books. I want to write many books, one after the other, about the land and sea. And our people and our spirits. And send them to Juneau and Anchorage and Canada and Washington and Seattle and the Lower 48, so kass'aqs can really understand about us and what we think. I want all the books to be free. All the books will be free so everyone can read them."

Nicolas looked past me with bright brown eyes. "I don't like to tell kass'aqs what I think. They change it all around. Then they tell other people something different. So I am writing books. In Yup'ik. And they can translate."

He shifted his weight on his cane. I felt I ought to say something— what could I say about books?—but he went on.

"Do you know there is two kind of love? There is love that come from heart and mind…" He pointed to his heart and then to his head. "It is like God's love. It is sincere. It is true. And there is love that come only from mouth and is not real love." He pointed to his mouth. "The man that leave a woman after she have his baby only loves from mouth. Everyone must love everyone else, like their own brother or sister, their own father or mother. Love is what will save us. If there is love, then there is no stealing and lying and cheating."

Nicolas cleared his throat loudly again and gave me a quizzical look. "Even you had nothing to eat, you would not starve. You would not starve, because Native people would feed you and share with you. You would not starve, even you didn't have one penny. Some *kass'aqs* is good, some is bad. I don't trust the bad ones, 'specially not these days. 1991 is not far. Native people must be careful these days, very careful. 'Specially this year."

I knew what Nicolas meant. Since moving to Tununak the previous fall, I had heard much about the Alaska Native Claims Settlement Act, a piece of legislation that I had not been aware of when I lived in Colorado. Passed into law in 1971, ANCSA grouped Alaska Natives into thirteen regional corporations and two hundred village corporations, including Tununak's TRC, the Tununermiut Riniit Corporation, Voices of the People of Tununak.

ANCSA represented a trade between Alaska Native people and the federal government of the United States. In exchange for giving up aboriginal claims to most of the state, Alaska Natives had been awarded $963 million and forty-four million acres of land. The act provided for a twenty-year waiting period, during which Natives were prohibited from selling their stock. The federal government hoped that Natives would become educated about the provisions of the law and that they would organize through the corporations and make informed decisions. In 1991, individual Alaska Natives as well as Alaska Native corporations would be able to sell their land if they wished.

Slowly, I had learned why many Native people, like Nicolas, were suspicious of ANCSA. Lawmakers had not realized that the hierarchical, profit-based nature of the corporate structure was incompatible with Alaska Native traditions of consensus decision-making and of sharing property. Furthermore, Western ideas of land boundaries and of ownership of natural resources were incompatible with Alaska Native practices of hunting and gathering and with Native attitudes toward stewardship of the land and sea.

The people of the Yukon-Kuskokwim Delta had named their corporation Calista. The Worker. Calista represented fifty-seven villages in the Delta, about 16,500 people. It was the most subsistence-based population in Alaska.

Now Nicolas leaned closer to me on his cane and peered from under his eyebrows, right up into my eyes.

"All the problems is getting worser and worser," he said. "In old days, Native people did not use money. They did not have money, not even one cent. They had never had money because they had never needed it. They could get all the food from land and sea. Money is not needed, money is useless. Even if a *kass'aq* would give me millions or trillions of dollars, a whole pile of money," he traced a pile on top of the freezer with his brown hands, "I choose the land. The land is precious, the sea is precious. It is worth more than money. It can feed all the people. I am worried about the land and sea."

Before I could comment, Athena came up behind Nicolas in her navy blue parka. Without looking at me, she huddled against his shoulder like a bundled bird and said something in Yup'ik, her wrinkled face hidden by fur. I caught one English word, *snowmachine.*

Nicolas and Athena talked back and forth, and Nicolas seemed to make a decision. Athena nodded her small, scarfed head, then shuffled back up the aisle past jars of Smucker's grape jam and red cans of Pringles potato chips.

"I go now," Nicolas said, turning down his hearing aid.

I reached out to shake hands.

Tucking his cane under his arm, he took my white hand in both of his and held it. Then he hobbled away.

I looked down at the top of the freezer, where Nicolas had traced the pile of money. Then I stood a minute, staring at my boots. There was nobody else in the store.

NOT TO TALK BAD OF
THE WEATHER

Jerah Chadwick

Avalanche of air
and sideways wet
snow breaks

around my sinking sprawl
home from a high-centered car,
my walking backward

through rip-tide surf.
I'm losing my land legs.
With each great storm

the roads, the well-lit
houses go. After 19 years
what little I know

of the village beneath
the pavement, the local
language few still speak.

*And there is no one to tell me
when the ocean will begin,* the inner
shift of weather.

My purchase on this place is whiteout.

FROM

THE STARS, THE SNOW, THE FIRE

ICE

John Haines

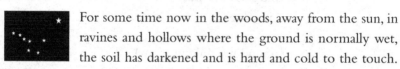 For some time now in the woods, away from the sun, in ravines and hollows where the ground is normally wet, the soil has darkened and is hard and cold to the touch. The deep, shaded mosses have stiffened, and there are tiny crystals of ice in their hairy spaces.

Water has sunken in the pools of the footpaths, in the high ridge trails the small potholes are ringed with transparent ice, or they filled with whitened splinters shattered by the foot of some passing animal. Ice thickened with leaves surrounds a circle of open water in the flowing pool of the creek below the house.

The waters are freezing. From the reedy shallows outward to the centers of the roadside ponds: black ice, clear and hard, with bubbles that are white; opaque patches of shell ice that shatter easily when stepped on. The last ducks that kept to the open centers of the ponds are gone. Clumps of stiff dry grass stand upright there, held fast, casting their shadows on the evening ice.

Now that the steady frost has come, I have been thinking about the river. It is time to take a walk over the sandbars and islands, while there is still so little snow. It is late October; the smaller channels of this broad and braided river have long since stopped flowing, and their remaining pools are frozen. Far out in mid-river, beyond the big, wooded island, a single large channel is now the only open water. The sound of that water, though distant, comes strong and pervasive over

146

the dry land dusted with snow: a deep and swallowed sound, as if the river had ice in its throat.

One afternoon I take the steep path downhill to the riverbed. I make my way across to the big island over sandbar and dusty ice, past bleached piles of driftwood and through waist-high willows and alders, to the gravelly, ice-coated shore of the open channel. I walk a short distance out on the shore ice and stand there, looking at the water. A little wind comes down the wide river, over the frozen bars, smelling of winter.

Free of its summer load of silt, the water is clear in the shallows, incredibly blue and deep in the middle of the channel. Ice is riding in the water, big rafts of it crowding each other, falling through the rapids above me and catching on the bottom stones. Here where the current slackens and deepens, the water is heavy and slow with ice, with more and more ice.

Call it mush ice, or pan ice. It forms at night and during the colder days in the slack water of eddies and shallows: a cold slush that gathers weight and form. Drifting and turning in the backwaters, it is pulled piecemeal into the main current and taken down.

Now on the heavy water great pans of ice are coming, breaking and reforming, drifting with the slowed current: shaggy donuts of ice, ragged squares and oblongs, turning and pushing against each other, islands of ice among lakes of dark blue water. Crowded shoreward by the current, they brush the shore ice with a steady "shsss" as they catch and go by. And with each sheering contact a little of that freezing slush clings to the outer edge of the shore ice. The ice is building outward, ridged and whitened, thickening with each night of frost, with each wave of shallow water that washes it.

As I look intently into the shallows, I see that boulder ice, a soft, shapeless and gluey mass, is forming on some large, rounded stones not far below the surface; the river is freezing from the bottom also. Now and then a piece of that water-soaked ice dislodges and comes to the surface, turning over and over. It is dirty ice, grey and heavy with sand, small stones and debris.

Where it gathers speed in the rapids above, the sound of all this ice and water is loud, rough, and vaguely menacing. As the cold gradually deepens and the sunlight departs in the days to come, the floating ice will become harder and thicker, and the sound of its movement in the water will change to a harsher grinding and crushing. Now in the slowed current before me, it is mostly that steady and seething "shsss" that I hear, and underneath it a softer clinking as of many small glasses breaking against each other.

Standing here, watching the ice come down, I recall past years when I came to a channel much like this one, in mid-October with only an inch or two of snow on the gravel bars, to fish for salmon. I had with me a long pole with a steel hook at one end. Standing very still and quiet where the current slackened against the ice, I watched for the glowing red and pink forms of salmon on their way upriver in the last run of the season. Sometimes I caught sight of one toward mid-channel, beyond reach of my pole; but often they traveled slowly along the edge of the ice, finning and resting, at times nearly motionless in the current. And carefully I extended my gaffhook along the ice edge behind the fish, and with a sudden, strong sweep and jerk I struck the fish through its body and flung it ashore.

The big hook made a nasty gash in the side of the salmon, and fish blood soon stained the snow where I piled them, one by one. If the fish happened to be a female heavy with eggs, the eggs sometimes spilled through the torn side of the fish, to lie pink and golden in the shallow snow with the glazed, mottled bodies of the freezing salmon.

There was something grand and barbaric in that essential, repeated act. To stand there in the snow and cold air toward the end of the year, with a long hook poised above the ice-filled river, was to feel oneself part of something so old that its origin was lost in the sundown of many winters: a feeling intensified, made rich by the smell of ice and cold fish-slime, by the steely color of the winter sky, and the white snow stained with the redness of the salmon: the color of death and the color of winter. And to all this was added the strong black of the ravens that gathered each evening as I was leaving the river, to clean the snow of the spilled eggs and blood.

I caught the big fish one at a time, watching and walking quietly along the edge of the ice, hour after hour. In a few days I had from two to three hundred salmon heaped in scattered mounds in the thin, dry snow of the sandbar, to be packed home a few at a time, heavy and frozen.

I see no salmon now as I stand here by this ice-filled channel, searching its green, bouldery shadows and bluer depths for a telltale flash of crimson. It may be that there is not a good run this fall, that I am too early or too late, or that the fish have taken another way upriver.

★

The sound of the water and the ice before me is one sound, familiar over the years. But there are other sounds of the ice, among them the strange and eerie moaning that comes from under the new ice of the pond when it is walked on, as if some sad spirit in the depth of the pond were trying to speak. In midwinter, a large sheet of ice will split with a rippling crack when the temperature suddenly changes or the ice bed shifts underneath, the ripple traveling fast with a winnowing sound at the end. And there are those small ticking sounds of the ice in the evening when the cold slides toward its deepest zero, as if a thousand hidden insects were chirping bitterly in chorus under the ice and snow. And, finally, the thundering crack and plunge of the shelf ice breaking off in the spring as the rising water wears away its support, a sound that can be heard for miles, like the detonation of a heavy building.

The ice sings, groans, howls and whistles like a living thing. Years ago while hunting caribou in the Alaska Range, I heard the oldest lament of the ice. It was early in October, and the slow freeze was coming down over the empty land and its many lakes. As I stood alone and listening by the roadside one afternoon, I heard on the nearly windless air, as if from the earth itself, a muted and forsaken moaning from the lakes and ponds. It was a sound out of prehistory, of something deeply wounded and abandoned, slowly giving up its life to the cold. There were fleeing ghost-fires on the tundra, white-maned shadows from the bands of caribou fleeing before something I could not see. Then distant shots, gunfire, the sound of a truck rattling by on the frozen road.

Here before me the river is still awake, still speaking in its half-choked mutter and murmur, still surging, pushing its ice-filled way across the open sand and gravel. But one day—it may be soon, or it may be very late, when the solstice sun clears the south horizon—the sound of all this surging and grinding, this shredding and crushing will stop. The great silence will have come, that other sound of the ice, which is almost nothing at all. This channel will have finally filled, the last open water will close, and the river will go under the ice. Snow will drift and cover the ice I stand on.

If I were to walk out here in midwinter, the only sound I would be likely to hear would be the wind, pushing snow across the ice. Only now and then, while walking over the frozen shallows, would I hear under my feet the sound of trickling water finding its way somehow through the ice. And later still, when ice has thickened to a depth of many feet on the deepest channel, I might hear far down in some snow-filled crevice the deep murmur and surge of the river running beneath me.

For the ice and the river under it are never still for long. Again and again throughout this long winter, water will find its way into the open, welling up from a seam in the ice, and spreading over the existing surface of ice and snow to freeze again in a perilous sheet. The wind will bring its dry snow to polish the new ice and turn it into a great slick and glare. Delicate flowers of frost will bloom upon it: small, glittering blossoms standing curled and fragile on the gritty ice, to be scattered by the first passage of air. And over the renewed expanse of ice there will be silence again, the silence of ice, unchanged since the first winter of Earth.

But all this is still to come, as it has come before. Winter is making its way across the land, over slope and plain, bog and high meadow, across lake and pond, outlet and feeder. It has progressed slowly this fall in an even, majestic tread, with a little more frost each night, a little less warmth each day. Meanwhile, the open water of the river flows at my feet, steady and heavy with ice, the deep sound of it filling the land-scape around me.

I turn and walk back to the home shore whose tall yellow bluffs still bare of snow I can see nearly half a mile to the north. I find my way as I came, over dusty sandbars and by old channels, through shrubby stands of willows. The cold, late afternoon sun breaks through its cloud cover and streaks the grey sand mixed with snow.

As it has fallen steadily in the past weeks, the river has left behind many shallow pools, and these are now roofed with ice. When I am close to the main shore I come upon one of them, not far from the wooded bank. The light snow that fell a few days ago has blown away; the ice is polished and is thick enough to stand on. I can see to the bottom without difficulty, as through heavy, dark glass.

I bend over, looking at the debris caught there in the clear, black depth of the ice: I see a few small sticks, and many leaves. There are alder leaves, roughly toothed and still half green; the more delicate birch leaves and aspen leaves, the big, smooth poplar leaves, and narrow leaves from the willows. They are massed or scattered, as they fell quietly or as the wind blew them into the freezing water. Some of them are still fresh in color, glowing yellow and orange; others are mottled with grey and brown. A few older leaves lie sunken and black on the silty bottom. Here and there a pebble of quartz is gleaming. But nothing moves there. It is a still, cold world, something like night, with its own fixed planets and stars.

CROSS TALK

Nora Marks Dauenhauer

When asked by the
census taker
how old she was
Gramma replied,
"Tleil dutoow, tleil dutoow."
The census taker says,
"Fifty two."

Note: Tleil dutoow; Tlingit, "It's not counted."

THERE IS NO WORD
FOR GOODBYE

Mary TallMountain

Sokoya, I said, looking through
    the net of wrinkles into
    wise black pools
    of her eyes.

What do you say in Athabascan
    when you leave each other?
    What is the word
    for goodbye?

A shade of feeling rippled
    the wind-tanned skin,
    Ah, nothing, she said,
    watching the river flash.

She looked at me close.
    We just say, *Tłaa.* That means,
    See you.
    We never leave each other.
    When does your mouth
    say goodbye to your heart?

She touched me light
    as a bluebell.
    You forget when you leave us;

you're so small then.
We don't use that word.

We always think you're coming back,
   but if you don't,
   we'll see you some place else.
   You understand.
   There is no word for goodbye.

WHAT TO BRING
FOR THE NEXT CENTURY

Joseph Enzweiler

A wilderness where you can mend,
a coat, one good pair of shoes,
money that grew in the shadow
of your work. Sew pockets

for simple things, a door key,
orchard wind, meadowlarks
that call from an island in traffic,
wool hat and folding knife,

memories of hay sun-driven,
sweat and the burn of twine.
Useless things, one patch of woods
where you can't be seen, blue horses

pastured in the sun, the greatest
meal you ever ate, one coldest night,
love letters and a book of matches,
the silence at evening that settles

into friends. Bring a hand
to raise by the road at dusk.
Already history has forgotten
your kindness. Bring it all the more.

Fountain pen, flashlight for the dark
to come, goldenrod, a book
to write dreams down. Toothbrush.
Love. Some extra pairs of socks.

PART V

Finding Self and Spirit

HOMESTEAD

John Haines

I

It is nearly thirty years
since I came over Richardson Hill
to pitch a bundle of boards
in the dark, light my fire
and stir with a spoon
old beans in a blackened pot.

II

What did I come for? To see
the shadows waver and leap,
listen to water,
birds in their sleep,
the tremor in old men's voices.

The land gave up its meaning slowly,
as the sun finds day by day
a deeper place in the mountain.

III

Green smoke and white ash,
the split wood smelling of honey.

And the skinned carcass of a fox
flung red in the snow, frost
flowering in the blue, flawed glass—
these are the images.

The canvas tent wall warmed
by a candle, my halfway house
of flies on summer evenings.

IV

One morning in my first winter
I met a tall man set apart
by the crazy cunning in his stare.

From him by tallow light
I heard his tales of Richardson
and Tenderfoot, names and antics
of the pathfinders and squawmen,
Jesus-workers, quick whores.

I followed where his hand
made a hill or a hollow,
saw their mark on the land,
the grass-grown scars,
fallen bailiwicks, and heaps
of iron scaling in the birches.

These shadows came and went.
One still September day
I knew their passing
left no more sound in the land
than a handful of berries
tumbled in a miner's pail.

V

From the spent dream behind me,
Dakotas, reeling Montanas...
came grass fires, and
a black hand mowing the plains.

The floor of the sky littered
with shackled farms,
dust through the window cracks,
a locust cloud eating the harvest.

California, pillar of sandstone,
Oregon still vaguely green—
these are the images.

And now on the high tundra,
willows and water without end,
come shade and a noise like death.

VI

Old ladders shorten, pulled down
in the sod, half-rotted houselogs
heaved by the frost; my hand
spans the distance I have come.

Out of a passion turned searing
and blind, like a theme
of bitter smoke, a deep blow
strikes at the granite roots.

By oil-light and the glint of coal,
forcing its way,
a rougher spirit invades the land,
this ruin carved by a plow.

VII

Here is the place I came to,
the lost bridge, my camp
made of shouldered boards
nailed to this hill, by a road
surveyed out of nowhere.

A door blows aside in the wind,
and a path worn deep to the spring
showers familiar leaves.

A battered dipper shines here
in the dusk; the trees stand close,
their branches are moving,
in flight with the rustling of wings.

FROM

TRAVELS IN ALASKA

John Muir

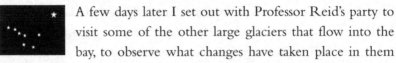A few days later I set out with Professor Reid's party to visit some of the other large glaciers that flow into the bay, to observe what changes have taken place in them since October, 1879, when I first visited and sketched them. We found the upper half of the bay closely choked with bergs, through which it was exceedingly difficult to force a way. After slowly struggling a few miles up the east side, we dragged the whale-boat and canoe over rough rocks into a fine garden and comfortably camped for the night.

The next day was spent in cautiously picking a way across to the west side of the bay; and as the strangely scanty stock of provisions was already about done, and the ice-jam to the northward seemed impenetrable, the party decided to return to the main camp by a comparatively open, roundabout way to the southward, while with the canoe and a handful of food-scraps I pushed on northward. After a hard, anxious struggle, I reached the mouth of the Hugh Miller fiord about sundown, and tried to find a camp-spot on its steep, boulder-bound shore. But no landing-place where it seemed possible to drag the canoe above high-tide mark was discovered after examining a mile or more of this dreary, forbidding barrier, and as night was closing down, I decided to try to grope my way across the mouth of the fiord in the starlight to an open sandy spot on which I had camped in October, 1879, a distance of about three or four miles.

With the utmost caution I picked my way through the sparkling bergs, and after an hour or two of this nerve-trying work, when I was perhaps less than halfway across and dreading the loss of the frail canoe which would include the loss of myself, I came to a pack of very large bergs which loomed threateningly, offering no visible thoroughfare. Paddling and pushing to right and left, I at last discovered a sheer-walled opening about four feet wide and perhaps two hundred feet long, formed apparently by the splitting of a huge iceberg. I hesitated to enter this passage, fearing that the slightest change in the tide-current might close it, but ventured nevertheless, judging that the dangers ahead might not be greater than those I had already passed. When I had got about a third of the way in, I suddenly discovered that the smooth-walled ice-land was growing narrower, and with desperate haste backed out. Just as the bow of the canoe cleared the sheer walls they came together with a growling crunch. Terror-stricken, I turned back, and in an anxious hour or two gladly reached the rock-bound shore that had at first repelled me, determined to stay on guard all night in the canoe or find some place where with the strength that comes in a fight for life I could drag it up the boulder wall beyond ice danger. This at last was happily done about midnight, and with no thought of sleep I went to bed rejoicing.

My bed was two boulders, and as I lay wedged and bent on their up-bulging sides, beguiling the hard, cold time in gazing into the starry sky and across the sparkling bay, magnificent upright bars of light in bright prismatic colors suddenly appeared, marching swiftly in close succession along the northern horizon from west to east as if in dili-gent haste, an auroral display very different from any I had ever before beheld. Once long ago in Wisconsin I saw the heavens draped in rich purple auroral clouds fringed and folded in most magnificent forms; but in this glory of light, so pure, so bright, so enthusiastic in motion, there was nothing in the least cloud-like. The short color-bars, appar-ently about two degrees in height, though blending, seemed to be as well defined as those of the solar spectrum.

How long these glad, eager soldiers of light held on their way I cannot tell; for sense of time was charmed out of mind and the blessed night circled away in measureless rejoicing enthusiasm.

In the early morning after so inspiring a night I launched my canoe feeling able for anything, crossed the mouth of the Hugh Miller fiord, and forced a way three or four miles along the shore of the bay, hoping to reach the Grand Pacific Glacier in front of Mt. Fairweather.

But the farther I went, the ice-pack, instead of showing inviting little open streaks here and there, became so much harder jammed that on some parts of the shore the bergs, drifting south with the tide, were shoving one another out of the water beyond high-tide line. Farther progress to northward was thus rigidly stopped, and now I had to fight for a way back to my cabin, hoping that by good tide luck I might reach it before dark. But at sundown I was less than half-way home, and though very hungry was glad to land on a little rock island with a smooth beach for the canoe and a thicket of alder bushes for fire and bed and a little sleep. But shortly after sundown, while these arrangements were being made, lo and behold another aurora enriching the heavens! and though it proved to be one of the ordinary almost colorless kind, thrusting long, quivering lances toward the zenith from a dark cloudlike base, after last night's wonderful display one's expectations might well be extravagant and I lay wide awake watching.

BRAIDED RIVER

Peggy Shumaker

Under the ice, burbot glide
as if giving birth
to silence.

Someone who held the auger straight
drilled clean through
to moving water,

set gear, then hurried home,
chilled blood pulling back
from the surface, circling deeper

toward the center, the sacred.
As all winter the heartwood
holds the gathered birch sap

still. Ours is only one bend
of a wild, braided river.

WHY SUBSISTENCE IS A MATTER OF CULTURAL SURVIVAL

A YUP'IK POINT OF VIEW

John Active

BLACKFISH

 Once there was a little blackfish swimming up a stream. Every so often he would swim up to the surface and look around.

The first time he had surfaced he saw a camp where people were living. The people there were very careless. Their camp was unkempt and their belongings were strewn around.

He noticed that when the people ate, they ate very carelessly. Bits of whatever they were eating would drop from their hands or out of their mouths as they talked, onto the ground.

The little blackfish heard much wailing and crying at this camp. Those cries were the weeping and wailing of the bits of food that had fallen to the ground.

The dogs were given the leftover scraps of food and these dogs would also leave uneaten bone and bits of food around the ground. These bits of food and bones were also crying.

The little blackfish said to himself, "I'll not swim into this man's fish trap. He's too careless with his food. I don't want my bones stepped on underfoot." The blackfish swam on.

By and by little blackfish came to another camp and there he also saw people eating. These people also were very unkempt and, just as at the first camp, were dropping bits of food onto the ground and throwing their bones to the dogs who were leaving them strewn on the ground. There was much wailing and weeping coming from these bits of food, too.

Little blackfish also noticed that the children were playing with their food, throwing bones at one another as in a game. He thought to himself, "I'll not swim into this man's fish trap. They are also too careless with their food. His children are playing with their food. I am not a game to be played with."

Blackfish swam on and soon he came to another camp. This next camp seemed to be deserted. There were no dogs about or people. But again little blackfish heard much wailing and weeping.

These cries were coming from the stores of many fish rotting in the fish cache. There were no cries coming from strewn-about bones and bits of food on the ground, but the cries were just as horrendous coming from the caches.

Little blackfish said, "I'll not swim into this man's trap. He must be greedy. For all those poor fish are crying and not being eaten. I don't want to be wasted. I'd rather be shared with others in need."

Soon blackfish came to another camp. He listened and there were no cries to be heard. A man, his wife, and two children lived there. Their father also had many dogs which were tied around the camp.

Blackfish noticed there were no bones or bits of food lying about, and, when the family ate, they ate very quietly, being careful not to drop bits of food on the ground. He also saw that they set the edible bones aside for the dogs, and those bones which they knew the dogs would not eat went to a separate pile.

When the family was done eating, their father took the leftovers for the dogs to them and placed them in the dogs' bowls. The other unedibles were taken aside, where people never walked, and buried there. There was no carelessness at their camp and indeed it was very quiet.

Little blackfish said to himself, "At last, a family which appreciates their food. They don't waste or leave bits of food or bones on the ground. They bury their unedibles so there is no crying and wailing at this camp."

Blackfish was overjoyed. He swam about immediately looking for the man's fish trap and, upon finding it, swam into it because he knew he would be eaten very carefully and his bones would not be strewn about on the ground.

LESSONS IN STORYTELLING

The preceding was a story my late grandmother, Maggie Lind, of Bethel, used to tell me when I was a child: her Yup'ik way of teaching me to be careful with my subsistence foods. I think you get the point. If you are wasteful you will become unlucky during your hunting and gathering because the animals will stay away from you. Might be a fable or might not.

Young Yup'ik people are taught by example and through story telling. Here's another regarding waste of subsistence foods and stealing. The late Jimmy Chimegalrea of Napakiak told this story at our kitchen table one day when visiting my grandmother. Chimegalrea was relating a story he had heard from another man, who had the following dream.

The man relates that he dreamt he was drift-netting on the Kuskokwim River. The man drifted and drifted and he didn't seem to have caught anything so he decided to take his net in.

As he pulled the net in there were no fish caught in the first half of the net, but then, near the end, he felt a tug and eagerly waited for the fish to appear.

When it did appear the man was horrified to find what appeared to be a salmon which was nothing but skin and bones but was quite alive.

The man was about to pull the fish into his boat when the fish spoke to him. It said, "Please wait a moment. I have something to tell you."

The fisherman sat down quite surprised and listened. "Look at me," said the fish. "I am skin and bones. This is because your people have been so wasteful. There is coming a time when we fish shall be scarce to you. The people have begun to use us to become rich (probably referring to the commercial fishing industry).

"We fish were not put on this earth to be used this way. We were placed here for you to eat. Look where it has led you. You fish us only to make money and some of you fish us only for our roe and throw the rest of us away.

"Listen, I hear crying and wailing coming from your fish caches. Many of us from last year hang rotting in them. Why should we make ourselves available to you when you waste us and only use us in this way?

"Go and tell your people there is coming a time when there shall be very few fish returning to this river, the Kuskokwim. Those of you who fish honestly for food must go and lock the doors to your caches. The days of want and stealing are coming. Many hearts will be broken when they find that their subsistence-caught fish have been stolen. Even their set nets will be taken without the asking. Be watchful. There, I have said it. Now you can take me if you want."

The man, needless to say, released the fish and told his story to Mr. Chimegalrea, who related it to us so we could pass it on to others who would listen.

Indeed, along the Kuskokwim river of late there has been some reported waste and stealing of fish from fish camps.

People have resorted to locking the doors to their fish caches as fish have been stolen from them, sometimes a family's whole winter's supply.

Only several years ago there was a chum salmon crash on the Kuskokwim and commercial fishermen were broke for a whole year. Even now, there is always the question of whether or not to have a commercial opening because of these low returns.

Elders say fish return to the rivers for a purpose: for us to eat. Not to make money off of, but for subsistence purposes.

They have always said, "While there are fish in the river, fish for them as much as possible. They will sustain you."

BEING A "GENUINE YUP'IK"

Now, in this cash economy some people fish commercially and others even go so far as to fish to sell them illegally. Unfortunately, those who know about people who do this turn the other way and pretend not to notice. This is not the Yup'ik way of doing things.

A cash economy and stealing are not a part of our culture. Subsistence is everything to us. Our traditions teach us this.

I am so very fortunate to have been raised by my grandmother. I am so happy to have had the opportunity to live with her and learn from her.

Maggie Lind was a "genuine Yup'ik," as she used to call herself, and I hope by remembering her teaching I too am a genuine Yup'ik. There are so many things that she taught me by her example that they are too numerous to mention. Perhaps a book might be in order.

Let me give you some examples of what I learned from her about being a genuine Yup'ik.

First and foremost: subsistence is our life. I used to go weeks on end out into the far reaches of the tundra with her to pick berries and watch my uncles hunt and fish.

For instance, when we went picking berries about fifty miles west of Bethel up into the Johnson River, a tributary of the Kuskokwim, we would travel by boat all day, and then somewhere in the Johnson River we'd veer off into one of the many small sloughs.

I would watch my grandmother as she sat at the front of the boat directing my uncle, who was running the outboard motor, to go this way and that, until she would point at the bank and tell him to stop.

I remember thinking to myself: berries don't grow here; there's no tundra. It's a swamp. We'd stop nonetheless and immediately my grandmother would take me and bring me ashore.

Then she would take me into the tall grass until we came to what appeared to be a small mound on the ground and say, "This is where my mother is buried. She was your great grandmother."

We'd linger there a moment and then return to the boat, where she would take out a lunch for us. Before saying grace, she would take a pinch of everything that we were going to eat. A pinch of bread. A pinch of butter or jam. A pinch of dried fish. A pinch of tea or coffee. A pinch of everything that we were going to have for lunch and then take these and go back up onto the land and bury them there.

She told me that she was feeding our ancestors, her family, who were buried there. She also said this was done for a good journey and for the abundance of the subsistence foods we were going after. Today, I still do this. It is my—our—tradition. It is a part of what makes me a "genuine Yup'ik."

I thank my grandmother who taught me these things, who taught me to appreciate our subsistence lifestyle. To take care; not to waste, but to share. To take care not to steal, but to provide for myself so I don't need to steal. To remember my elders, those living and dead, to share with them also. To be watchful at all times that I do not offend the spirits of the fish and animals that I take for food.

To give the beaver or seal that I catch a drink of water so its spirit will not be thirsty. To take from the land only what I can use and to give to the needy if I have enough to share.

Today Yup'ik elders shake their heads and say we Yupiit are losing our culture. Our subsistence lifestyle IS our culture. Without subsistence we will not survive as a people. We Yupiit are different from the many other Native groups in Alaska.

If our culture, our subsistence lifestyle, should disappear, we are no more and there shall not be another kind as we in the entire world.

DECEMBER: FOR SPIRIT

John Morgan

Toward the end of the year—perhaps
this is always the case—I'm

looking for a sign. The mountains, like a
massive wave, rush upon the land.

And striking from below the southwest flange,
sunlight flames the upper sky. Darkness

flows from the east at three in the afternoon.
This month, except for bombs and

hijacked planes, I'd be in Israel.
Is one place better than the next?

Like minor stars three snow-machines
approach downriver with swift, silent speed.

We've trotted to the slough and back.
Overdressed, in double-insulated mittens

and down pants, I watch you chew the snow,
wearing the comfortable hair of a dog.

Hot breath fogs my glasses, while you
nip a thorny branch whose brittle

bract enfolds the rose. In sixteenth-century
Palestine, young rabbis paced the graveyards

of the ancient Torah-tellers, smelt the tar-smell
of redemption burning in their templed hearts.

They knew, no less than Christians do,
this world must be remade. Is it

too late? The other night, at twenty-eight below,
a green aurora branched across the sky.

I watched the sickle moon dip toward
the range. Orion bristled overhead,

jeweled sword, and golden belt of stars:
his state was all the wide and snowy west.

Now that the year is almost dead, have I
done what I set out to do? How have I changed?

At four, the evening star shines through,
the southwest rim is still in flames.

BAMBOO FLY ROD SUITE

REFLECTIONS ON FISHING
AND THE GEOGRAPHY OF GRACE

Frank Soos

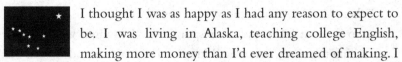 I thought I was as happy as I had any reason to expect to be. I was living in Alaska, teaching college English, making more money than I'd ever dreamed of making. I was just sitting in my office minding my own business. If anybody had asked me I might have said I was free of want, free of desire. One of the guys I work with, Eric Heyne, came by with a faded blue cardboard tube. I had a feeling—the kind of feeling you get when somebody you work with casually drops by in the middle of the day— that whatever he wanted was going to involve effort, a favor of some kind I was about to get roped into. I put on a dangerous face, dragged the corners of my mustache down. But Eric didn't seem to notice. He screwed the cap off the tube and pulled out a long brown sack, all the while talking about this bamboo fishing rod. I told him I didn't know anything about bamboo rods. Which was kind of true. I didn't know much except that with the possible exception of a BMW motorcycle there was no thing in the world I might have wanted more.

As a six-year-old in Virginia standing on the bank of the lake backed up behind Falls Mills Dam where my parents brought us to fish with our worms and bobbers, I saw a man—Dr. Ballard, our town's GP—as he stood in his flat-bottomed skiff casting a popping bug to the edge of a raft of lily pads. He had a sidearm delivery, and the long line whipped out toward me, snakily, enticingly, then pulled back, then came again. Then finally it settled itself on the flat water. Dr. Ballard

flipped the tip of the rod, and from halfway across the lake I could hear
the lure gurgle and pop. We had no boat, and I was too young to
manage my casting reel, too inexperienced to ride my thumb on the
arbor to prevent backlashes from building in my line. My dad cast for
me, and I learned to watch my bobber and wait.

Eric had already taken the fly rod to a fishing tackle store where
the guy had told him his pole was worthless. About all it was good for
was a wall hanging, a conversation piece, something else to stick in the
corner. Eric thought he had enough junk to stick in corners, and I
said I did too. But he said I could have it if I wanted it, could take it
in to another shop for a second opinion. I applied my mother's
famous axiom: If somebody gives you something, take it; if they hit
you, run. [...]

When I said I didn't know anything about bamboo rods, I was
trying to slip out from under a responsibility I thought would come
from telling the truth, that what I knew about bamboo rods was in the
wanting. I had probably wanted one as long as I had been fly-fishing—
since I was twelve years old. I'd never thought I'd own one because I
had priced them in an Orvis catalogue. I can't remember how much
they cost, only that the figure was beyond what I'd imagined ever
paying for a fishing rod, or anything else my twelve-year-old self could
conceive of wanting, for that matter.

Yet I did want such a rod. Laid out handsomely in the catalogue
display, such rods invited me to take them up, to handle their cigar-
shaped cork grips, their clean amber grain, and the lighter bursting nodes
of the cane. I saw how in taking up such a rod I might be changed into
the man in the boat. Hadn't that man himself been changed from the
sometimes-sinister guy humming his little tune to cover the sounds of
the sterilizer door clanking open and the hypodermic being prepared to
some magical figure capable of standing up in a boat, of almost walking
on water? Casting his fly rod, he had made himself beautiful. Beauty. It
was a word you didn't hear much growing up in a coal camp.

Somewhere among the junk gathered in a catchall box on top of my
dad's dresser there can still be found a key chain with a St. Christopher's
medal and a key to the chained oars of a rowboat, a boat perpetually on
loan to us during my high school years. Somewhere in a damp basement

corner stands my dad's cheap fiberglass fly rod. I own a couple of cheap ones myself and one pretty good graphite rod. Now I even own a BMW bike, though it is covered by a plastic tarp and sitting on my aunt's porch back in Virginia. I have sought a narrow satisfaction of my wanting.

I took a closer look at the rod. The guides and tip-tops were rusting and some were missing from the fraying wraps. But it was all there, four pieces, two tips of the same length. *Shakespeare Au Sable* was printed on the tube and *Shakespeare* on the label on the butt section of the rod, and I knew Shakespeare. In the hillbilly fishing world of my boyhood, Shakespeare was top-of-the-line gear. Didn't Fuzzy Elmore himself use nothing but?

I took the rod home and put it in my basement. I left it there maybe four years without thinking about it too much. I think I left it alone for so long because I was a little afraid of it. What if Eric Heyne decided one day that he wanted this fishing rod back? What if in trying to make it fishable I only screwed it up? I thought of the rod in this way as something like an exhumed mammoth's tusk waiting to be carved. Once it was done, done well or done poorly, it was finished. There could only be so many out there, couldn't there? And finally, I wondered what if I did fix it all up and fished with it and liked it and *then* Eric came around and wanted it back? I thought I would be honor-bound to return it. Maybe it was better not to actually allow myself to own it at all but to just let it inhabit my house, a ghostly promise of all my fishing wishes. [...]

We have no cathedral-scale shopping malls in Fairbanks, Alaska. People in need of the pinball experience of a mall shopping orgy must travel to Anchorage or the Lower 48. But we do have the postal service and, through it, a vast and interconnected array of goods available through catalogues. It is from these that I discover all my needs: custom-fitted neoprene waders in a variety of thicknesses, jaunty fishing hats, increasingly elaborate fishing vests. All the doodads and odds and ends to stuff in all those vest pockets. And rods and reels at breathtaking prices. It's in the pages of these catalogues I see I can still buy a newly made split-bamboo rod with two tips beginning at around fifteen hundred dollars.

What am I saying when I laugh and flip the catalogue in the trash and I just say "no"?

It's a harder question than it looks to be. It is the question of my life. How to have the beauty of the man in the boat—the long graceful casts, the rod catching the sunlight as the bamboo flexes, the absolute stillness of the lake—and have it honestly come by? For who would choose a world devoid of beauty—or of desire?

Our basement has taken to flooding on a semiannual basis. This last time, while I was down there moving everything that could be damaged up out of the water, I came upon the blue cardboard tube. My first fear was that I'd finished off the neglectful job somebody else started on this rod and it would now be ready for the Dumpster. But it was fine; it wasn't even damp. I carried it up out of the basement, took it out of its tube and bag, left the four sections sitting in the corner of the living room for a few weeks, thinking that through merely looking at it I would get annoyed at the clutter and motivate myself to do something with the rod.

I took it to the Fly Shop, where a couple of state troopers were deep in a fly and tackle conference with Howie, the owner. I'd put the rod back in its tube and had been driving around with it stashed behind the seat of my truck for a week or so. Spring was coming in, and I guess I was beginning to get worked up about it. I pushed into the conversation, put my rod tube on the counter and began to open it up. The troopers starting guessing what I was going to show them.

"It's a bait casting rod."

"It's some sort of collapsible net or something."

"No, no," I said. "It's an old bamboo fly rod."

"Oh yeah?" they said. Nobody in Alaska fishes with bamboo much, nobody I know but me, and at the time I was a committed doubter. A modern graphite rod, the kind Howie sells, so light, quick, and powerful, could almost be classified as a weapon. It will throw a line across a big Alaskan river; it will help you play in the most ornery of salmon right to your ankles.

I stood away from the pieces of the rod spread across the counter. I still wasn't sure I was willing to claim this thing as my own. A guy wants to watch himself in a place like the Fly Shop, in any sort of guy place—pool rooms, car lots, the high-up bleachers at ball games. To be secure in the company of men is, above all, never to appear foolish. Most likely the rod was junk, and how would I look thinking it could be anything else?

Well, Howie thought it wasn't so valuable that you'd be afraid to fish with it, though he wouldn't use it for anything bigger than trout and grayling. "Fix it up. You'll have some fun with it." I matched up the rusted guides with some brand-new chrome ones and left the shop.

In the Fly Shop, I had seen the promise of the bamboo fly rod's grace. I went back to my truck grinning like a dope in my self-satisfaction, picturing myself already casting this elegant old rod, and replaying Howie's advice on how to fix it, how to fish it. And then I stuck on his line about value. Exactly how valuable was it? And what did he mean by valuable anyway? One way to think of the value of my fly rod was in terms of the work and materials that went into it, the effort I would have to put into it to return it to use. Howie's certification, I decided, was not so much a measure of its monetary value, but of its usefulness, its potential for real fishing. I let myself relax a little because I found I truly wanted this fly rod. Having invested ten bucks or so in its restoration, I couldn't give it up now.

Then something worse happened. I considered the miracle of this rod. How I'd sat in my office so small that the only way to assemble a nine-foot fly rod was on the diagonal, and suddenly I was blessed with a nearly perfect, nearly fishable bamboo rod. I considered that if it came to me so innocently unannounced, then the world must be full of more of them. The attics, garages, and basements of America would be full of these wonderful rods, and some on-the-ball person could get them for free, or next to it. Yard sales, flea markets, estate auctions ought to be teeming with them. If this rod was a nine-foot, six-weight, maybe I should get ahold of a seven-and-a-half-foot, four- or five-weight, maybe an eight-footer, maybe a tiny three-weight. I wanted them all. [...]

Clearly my rod was not worth thousands or even one thousand dollars. That, I thought, would be, in both Howie's mind and my own, too pricey to fall in a creek with. Because I could still fish with it, it had a truer value as a tool. But like certain baseball cards, glass telephone pole resistors, and other popular collectible junk, a fishing rod too can be made valuable because enough people get together and agree. I considered: I had driven it around in my unlocked truck. It could have been stolen. Yet by simply owning this bamboo fly rod, I might become the envy of my friends. The rod would be made useless, then. Valuable, but useless. But if it were less valuable—say in the hundreds—shouldn't I just give it back to Eric now?

Isn't it all just a trick of the mind? A trick that says having is enough? A seduction by the immediate, by what can be held in the hand, by what can be shown as proof? The rod in its current condition was useless, a bundle of sticks. What Howie saw in it was what it might be on the river someday, a fly rod put to its best use by fishing it. [...]

Here's another thing I grew up hearing my mother say: "You don't need *that*," whatever *that* may have been—another model airplane, fishing lure, or odd article of clothing that struck my fancy. Hearing her words usually made me want whatever it was that much more. Years later, there would be a popping lure, yellow head with a white and green polka-dotted body, lying unused in a tray of my tackle box. If my mom recognized it and saw that it had never been in the water, she would say with a certain righteous pleasure, "And you had to have it."

Along the banks of my boyhood lake, dragonflies buzzed the air, indifferent to the distinction between water and land, indifferent to the limits of where a kid could and couldn't go. We called them snake doctors, though we rarely saw snakes and never thought at all about how dragonflies might have doctored any snaky diseases. Shiny, skinny and iridescent, scary, you didn't want one of them to get too close to you, to try to land on you. They darted and hung, sometimes singly, sometimes stacked in pairs. It was a long time later when I understood this was sex, sex flying though the air. But wasn't sex all over them? Wasn't it all over their snake patients, all tongue and slither, demanding that I acknowledge the current of desire running through them, through the world? Didn't they have an animal sense that I feared it? Desire could ruin you—look at the dragonfly carcasses scattered all around the lake. It could change you too, like the snake that left its spent skin along the thwarts and oarlocks of the half-rotten rowboat. [...]

I went home from the Fly Shop and stared at the blue tube for a couple of more weeks, thought wishful thoughts about its contents, then slowly started stripping the rod for restoration. Before I could finish it, before I could actually fish with it, my wife and I went to

Texas to see to her scholarly research. Fresh from Alaska, I saw Texas as a living monument to wanting everything. I understood this when we stood on a single floor of a department store where three acres or so of party dresses stretched out before us. The dresses were packed onto their racks so tightly that it would take the help of a salesperson to pull a few free to try on.

The fishing supply corner of Ched's, where I did my shopping as a boy, foresaw the Texas principle. In a ten-by-ten-foot area were cards full of spinners and spoons, jigs and dry flies sold in pairs inside tiny plastic boxes. The rocky rivers and weedy lakes of the southwest Virginia mountains would take all the equipment you could throw in them. Seeing all those lures, and picturing themselves caught up short when the fish were on the bite, men stocked up their tackle boxes by the fistful.

Once, the company store in our town sold a few dozen dresses on a wholly different premise—that a woman could safely buy a dress and be fairly sure nobody else in town would have one like it. At least, there was the illusion of individuality. In that small corner of Ched's and in the shopping malls of Texas, though, something different took hold. Here were goods so thick they ought to be carried out in wheelbarrows. Such plenty encouraged a wild spirit of duplication. Everybody ought to have everything.

"You can only fish with one at a time" was what my mother said. She had never seen Fuzzy Elmore hunting the largemouth bass. Fuzzy Elmore had a sheaf of identical Shakespeare Wonder Rods arrayed in the stern of his boat, each set up with a different lure, and I saw that here was another principle: Be prepared for all contingencies.

I went to a couple of Texas-sized flea markets, read the want ads, went to likely looking estate sales and antique auctions. There I saw confirmed what I already believed, that people are like locusts. Once provoked, they will consume everything in sight—cups with broken handles, dying potted plants, worn shoes that don't really fit—with no thought as to what good any of it might finally do them. At one flea market, my wife bought some cowboy boots; I bought a racquetball racket. I found no bamboo fly rods, and not finding them seemed to only heighten my wanting. I had to have more. [...]

I went to the fly-fishing store in Austin, a small, unassuming place located upstairs from the High Times Tea Room and Brain Gym. A Range Rover was parked outside, and inside the store, its owner and his pal were pricing their first-ever fly outfits. The guy running the store was loading them up with the most expensive gear he had to offer, and they weren't flinching. I knew what would happen to all that gear, and the salesman probably did too. These two middle-aged guys' idea of fishing up to this moment was cruising a reservoir, flipping lures out of an overpowered, sparkle-painted bass boat. They would never put in the time to learn fly-fishing, and being too vain to fish badly in public, they'd soon ditch their fancy new gear in a closet.

When I got my chance, I asked the guy where I might look for older bamboo rods. He said they didn't deal in bamboo rods. I told him about my own rod and my start on its restoration.

"Yeah, well, that's a production rod. I see a couple of those a month. They're kind of heavy and slow."

"Oh," I said. "I was hoping to find a smaller rod that'd take a lighter line."

"So is everybody," he told me. And he gave me a newspaper full of bamboo rods in various states of repair and disrepair, all for sale.

Now I knew. I knew "production rod" was a mild insult in the world of bamboo rods. It was like owning a Ford or Chevrolet in the company of people who drove Jaguars. And I knew that the guy who'd told my colleague the rod was worthless also was right in his way. A Shakespeare rod like mine in excellent shape was worth about what I would have put into the restoration: new guides, wraps, varnish, and time—provided my time were worth about a dollar an hour. The only way it would be worth having was to fix it up, take it to the river and put it to use. [...]

I cherish certain prejudices about fly-fishing. One is that fly-fishers are better people all around—more inclined to put their fish back in the river, less inclined to leave their litter on the banks. Your better fishing people are fly-fishers. Doesn't that notion come from the old four-porthole Buick crowd, though? Fly-fishers are better people simply because they're drawn from a better class of people, a more monied class?

Could it be that a fly-fisher studies the natural world, the world of fish and the bugs they eat, the places they live and cannot live until it must become clear to him that he's a part of it all, part of great nature too? I want to believe this. Fish are greedy rascals, as greedy as people. Fear of getting eaten is all that keeps their greed in check. Each fish we catch is a fish that has allowed its greed to overcome its sense of caution.

Like all the rest of America, I have been successfully conditioned to want everything. But thanks to my mother and father, I have been conditioned more strongly in the ways of cheapness. My basement is filled with the by-products of greed and cheapness—cardboard boxes the computer came in, the stereo came in; trash bags filled with accumulated foam peanuts; scrap lumber; bins of nuts, bolts, and screws, many picked up out of the roadway. I can't throw them away because, as Mom says, "Better to have it and not need it than to need it and not have it." Keeping this junk around has one good end: it triggers momentary attacks of revulsion at having so much stuff. I cannot throw it away, but just looking at it wears me out. I give up on wanting more.

Out fishing for trout, I find the river full of dead king salmon. These swam—and have consumed themselves in the swimming—a couple of hundred river miles to get here. They have changed from silver-bright to a deep glowing red to a mottled and tattered dun, their flesh rotting off them even as they lived. Their carcasses lie on the banks, ride in the eddies, jam between river rocks like water-logged tree limbs. They've done what they came here to do.

I could never drop two thousand dollars in a day on fishing tackle like the two rich Range Roving Texans. What, though, is so bad about that? There are worse things to spend money on. And since they'll most likely never wind up crowding my favorite fishing holes, why should I care? Sometime up the road, their mint-condition late-twentieth-century equipment will be a bargain to be found in another collectors' newsletter.

This cheapness is not a virtue. It's niggling and dangerous and causes a person to drive on bald tires, to go too long between oil changes and delay painting the house until it needs scraping and a new undercoat too. It causes me to buy things I don't particularly need because they are on sale and I cannot resist this fraudulent way of saving. In this way I prove I am as dumb as a fish. We all are. We always have been.

And yet there is this to be said about my wanting. It is a good, necessary thing. A thing I'm afraid no fish can understand. Beauty, grace, desire—elements of the human animal's world—what is life without them? I am thinking of a grayling, oblivious to its wonder-working ways, holding in the current where Cripple Creek dumps into the Chatanika River. Moving out into the faster water to take a fly, it is a fish living its fishy life.

Caught and in my hand, the fish is a miracle of calico blue with spotted circles down its sides. Sunlight shakes rainbowed iridescence from its scales. Its long dorsal fin trails like a pennant, and in its other fins, rays of turquoise and orange shoot through the black. [...]

A cast of my bamboo rod has directed me to this place, this moment, this fish. And I find that it is not in the having but in the using of this rod that I have found a way to live with my wanting. Catching this grayling has let me see again the beauty in the world; it has done me some good. I let the fish slip back into the water and it settles to the bottom, near my feet, confused and worn out. In a few minutes it will be back in the water column again, feeding. I will move on up the river, casting under the cut banks, into the eddies, and behind the sweepers. To be out on the river is enough.

PART VI

Feminine and Masculine Unbound

NAWALASKAM AGAGAA: WOMAN OF OUNALASHKA

Jerah Chadwick

—Webber drawing, 1778, upon the original's return
to Unalaska after 222 years

We'd known you only from etchings,
edition after edition of Cook's visit
as if described by someone
to someone and so on. So different

your face, not forced into some
mannered pose, no stylized aboriginal,
dulled eyes or prim
out-thrust chin. With high collared

suk, chin and cheek tattoos
distinct as the loose strands
of this drawing, your human hair.
You look with hesitant smile,

a woman stepping out of history,
written by certain ones
for certain ones, a woman sent
to greet strangers as was custom,

as women before were
also sent, offering hospitality

to those who would bring disease,
death. What your people endured

the first twenty-three years
of contact can only be guessed,
what you endured after
standing for this quick sketch.

Note: *Suk* is a woman's parka.

FROM

WORKING ON THE EDGE

SURVIVING IN THE WORLD'S MOST DANGEROUS PROFESSION:
KING CRAB FISHING ON ALASKA'S HIGH SEAS

Spike Walker

 Only twenty years old, Susey Wagner was an attractive 135-pound brunette. She'd grown up in the Santa Cruz Mountains of California and had never been more than an hour from home when she first decided to escape north to Alaska. Eighteen at the time, Susey had grown tired of the Cloud-9 truck stop clientele, where, while still in high school, she earned minimum wages cooking and serving up food, beer, and wine.

From the beginning, she knew she would never be satisfied with just existing or only getting by. It was important to her to get somewhere, to achieve something and do it on her own.

The day Susey received her high school diploma, she moved out of her parents' house and away from her five brothers and sisters. She supported herself with a $3.25-an-hour job, while on the side she hired out as a baby-sitter and sold her own handmade pottery at flea markets.

Only days after arriving in Kodiak, Susey found a job in the local Skookum Chief Cannery. When she discovered that the cannery would allow you to work as many hours as you could remain standing on your feet, she thought she had died and gone to heaven. The opportunity to get ahead was everywhere, and Susey was soon taking home three hundred dollars a week.

For an entire year, Susey bunked at the Skookum Chief Cannery. She began, as did every new cannery worker, by butchering and packing crab on the processing line. But she was interested in taking a more physically demanding role and soon got assigned to off-load crab boats. It didn't take Susey long to realize that the plum off-loading job was to run the crane mounted on top of the dock. Seated inside in the dry protection of an enclosed cabin, its operator lowered and raised brailers (baskets) full of crab from the holds of crab boats tied to the Skookum Chief docks. Susey was determined to win that coveted job, but when she approached the dock foreman, he flatly refused. Later, when she went off shift, he made it clear to everyone that he didn't want any *woman* running that crane.

Susey was stubborn, and she bided her time, becoming friends with the main crane operator. Often, after she had finished pitching a brailerful of crab, while her male coworkers took their usual well-earned break, Susey would climb out of the boat's hold and scale the thirty feet of ladders to the dock up top for a chance to run the crane, if only for a few moments. If the foreman was nowhere near, the crane operator often would give her his seat and stand beside her and give her lessons.

When the crab-stuffed brailer had been hoisted up onto the cannery dock, Susey would lower another empty brailer into the ship hold far below. She would then race back down the dockside ladder, swing down into the crab hold, and begin tossing crab into the next brailer as fast as her hands could fly. Through such tireless persistence, extra effort, and hustle, Susey gradually learned to operate the crane.

Then one windy, rain-washed night, the crane operator broke his ankle, and no one but Susey knew how to run the crane. The cannery foreman had left specific orders that Susey not be allowed to run the crane. He "didn't want any foul-ups!" But he was gone at the time, and there was an impatient skipper stalking the docks with 65,000 pounds of tanner crab growing weaker in his live holding tanks with each passing hour. So Susey climbed up into the cabin of the crane, sat herself down in front of the controls, and went to work.

She was still hard at work off-loading the ship when the cannery foreman reappeared. It was a cold and rainy night, and the windows of the crane's cabin were fogged up—with the exception of the rag-wiped hole through which Susey watched and made her calculations—and the foreman didn't notice her. In fact, the cannery foreman didn't even learn of the crane operator's injury for some time. When he did, he inquired as to who, exactly, *was* running the crane.

"What?" he cried when he discovered that his orders had been ignored.

"But I wouldn't worry," one cannery worker offered. "She's doing fine! Hell, she's been running it for the past five hours! She's nearly done now. She's off-loaded the whole ship!"

The cannery foreman grew quiet and said nothing, but from that day on, Susey ran the crane.

Soon, however, Susey's attention turned toward the excitement—and money—of going to sea, and she set herself a new goal, one that had never been accomplished before by a woman: to win for herself a berth aboard a ship in the king crab fleet.

In the beginning, she freely admits, she lucked upon a fine teacher—her future boyfriend and a longtime fisherman, Danny O'Malley. It was O'Malley who first opened the way for her to go to sea. He worked on the ninety-foot crab boat *Atlantico* (skippered by Bill Jacobson). When the opportunity for her to go along on a free trip presented itself, she jumped at the chance.

Once at sea, Susey watched carefully, absorbing the crew's every move. She noticed how they manhandled the huge 750-pound crab pots, but soon realized that the work required more than brute strength. It also involved stamina, positioning, and technique, things Susey thought she could manage in time. The bulk of the work on deck involved coiling lines, tying knots, pitching crabs, chopping bait, and filling bait jars—as well as getting along with those around her.

Susey also paid close attention to the deck lingo and sometimes felt she was learning a foreign language. When the *Atlantico* docked in Kodiak at the end of that first journey to sea, skipper Bill Jacobson called down from the wheelhouse for her to secure the hawser line to the cannery piling. Susey could only shrug her shoulders. She honestly had no idea what the man was talking about. What was a hawser? And what was piling?

But Susey soon learned, and the next time the *Atlantico* tied up dockside, the skipper didn't have to say anything.

Susey went to sea for an entire month without pay—just for the experience. She worked outside on deck right along with the rest of the crewmen. Afterward, back inside the wheelhouse, she cleaned the galley, washed the cupboards, and swept and scrubbed the floors. She learned early on that when a good deckhand saw something to do, he or she went to it and didn't walk on and leave it for the next guy to do.

She worked hard and tried not to complain, and by the end of the month, she had improved dramatically on deck. She intentionally avoided the bull-like job of pushing pots, but in all other areas she worked right along with the rest of the crewmen. Life at sea was new and intriguing, but it was more than that, those who were with her in the beginning will tell you.

Watchful of Susey thoughout her apprenticeship, *Atlantico* skipper Bill Jacobson recalls that she was "genuinely curious" about the sea around her. She took naturally to the knots, the navigation, and the endless work. She maintained a good attitude and managed to blend in with the men. Somehow, Susey fit.

Then one day, she remembers, an *Atlantico* crewman "slipped on the dock, of all places," and injured himself. Bill Jacobson took on Susey as the man's temporary replacement—at 4 percent of the crab boat's gross, a half share.

As one of the first skippers to do such a thing, Jacobson caught a lot of static. One couldn't call it flak so much as an attitude, a general disbelief. Everyone thought a woman wasn't physically capable of deck work. It was a male culture, and a man's work. The attitude shared by many of the fishermen Susey encountered was a direct "throwback to the Middle Ages," she recalls. But Susey remained.

During her first trip out as a half-share crewwoman, she worked twenty-two hours with hardly a break. Then the weather grew danger-ously rough. The size of the waves dumfounded her. Susey was terrified.

"You've been doing this for seven years?" she asked her boyfriend, Danny O'Malley. He nodded. "Hey, I'm telling you, as soon as this damned ship gets back to port, I'm getting off. And I'm not coming back out here again, I can tell you that!"

Susey was sure of it: These men were out of their ever-loving, oceangoing minds! The storm passed, though, and when three days later the *Atlantico* returned to port and Susey collected two thousand dollars for her efforts, she thought again. The *Atlantico* would be leaving the following morning at first light. The job was still hers.

Then, as she held the check, she made an astounding discovery. She noticed that not one cent had been deducted from her check—not IRS, nor Social Security, nor Employment Security, nor union fees, nor state taxes. The government looked upon fishermen (and fisherwomen) as self-employed workers. Susey was galvanized. At long last, she sensed financial independence. She was young and single, and dependent upon no one. There was no describing such a feeling. When the ship left again at dawn, Susey was on it.

On deck at sea, Susey's "secret weapon" was a stubborn refusal to let the physical demands of the work defeat her. Through the weeks and months of work it took to get where she had, she had come to believe that it was "mostly mental."

"Move quick, and keep moving!" was her motto on deck. Whenever her back knotted unbearably or her knees grew shaky with fatigue and threatened to collapse from under her, she would recall what she had been through and what she had left. She would remember the long hot months in the Sacramento Valley, and she could picture the white stucco greasy spoon café where she had waited tables for twelve sweaty hours a day, enduring rudeness and ten-cent tips with the same philosophic smile.

It was during her second trip to sea aboard the *Atlantico* that Susey was forced to prove herself. They were stacking gear (hauling crab pots on board and storing them on deck) in heavy seas off the Portlock Banks when by a quirk of chance and circumstance, she found herself alone on the pitching, rolling deck, clinging to one of the giant eight-foot-tall, 750-pound crab pots. With the rest of the crew involved in coiling and other important matters, Susey knew she was faced with a decision.

She either could cling to the giant crab pot and wait for help or she could try pushing it across the deck by herself. At the time, she recalls, the pitch and roll of the boat was "perfect for pushing" if, that is, one knew when to push and how to go about it. With her adrenaline pumping, Susey made her decision. Bending forward at the waist, she stooped under the horizontal middle support bar of the pot and moved forward until it came to rest behind her head and across her shoulders. Like a weight lifter, she squatted low and, most important, timed her next move perfectly with the roll of the boat. At the critical moment, she pushed with everything she had.

With her legs pumping hard, Susey screamed as she drove ahead. She was sure someone had joined her in the effort and was now behind her, pushing with her. But when she stopped, she found herself standing at the far end of the deck. And when she stood up and glanced around her, she found she was all alone. She had pushed the largest of Alaskan king crab pots the entire length of the deck, and she had done it by herself.

It was a feat that did not go unnoticed, for when she raised up and turned to look around, she saw her male crewmates standing silent and frozen in place, staring dumbfoundedly at her from the opposite end of the deck.

Toward the end of the trip, one crewman came up to her and remarked, "You know, we didn't think you would be able to hold your own like you did. You really did good, young lady. Honestly, we didn't think you'd make it!"

As the *Atlantico* drew near town, deck boss Danny O'Malley yelled to her. "You know, Susey," he said, "they ruined a hell of a man when they cut the balls off you!" O'Malley never was one to tiptoe around a thing.

HARRY

Phoebe Newman

Hardly a day goes by
that I don't think of him
lying so still
with his thumbs curving outward,
his fingers flat
against the mattress.
I think of him even
while I am climbing
the mountain, staring
at the huge green spruce,
their trunks green
with moss and lichen
and rich ferns uncurling
all along, the fragrance
of water everywhere.
I imagine that he smells water
inside his dreaming,
that he is still twenty-three,
a magical age for a man,
watching the waves grow higher
and higher around the boat,
suddenly knowing
that his disbelieving gaze alone
cannot stop the swelling, the noise,
nor can his fervent, blasphemous prayers.
I think of him when I smell

black water, the fierce
blackness of bear. I imagine
the water swirling across his feet,
loosening them from the deck,
the dull weight of his fearful body
swept lightly into the sea,
the cascades of bubbles rising
from his surprised mouth, his
dancing hair, his palms pushing
against the downward thrust
of the storm. I imagine
his father's face filled
with rain and grief, trying
to see him, trying to find him
huddled within the swells,
cradled in some gentle pocket
of current, and seeing nothing
but the stinging rain, his
tears and curses soundless
in the surprising, sudden darkness
until something flashes, and it is
a leg or an arm, a piece of flannel
or a boot, and the two men left on board
grab the gaffs and swing madly
at the thing, rising and falling,
swirling away and near, until one
finds hold and they pull and pull,
then make the long cold journey home,
silent and staring at Harry,
who is leaking Pacific from his ears
and his nose, his jaw slung open
with surprise even now, eight years later,
in the narrow bed in this yellow room
where we move with careless gestures,
with open eyes and wonderings,
discussing the pallor of his skin,

the wonderful green tinge
of his eyelids, the stillness,
how absolutely undemanding
the body can be,
near drowned,
simply longing for sleep.

RAISING OURSELVES

A Gwich'in Coming of Age Story
from the Yukon River

Velma Wallis

 Back in Fort Yukon, my mother was drinking more. For the first time in her life, she could walk away from her responsibilities. Drinking made it possible for her to ignore the needs of her children.

I tried to stay in school, but whenever Mom was not home I found tasks that demanded my attention. The house needed cleaning. Meals needed cooking. Clothes needed washing. The more housework there was to do, the less important school seemed.

By then I had become shy around my peers. Staying home was easier than having to face old friends who had changed beyond recognition. Part of me wanted to act grown-up too, but without the drinking and smoking. So I tried to bypass my teenage years and move directly into my mother's position. I felt that this would insulate me from the changing world outside. I would stay home and play house.

Two teachers who did not want me to quit school sent books down to the house so that I might study at home, but I was a lost cause. As my mother was drawn into alcoholism, I played her role in the family.

I was glad to be the pretend mom. There was Barry, who would always seem older than I was, and at times when I became a recluse, he would act as the go-between for the world and I. Billy, Brady, Benny, and Becky were the younger ones that Barry and I cared for when Mom was not around.

Since childhood, my mother had done everything for Barry and me. Now it was time for us to do things on our own. When I cooked my first hamburger patty, it shrank to a fraction of its original size. We pondered how to keep it from getting so small as we ate the tiny burgers along with the flaky instant mashed potatoes that I never mixed well enough.

My mother never used a cookbook. Even when making bread she would dig out her big bowl and proceed to add all of the ingredients by memory. When I cooked, I had to recall what I had seen her do. My siblings would try to help.

Once I tried to cook duck soup, and my older brother Johnny, who was visiting that day, taste-tested it. He kept shaking his head as if trying to pinpoint the cause of its funny flavor. Finally he said, "Oh, I know what's going on!"

"You forgot to singe off the feathers," he explained, pulling a couple duck feathers out of his mouth. He could have helped with the cooking, but he and the two other older brothers, Jimmy and David, had their own lives and we hardly ever saw them.

After my father died, the food he had caught and stored the season before slowly ran out, and my mother applied for food stamps. It took us a while to adjust to Mom's decision to use the vouchers, remembering how my father had frowned upon the idea.

In the past, Uptown people came down to ask my father for fish and meat. My father was always generous, so even after his death the women from Uptown asked for food. I would get angry and swear a blue streak at them. Could they not see that without my father we no longer had any wild food in our freezer?

We were lucky that my father had a few friends who remembered him. Every Christmas morning, Sampson Peter Jr. from Uptown came down to give us two large king salmon. We looked forward to this feast, for our diet now consisted of what our monthly food stamps could buy at the store. We bought wieners, hamburger, and chicken, as well as staples like sugar, tea, macaroni, rice, butter, Pilot Boy crackers, and grease.

Our meals were not balanced, for we would devour all the crackers with tea in a matter of days. Our bodies were always craving food, and most of the time we ate poorly and gained weight.

★
* ★
* ★ ★
* ★

In the years she drank, my mother made it her pattern to drink for two weeks straight every month. For the other two weeks that she was sober, my mother shopped, filling the cupboards and the freezer with food. She would bake loaves of bread and a big pan of biscuits for us. After doing all of this, she got a certain look in her eyes, and we knew her time on the streets was fast approaching. Her two weeks of sobriety usually ended with her putting on her jacket, telling us that she was going to go visiting and would be back shortly. Often two full weeks would pass before she returned.

Sometimes she returned home drunk and fought with us. She accused us of stealing her wine and her food stamps, and would try to bully us as my father once did. She cried about the past, and then threatened that if we didn't shape up she would throw us out of the house. The list of what she said and did was long, and most of the time we learned to listen to her, knowing it was only the drink that made her do those things. But when she brought home her street friends and they tried to use the house for drinking, I would have to fight them all. Then my mother and I would literally have a fist fight. When she managed to hit me, I felt like I hated her.

Once one of her friends had diarrhea all over the place, and I had to clean our house from ceiling to floor to get rid of the smell. I cleaned up her friend and ushered all of her friends out of the house, even though they looked like they needed to be hospitalized, they were so ill from drinking. Those were the times I wished they would all die, including my mother. I rationalized that they were better off dead.

When she sobered up, we loved her as if nothing had happened. But I was fast growing into a hateful teenager. I hated alcohol with a passion. I would rather die than touch the stuff.

★
* ★
* ★ ★
* ★

The 1970s were a time when everyone in Fort Yukon seemed to be drinking. A whole generation of us spent our teenage years with no concept of rules, discipline, or order. Nor did we feel safe at any time of day.

One night, a drunk crept into the house and sat by the couch where I was sleeping. When I woke I escorted him out of the house. From then on, the doors were kept locked.

Often a neighbor would come running wild-eyed to tell us about someone being killed or maimed uptown. We all seemed addicted to bad news. If someone didn't get killed, raped, or stabbed Friday or Saturday night, then on Sunday night people would suffer from withdrawal.

Even my older brothers joined in the fray of violence. One of my older brothers once came from Uptown staggering drunk and decided to bother us. He started a chainsaw and began to chase us with it. We were horrified. Not knowing what kind of drugs he was on, we ran for our lives to the nearby clinic to call the police. The nurse on duty was a crusty old soul who had been there for more years than she cared to count, and when we begged to use her phone she became disgusted with the whole situation.

"You people never learn!" she said, slamming the door in our faces.

We stood on the porch and wondered who else we could turn to for our protection as the cold winter wind touched our faces in the night. We knew then that no one could or would protect us. Even if the police showed up, they were just as burnt out and bitter as the nurse, so we had to hide until our brother sobered up.

Another time this brother got drunk and kicked down the door of our cabin, acting as if he would stab me. My mother, who was also drunk, went down on her knees and begged him not to do it. I stood there hoping he would.

In time I came to hate my older brothers. It riled me to no end that when they were sober they did not seem to remember the terrors they had inflicted on the rest of us.

Christmas always meant hardship for me. One Christmas when my father was still alive, I caught my younger siblings eating the scraps that I had scraped into a pan as I cleaned the mounds of pots, pans, and dishes. I cried as I watched them eat the scraps, but there was nothing I could do—they were hungry and there was nothing else to eat.

Barry and I tried to make Christmas festive for the younger ones. We never had money for presents, but our sister Linda, the only sister still living in town, made sure we each had a gift and some candy. Despite the fact that she supported her family of four, she always tried to help us no matter how it strained her budget.

Only once did Barry and I plan a month ahead and order a few gifts for the kids from the Sears Roebuck catalog. We sat on pins and needles, right up until midnight on Christmas Eve. The postmaster was a young man who understood our plight. He kept the post office open late for those who were still waiting for our packages to arrive. I thought it akin to a miracle when our box arrived that night.

It got to the point that the less we had in the way of a family, the more we tried to fill the void with material goods. Christmas became an obsession. Barry and I dreamed of having a good Christmas, which meant a sober mother and a time of togetherness like our family once had. When things did not work out that way, we would just call it a bad Christmas.

When I was sixteen, I worked for a program called Homehelpers. My job was to clean the house of an old woman named Blanche Strom.

Blanche was confined to a wheelchair. She reminded me of an owl with those watchful eyes that neither smiled nor acknowledged you in any way. She wanted her house sparkling clean, and she missed nothing. More than once she took the mop out of my hands and showed me how to mop the floor properly.

"You kids today just want everything easy," she barked at me as she briskly mopped the floor. She did not seem to need any help as she wheeled herself about, showing me how she wanted her dishes washed and her floors cleaned. It seemed that the only thing she couldn't do was empty her chamber pot outside.

One day, Blanche sat eyeing me as I mopped her floor. Sweat dripped down my nose, and my face was red with exertion. I was trying to get the job done quickly so I could escape her scrutiny.

"How come you guys never use your father's land?" she asked.

I did not know how to respond. I had not thought about my father's trapline since Itchoo had tried to save her tree years before.

The old woman persisted.

"Don't you know that if you don't use that land, it will be taken over by others?" she demanded.

I nodded, but I did not care.

"Your grandmother Martha Wallis used that land too. You guys should use it instead of wasting it. Already I hear that a young man is taking over your land. You need to use that land before it's too late."

I finished mopping and nodded my head as if I intended to take her advice. In reality I just wanted to go home.

A day later Blanche died. She had seemed perfectly lively the day before. I could not bring myself to collect the pay owned to me, for in some ways she had given me the first inkling of respect that I had had in years.

Later I questioned Jimmy about the land. Jimmy, who was four years older and once had been my tormentor, was now the quiet brother. He didn't say much, but what he did say always made complete sense.

"There's nothing there," Jimmy said. "It's all burnt out. Me and Alex tried to trap there, but there's nothing to trap so we just left."

"Take me up there," I told my brother.

At first he thought I was joking. When he realized that I was serious, he told me to pack. He would take me to my family's trapline.

Being on my own as a teenager allowed me to recklessly do whatever popped into my mind. Jimmy was used to my adventurous spirit, and he knew once I decided on something it would be a waste of time trying to change my mind.

I wanted to learn to trap and to live off the land. The younger kids were bigger now, and we all had learned to become latchkey kids, independent in our own way. Billy and Brady had begun the early stages of dropping out of school. As my mother had tried to keep Barry and me in school to no avail, I tried to do so with them but I never bothered them too much about school because they hauled firewood and snared rabbits when they weren't in school. Without them, we would not have had firewood or rabbit meat. The younger children, Benny and Becky, were able to care for themselves too.

Blanche had set in my mind a romantic notion about Itchoo's land. I was intrigued that it belonged to us, for we had nothing. Fort Yukon had become quite predictable. I wanted to know what was out there. My mother had always spoken fondly of the land she and my father had lived upon in the first years of their marriage. They had many adventures up there, and the fur had been plentiful. I wanted to be a trapper like my father and grandmother.

Many times I had watched my father pack for a trip into the woods. Trying to remember what he had taken, I gathered up all the necessary supplies: Swede saw, ax, knife, file, lots of matches, first-aid kit, camping candles, flashlight, a wooden grub-box filled with kitchen implements, and a couple cardboard boxes filled with store-bought food, plus my clothes and books.

I asked my younger siblings if they wanted to join me on this adventure, and only Billy, who was two years younger, volunteered. Billy was a reluctant participant in all of my endeavors only because he was tender-hearted toward those who come up with nutty ideas. He must have felt sorry for his goofy older sister who always tried crazy things. He said he knew how to trap. But he wanted to join up with me later, for he said he would have to gather his own supplies and find some dogs. So I felt I was set for the winter.

Together, Jimmy and I piled all the supplies on the narrow toboggan and strapped them down. We were ready to head out into the woods.

LOVE SONG[*]

Semyon Pan'kov

My breath, I have it here![1]
My bones, I have them here!
My flesh, I have it here!
With it I seek you, with it I find you.
But speak to me, say something nice to me!

Ánĝing anĝix̂takúqingáan wáya!
Qagnáning qagnax̂takúqingáan wáya!
Úlung úlux̂takúqingáan wáya!
Ímin ilgáasadang, ímin ukúusadang.
Táĝa núng tunúda, iĝamánan núng hída!

---

*The Eastern Aluet words to this song were published in 1846 in a collection of songs gathered by the Russian Orthodox priest and missionary Ivan Veniaminov. A footnote in that collection states that these songs were collected, written down, and translated into Russian by an Unalaskan interpreter, the Aleut Semyon Pan'kov. In 1909–1910, the song appeared in English in a collection gathered by Waldemar Jochelson.

[1]Each line of the song was sung twice.

SHADOWS ON THE KOYUKUK

Sidney Huntington

In 1900 or 1901, my mother married Victor Bifelt, a Finn who, like about a thousand other gold rushers, had left the Klondike to prospect and trap in the Koyukuk country, where gold had been found several years earlier. "Marriage" in the Koyukuk in those days consisted of choosing a partner and living together. If the relationship was good, it lasted; if not, it dissolved. At that time, whites lived with Koyukon women and there were no bad feelings; only the missionaries resented the practice. Although rough-spoken, Bifelt treated my mother well, and the couple had two children, Fred and Edith.

They settled in Hogatza country, where they built a log cabin two miles below where Hog River runs into the Koyukuk, and Victor began trapping. He enjoyed living off the land, but he wanted the whole country to himself and didn't respect the claims of others.

Their nearest neighbors were at Hog River, where Ned Regan, another white, lived with my mother's mother, Old Mama. These two had a daughter, Eliza, whose son, George Attla, would one day become one of Alaska's most famous sled dog racers. Ned trapped from his Hog River cabin.

Victor and Ned soon began quarreling over trapline rights. Koyukon Indians often spend a winter, or even years, in close vicinity of friends or family without conflict, but these two hard-headed white men were different. Since they both sold firewood to steam-boats plying the Koyukuk River and were trapping in the same region, they regarded each other as competitors and their dispute became a bitter feud.

Bifelt accused Regan of trying to take over his trapline and ordered him off, but Regan refused to leave. "I'm going to kill Regan," Victor told my mother one day, after the two men had clashed. Frightened, the next day while Victor was away, my mother hurried to Hog River to warn Old Mama. "Get out of here, Mama," she warned. "I think Victor is going to shoot Regan." Old Mama, capable of living from the land as were all Athapaskan women of her generation, fled and set up camp some distance away.

She also told Regan about Victor's threat. "I'll take care of myself," Regan said, and my mother ran home.

The murder must have taken place a short time later. Regan saw Bifelt coming, and when Bifelt walked through the door of his cabin, Regan blasted him at point-blank range with a double-barreled shotgun.

Details have dimmed with time, but I believe Regan buried Bifelt before he went to the Yukon River village of Nulato to turn himself in. The local marshal took Regan to Nome, the center of legal matters in those gold rush days.

The following summer, two deputies arrived to take Anna to Nome as a witness at the trial set for February of the next year. They had to leave quickly before the winter freeze closed their watery route. Anna was distraught at having to leave her children with Old Mama for the many months that she would be gone. Also, she dreaded going into forbidden Eskimo territory. All her life she had heard of the savagery of the Eskimos, who always killed Athapaskans who ventured into their country, with the truce between her father and Schilikuk being one of few exceptions.

My mother was a small woman (about ninety pounds) but she was strong and courageous. With the deputies, she traveled by river steamer down the Koyukuk and Yukon rivers to St. Michael, near the mouth of the Yukon. From there they crossed Norton Sound on the last steamboat of the year, arriving at Nome in September 1904. Theirs was a trip of about 1,000 miles, although the distance was only 320 miles as the raven flies.

Nome was then a chaotic boomtown filled with gold rushers. Tents stretched along the beach in a solid row for five miles. The air was filled with sounds of hammering and sawing, as residents prepared for the coming subarctic winter. To Anna, who had spent her life in the wilderness, twenty-five people was a crowd; Nome, with its 15,000-plus people was a nightmare. The court found a couple to feed and house Anna until the trial. Throughout the five-month wait, she was homesick and lonely.

At the trial, she was the only witness. She knew little English and the court could find no one to translate her Athapaskan. Regan, who pleaded self-defense, was found innocent and released.

After the trail, Anna insisted on returning home to her children immediately. The judge explained that the court would pay her way back by the same river route she had come, but that she would have to wait until breakup in the spring. Until then, the way was locked in ice and snow, and boats were useless.

So a determined Anna decided to walk overland. The distance was at least 400 miles, the midwinter weather was severe, she didn't know the way, and she'd be crossing Eskimo country.

There was no stopping her, so the judge gave her a document explaining that she was a responsibility of the court and was going by foot from Nome to her home on the Koyukuk River. It warned that anyone who harmed her would be punished by the United States government, and concluded, "The court will appreciate any help or guidance this woman receives."

"Show this to people. They will help," the judge promised.

Although Anna didn't know the route across the windswept, mostly treeless coastal land, she knew that Schilikuk lived on the Kobuk River, which she had learned was somewhere beyond Candle, on the north side of the Seward Peninsula. So she set out to walk to Candle.

The well-traveled, snowy trails between Nome and Candle were packed, so Anna did not need snowshoes. When she became confused, she waited until someone came along and showed them her note. Each time she received directions.

She walked from sunup until dark. Each night she wrapped herself in a blanket and burrowed into a snowbank for the insulation it provided, or shivered near a small fire. She stopped at roadhouses along the way for food and rest. Invariably, when the owners read her note, they refused the gold coins she offered in payment. Usually they tried to dissuade her from continuing her long, dangerous journey, but when they sensed her determination they gave her food, matches, and other supplies. Soon word spread along the trail about the tiny Indian woman who was returning to her family in the distant Interior.

Anna's moccasins were worn out when she reached Candle near the end of March. A miner and his wife took her into their home, and she made several new pairs of moccasins while regaining her strength. In late April, the Koyukon "month of the spring crust," she set out again, now on snowshoes, with a small pack on her back, walking north and east into country with no human trails.

In May, the Koyukon "month boats are put in the water," near the Arctic Circle light floods the land around the clock although snow still lingers. Anna traveled mostly at night when it was cool and the snow was crisp and frozen and easy to walk on, and she rested during the warm days when the snow became too mushy to support her. Rivers were still frozen, so she had no difficulty crossing them.

Using the sun as her guide, she traveled toward where people had said the Kobuk River lay. Spring storms delayed her, but she pressed on, some days traveling only a few miles. A lone prospector she encountered gave her several ptarmigan and some matches. He was the last person she saw for weeks. Days passed in a blur.

Breakup came in June, and the ice in the Kobuk River went out. This is a major turning point in the North, for without ice on the rivers, travelers must build rafts to cross deep rivers. Bogs, frozen and level in winter, become impassable, and travelers must detour around them. Anna walked upstream, following a bank of the deep and swift Kobuk as the easiest and most direct route into the mountains that separate the coast from the Interior. For food she snared rabbits, ate roots, and found berries of the previous year that became exposed when the snow melted. In this Koyukon "month when everything grows," swarms of mosquitoes hatched, adding to her hardship.

One July morning she awoke to see an Eskimo boy staring at her from a few feet away. In a moment he was gone. With a sinking heart, she remembered his look of elation. Weary and weak from hunger, she was sure that he would return with other Eskimos to kill her.

Soon a small band of Eskimos called to her from a distance. Anna thought that her end had come. She didn't try to escape, for she knew it was hopeless. When the Eskimos neared, her heart leaped, for with the boy she had seen, and several other Eskimos, was Schilikuk, the trader friend of her father.

His words warmed her heart. "I saw your father two months ago. He had word you were walking home and asked me to watch for you. My son has been waiting for you along the river every day."

Anna rested, regaining her strength in the home of the hospitable Eskimo. "You had better stay with me until March, when your father and I trade again," Schilikuk told her one day. "You can go with me to the trading place."

"No. I must get back to my children. I've been gone nearly a year now. I won't wait until March," she declared.

Schilikuk, seeing her determination, persuaded her to stay at least until snow came again and the rivers froze so she could travel more easily. Each winter he trapped at the head of the 100-mile-distant Pah River. Anna agreed to wait and go with him to the Pah. From there she faced a ten-day walk across the mountains to the Hogatza River and her father's home.

Fall came, and finally, snow fell and the rivers froze. The Eskimo family loaded sleds, harnessed dogs, and started the journey to the headwaters of the Pah. Several times they stopped for a few days to hunt caribou. They reached the trapping grounds in November.

A few days later the old Eskimo walked with Anna to the top of the low divide that separates the coast from the Koyukuk drainage of Interior Alaska. He pointed across No Man's Land toward the distant Hogatza River, saying, "There is your home. You'll have to go alone from here. I don't dare take you any farther."

She was dressed in warm furs. Her pack held caribou meat and dried fish, warm blankets, matches, and an axe. On her small feet she wore moccasins she had made for herself and snowshoes made by Schilikuk. After thanking him, she set out alone down the slope, bravely heading for the spruce forests of Koyukuk country.

Now she was in the kind of land she knew. Timber was abundant, so firewood and shelter were easy to find. She spent the nights next to the trunks of big spruce trees, sheltered by thick green branches and warmed by fires she built of dead lower limbs. Green spruce branches, piled deep, insulated her from the snow and provided her with a comfortable bed.

After ten days of solitude, Anna came upon snowshoe tracks. She followed them for a day until, suddenly, she recognized the place: she was only five miles from her father's winter cabin. She stopped and forced herself to eat, because she wanted to walk to her father with her head up, strong and proud, not tottering as if exhausted from her long trek.

As Anna approached the cabin, chained sled dogs set up a clamor. The door was flung open, and a man stepped out, rifle in hand.

"Who comes?" he called in the Koyukon Athapaskan.

"It is me, Anna," she replied in the same tongue.

The man was Hog River Johnny, her brother. Their reunion was joyous, for the two were close. When she told of her long solo trek home, he could scarcely believe it.

"Tell me again," he asked, wanting to hear repeatedly about various adventures she had experienced.

The reunion was tinged with sadness, for her father had died the previous summer. But her children were well. News of Anna's overland journey from Nome spread swiftly by moccasin telegraph. No Koyukon hunter, much less a slip of an unarmed woman, had ever dared to traverse the forbidden Eskimo land to the west. Not only had she braved the fierce Eskimos, she had traveled on foot for hundreds of miles, much of it alone, during parts of two winters. She was regarded with awe by the close-knit Koyukon people for years.

My uncle Weaselheart, another of my mother's brothers, once told me that the family was convinced that my mother would never return. When they learned that she had started her long trek, they thought she would be seized by some Eskimo wanting a woman. Such an act would have been much easier than the raids that Eskimos once made into Koyukuk country to steal women. Many tales of such raids were told and retold among the Koyukon people, and, of course, those raids perpetuated the traditional war.

Weaselheart also told me that for the help Schilikuk gave Anna, our family rewarded him with many gifts, including a large pile of wolverine furs of the finest quality.

Ned Regan returned to the Koyukuk, wanting to take up with Old Mama where he had left off, but she would have nothing to do with him. The Indians of the Koyukuk felt that his killing of Victor Bifelt had been too cold-blooded, and it made them uneasy around him. He left the Koyukuk never to return.

During my three-quarters of a century, I have watched with pleasure as the ancient hostility between the Koyukon Athapaskans and the Eskimos has gradually disappeared. Today there is only friendly rivalry between our peoples. And the legend of the long overland journey made by my mother from Nome to the Koyukuk is still recounted by the Koyukon people.

A COLD DAY FOR MURDER

Dana Stabenow

They came out of the south late that morning on a black-and-silver Ski-doo LT. The driver had thick eyebrows and a thicker beard and a lush fur ruff around his hood, all rimmed with frost from the moisture of his breath. He was a big man, made larger by parka, down bib overalls, fur mukluks and thick fur gauntlets. His teeth were bared in a grin that was half-snarl. He looked like John Wayne ready to run the claim jumpers off his gold mine on that old White Mountain just a little southeast of Nome, if John Wayne had been outfitted by Eddie Bauer.

The man sitting behind him and clinging desperately to his seat was half his size and had no ruff around the edge of his hood. His face was a fragile layer of frost over skin drained a pasty white. He wore a down snowsuit at least three sizes too big for him, the bottoms of the legs coming down over his wingtip shoes. He wasn't smiling at all. He looked like Sam McGee from Tennessee before he was stuffed into the furnace of the *Alice May*.

The rending, tearing noise of the snow machine's engine echoed across the landscape and affronted the arctic peace of that December day. It startled a moose stripping the bark from a stand of spindly birches. It sent a beaver back into her den in a swift-running stream. It woke a bald eagle roosting in the top of a spruce, causing him to glare down on the two men with malevolent eyes. The sky was of that crystal clarity that comes only to lands of the far north in winter; light, translucent, wanting cloud and color. Only the first blush of sunrise outlined the jagged peaks of mountains to the east, though it was well past nine in the morning. The snow was layered in graceful white curves beneath the alder and spruce and cottonwood, all the trees except for the spruce spare and leafless, though even the green spines of the spruce seemed faded to black this morning.

"I gotta take a leak," the man in back yelled in the driver's ear.

"You don't want to step off into the snow anywhere near here," the driver roared over the noise of the machine.

"Why not?" the passenger yelled back. A thin shard of ice cracked and slid from his cheek.

"It's deeper than it looks, probably over your head. You could founder here and never come up for air. Just hang on. It's not far now."

The machine lurched and skidded around a clump of trees, and the passenger held on and muttered to himself through clenched teeth. The big man's grin broadened.

Without warning they burst into a clearing. The big man reduced speed so abruptly that his passenger was thrown forward. When he hauled himself upright again and looked around, his first impression of the winter scene laid out before him was that it was just too immaculate, too orderly, too perfect to exist in a world of flawed, disorderly and imperfect men.

The log cabin in the clearing sat on the edge of a bluff that fell a hundred feet to the half-frozen Kanuyaq River below. Beyond the far bank of the river the land rose swiftly into the sharp peaks of the Quilak Mountains. The cabin, looking more as if it had grown there naturally rather than been built by human hands, stood at the center of a small semicircle of buildings. At the left and slightly to the back there was an outhouse, tall, spare and functional. Several depressions in the snow around it indicated it had been moved more than once, which gave the man on the snow machine some idea of how long the homestead had been there. Next was a combined garage and shop, through the open door of which could be seen a snow machine, a small truck and assorted related gear. He found the sight of these indubitably twentieth-century products infinitely reassuring. Next to the cabin stood an elevated stand for a dozen fifty-five-gallon barrels of Chevron diesel fuel, stacked on their sides. Immediately to the right of the cabin was a greenhouse, its Visqueen panels opaque with frost. Next to it and completing the semicircle stood a cache elevated some ten feet in the air on peeled log stilts, with a narrow ladder leading to its single door.

Paths through the drifts of snow had been cut with almost surgical precision, linking every structure to its neighbor. The resulting half-circle was packed firm between tidy berms as level as a clipped hedge. One trail led directly to the wood pile, which the man judged held at least three cords, split as neatly as they were stacked. Another pile of unsplit rounds stood next to the chopping block.

There were no footprints outside the trails. It seemed that this was one homesteader who kept herself to herself.

The glow of the wood of each structure testified to a yearly application of log oil. There wasn't a shake missing from any of the roofs. The usual dump of tires too worn to use but too good to throw away, the pile of leftover lumber cut in odd lengths but still good for something, someday, the stack of Blazo boxes to be used for shelves, the shiny hill of Blazo tins someday to carry water, the haphazard mound of empty, rusting fifty-five-gallon drums to be cut into stoves when the old one wore out, all these staples were missing. It was most unbush-like and positively unAlaskan. He had a suspicion that when the snow melted the grass wouldn't dare to grow more than an inch tall, or the tomatoes in the greenhouse bear less than twelve to the vine. He was assailed by an unexpected and entirely unaccustomed feeling of inadequacy, and wished suddenly that he had taken the time to search out a parka and boots, the winter uniform of the Alaskan bush, before making this pilgrimage. At least then he would have been properly dressed to meet Jack London, who was undoubtedly inside the cabin in front of him, writing "To Build a Fire" and making countless future generations of Alaskan junior high English students miserable in the process. He would have been unsurprised to see Samuel Benton Steele mushing up the trail in his red Mountie coat and flat-brimmed Mountie hat. He would merely have turned to look for Soapy Smith moving fast in the other direction. He realized finally that his mouth was hanging half-open, closed it with something of a snap and wondered what kind of time warp they had wandered through on the way here, and if they would be able to find it again on the return to their own century.

The big man switched off the engine. The waiting silence fell like a vengeful blow and his passenger was temporarily stunned by it. He rallied. "All this scene needs is the Northern Lights," he said, "and we could paint it on a gold pan and get twenty bucks for it off the little old lady from Duluth."

The big man grinned a little.

The smaller man took a deep breath and the frozen air burned into his lungs. Unused to it, he coughed. "So this is her place?"

"This is it," the big man confirmed, his deep voice rumbling over the clearing. As if to confirm his words, they heard the door to the cabin slam shut. The other man raised his eyebrows, cracking more ice off his face.

"Well, at least now we know she's home," the big man said placidly, and dismounted.

"Son of a bitch, what is that?" his passenger said, his face if possible becoming even more colorless.

The big man looked up to see an enormous gray animal with a stiff ruff and a plumed tail trotting across the yard in their direction, silent and purposeful. "Dog," he said laconically.

"Dog, huh?" the other man said, trying and failing to look away from the animal's unflinching yellow eyes. He groped in his pocket until his gloved fingers wrapped around the comforting butt of his .38 Police Special. He looked up to find those yellow eyes fixed on him with a thoughtful, considering expression, and he froze. "Looks like a goddam wolf to me," he said finally, trying hard to match the other man's nonchalance.

"Nah," the big man said, holding out one hand, fingers curled, palm down. "Only half. Hey, Mutt, how are you, girl?" She extended a cautious nose, sniffed twice and sneezed. Her tail give a perfunctory wag. She looked from the first man to the second and seemed to raise one eyebrow. "Hold out your hand," the big man said.

"What?"

"Make a fist, palm down, hold it out."

The other man swallowed, mentally bid his hand good-bye and obeyed. Mutt sniffed it, looked him over a third time in a way that made him hope he wasn't breathing in an aggressive manner, and then stood to one side, clearly waiting to escort them to the door of the cabin.

"There's the outhouse," the big man said, pointing.

"What?"

"You said you wanted to take a leak."

He looked from dog to outhouse and back to the dog. "Not that bad."

"That's some fucking doorman you've got out there," he said, once he was safely inside the cabin and the door securely latched behind him.

"Can I offer you a drink?" Her voice was odd, too loud for a whisper, not low enough for a growl, and painfully rough, like a dull saw ripping through old cement.

"I'll take whatever you got, whiskey, vodka, the first bottle you grab." The passenger had stripped off his outsize snowsuit to reveal a pin-striped three-piece suit complete with knotted tie and gold watch attached to a chain that stretched over a small, round potbelly the suit had been fighting ever since his teens.

She paused momentarily, taking in this sartorial splendor with a long, speculative survey that reminded him uncomfortably of the dog outside. "Coffee?" she said. "Or I could mix up some lemonade."

"Coffee's fine, Kate," the big man said. The suit felt like crying.

"It's on the stove." She jerked her chin. "Mugs and spoons and sugar on the shelf to the left."

The big man smiled down at her. "I know where the mugs are."

She didn't smile back.

The mugs were utilitarian white porcelain and the coffee was nectar and ambrosia. By his second cup the suit had defrosted enough to revert to type, to examine and inventory the scene.

The interior of the cabin was as neat as its exterior, maybe neater, neat enough to make his teeth ache. It reminded him of the cabin of a sailboat with one of those persnickety old bachelor skippers; there was by God a place for everything and everything had by God better be in its place. Kerosene lamps hissed gently from every corner of the room, making the cabin, unlike so many of its shadowy, smoky little contemporaries in the Alaskan bush, well lit. The plank walls, too, were sanded and finished. The first floor, some twenty-five feet square, was a living room, dining room and kitchen combined; a ladder led to a loft that presumably served as a bedroom, tucked away beneath the rear half of the roof's steep pitch. He estimated eleven hundred square feet of living space altogether, and was disposed to approve of the way it was arranged.

An oil stove for cooking took up the center of the left wall, facing a wood stove on the right wall, both of them going. A tall blue enamel coffeepot stood on the oil stove. A steaming, gallon-size teakettle sat on the wood stove's large surface, and a large round tin tub hung on the wall behind it. A counter, interrupted by a large, shallow sink with a pump handle, ran from the door to the oil stove, shelves above and below filled with orderly stacks of dishes, pots and pans and foodstuffs. A small square dining table covered with a faded red-and-white checked oilskin stood in the rear left-hand corner next to the oil stove. There were two upright wooden chairs, old but sturdy. On a shelf above were half a dozen decks of cards, poker chips and a Scrabble game. A wide, built-in bench ran along the back wall and around the rear right-hand corner, padded with foam rubber and upholstered in a deep blue canvas fabric. Over the bench built-in shelves bore a battery-operated cassette player and tidy stacks of cassette tapes. He read some of the artists' names out loud. "Peter, Paul and Mary, John Fogerty, Jimmy Buffet," he said, and turned with a friendly smile. "All your major American philosophers. We'll get along, Ms. Shugak."

She looked perfectly calm, her lips unsmiling, but there was a feeling of something barely leashed in her brown eyes when she paused in her bread making to look him over, head to toe, in a glance that once again took in his polished loafers, his immaculate suit and his crisply knotted tie. He checked an impulse to see if his fly was zipped. "I wasn't aware we had to," she said without inflection, and turned back to the counter.

The suit turned to the big man, whose expression, if possible, was even harder to read than the woman's. The suit shrugged and continued his inspection. Between the wood stove and the door were bookshelves, reaching around the corner of the house and from floor to ceiling, every one of them crammed with books. Curious, he ran his finger down their spines, and found *New Hampshire* wedged in between *Pale Gray for Guilt* and *Citizen of the Galaxy*. He cast a glance at the woman's unresponsive back, and opened the slim volume. Many of the pages were dog-eared, with notes penciled in the margins in a small, neat, entirely illegible hand. He closed the book and then allowed it to fall open where it would, and read part of a poem about a man who burned down his house for the fire insurance so he could buy a telescope. There were no notes on that page, only the smooth feeling on his fingertips of words on paper worn thin with reading. He replaced the book and strummed the strings of the dusty guitar hanging next to the shelving. It was out of tune. It had been out of tune for a long time.

"Hey." The woman was looking over at him, her eyes hard. "Do you mind?"

He dropped his hand. The silence in the little cabin bothered him. He had never been greeted with anything less than outright rejoicing in the Alaskan bush during the winter, or during the summer, either, any summer you could find anyone home. Especially at isolated homesteads like this one.

He swung around and took his first real look at the woman who wasn't even curious enough to ask his name. The woman who, until fourteen months ago, had been the acknowledged star of the Anchorage District Attorney's investigative staff. Who had the highest conviction rate in the state's history for that position. Whose very presence on the prosecution's witness list had induced defense lawyers to throw in their briefs and plea-bargain. Who had successfully resisted three determined efforts on the part of the FBI to recruit her.

Twenty-nine or thirty, he judged, which if she had had a year of training after college before going to work for Morgan would be about right. Five feet tall, no more, maybe a hundred and ten pounds. She had the burnished bronze skin and high, flat cheekbones of her race, with curiously light brown eyes tilted up at her temples, all of it framed by a shining fall of utterly black, utterly straight hair. The fabric of her red plaid shirt strained across her square shoulders and the swell of her breasts, and her Levis were worn white at butt and knees. She moved like a cat, all controlled muscle and natural grace, wary but assured. He wondered idly if she would be like a cat in bed, and then he remembered his wife and the last narrowly averted action for divorce and reined in his imagination. From the vibrations he was picking up between her and the big man he would never have a chance to test his luck, anyway.

Then she bent down to bring another scoop of flour up from the sack on the floor, and he sucked in his breath. For a moment her collar had fallen away and he had seen the scar, twisted and ugly and still angry in color. It crossed her throat almost from ear to ear. That explains the voice, he thought, shaken. Why hadn't she gone to a plastic surgeon and had that fixed, or at least had the scar tissue trimmed and reduced in size? He looked up to see the big man watching him out of blue eyes that held a clear warning. His own gaze faltered and fell.

But she had noticed his reaction. Her eyes narrowed. She lifted one hand as if to button her shirt up to the collar, hesitated, and let it fall. "What do you want, Jack?" she said abruptly.

The big man lowered his six-foot-two, two-hundred-and-twenty-pound frame down on the homemade couch, which groaned in protest, sipped at his coffee and wiped the moisture from his thick black mustache. He had hung his parka without looking for the hook, found the sugar on the right shelf the first time and settled himself on the softest spot on the couch without missing a beat. He looked relaxed, even at home, the suit thought. The woman evidently thought so, too, and her generous mouth tightened into a thin line.

"Parks Department's lost a ranger," the big man said.

She floured the counter and turned the dough out of the pan.

The big man's imperturbable voice went on. "He's been missing about six weeks."

She kneaded flour into the dough and folded it over once, twice, again. "He couldn't have lost himself in a snowstorm and froze to death like most of them do?"

"He could have, but we don't think so."

"Who's we?"

"This is Fred Gamble, FBI."

She looked the suit over and lifted one corner of her mouth in a faint smile that could not in any way be construed as friendly. "The FBI? Well, well, well."

"He came to us for help, since it's our jurisdiction. More or less. So as a professional courtesy I sent in an investigator from our office."

The woman's flour-covered hands were still for a moment, as she raised her eyes to glance briefly out the window over the sink. Gamble thought she was going to speak, but she resumed her task without comment.

The big man looked into his coffee mug as if it held the answers to the mysteries of the universe. "I haven't heard from him in two weeks. Since he called in from Niniltna the day after he arrived."

She folded another cup of flour into the dough and said, "What's the FBI doing looking for a lost park ranger?" She paused, and said slowly, "What's so special about this particular ranger?"

The big man gave her unresponsive back a slight, approving smile. "His father."

"Who is?"

"A congressman from Ohio."

She gave a short, unamused laugh and shook her head, giving the suit a sardonic glance. "Oh ho ho."

"Yeah."

Gamble tugged at his tie, which felt a bit tight.

"So you sent in an investigator," she said.

"Yes."

"When? Exactly."

"Two weeks and two days ago, exactly."

"And now he's missing, too."

"Yes."

"And you don't think both of them could have stumbled into a snowdrift."

"No. Not when the investigator went in specifically to look for the ranger."

"Maybe it was the same snowdrift."

"No."

"No." She worked the dough, her shoulders stiff and angry. "And now you want me to go in."

"The feds want the best. I recommended you. I told them you know the Park better than anyone. You were born here, raised here. Hell, you're related to half the people in it."

She sent him a black, unfriendly look, which he met without flinching. "Why should I help you?"

He shrugged and drained his cup, and stood to refill it. "You've been pouting up here for over a year. From what I read outside just now you haven't left the homestead since the first snow." He met her eyes with a bland expression. "What's next? You going to give the spruce trees a manicure?"

Her thick, straight brows met in a single line across her forehead. "Maybe I just like living alone," she snapped. "And maybe you should get out of here so I can get on with it."

"And maybe," he said, "you could use a little excitement right about now. At least looking for a couple of missing persons would give you the chance to talk to someone. Taken a vow of silence, Kate?" In spite of his outward appearance of calm, the big man's tone was barbed.

Her hands stilled and she fixed him with a stony gaze. "Dream on, Jack. I've got my books and my music, so I'm not bored. I run a couple traps, I pan a little gold, I bag a few tourists in season and raft them down the Kanuyaq, so I'm not broke. I guided a couple of hunting parties this fall and took my fee in meat, so the cache is full. I won't starve." The corners of her mouth curled, and she added, her words a deliberate taunt, "And Ken comes up from town every few weeks. So I'm not even horny."

The big man's jaw set hard, but he met her eyes without flinching. Gamble shifted in his seat and wished he'd never insisted on coming with Morgan to this godforsaken place, living legend or no. He cleared his throat gently. "Listen, folks," he said, examining his fingernails. "I get the feeling that if I weren't here the two of you would either duke it out or hit the sack or maybe both, and maybe that would be a good thing, but at this moment I don't really give a flying fuck about you or your personal problems. All I want is to get the Honorable Marcus A. Miller, representative of the great state of Ohio, off my goddam back. Now, what do you say?"

The flush in her cheeks could have been from the heat of the stove. She held the big man's gaze for another long moment, and then whipped around and kneaded vigorously. "There's nothing you have I need or want, Jack, so don't ask me for any favors. You won't be able to pay them back."

The fire crackled in the wood stove. Kate divided the dough into loaves and opened the oven on the oil stove to check the temperature. Gamble got up and refilled his coffee cup for the third time. The big man stirred, and said into the silence, "You busted that bootlegger for the Niniltna Corporation."

There was a brief pause. "That was different."

"Kate—"

"Shut up about that, Jack. Just—shut up about it. Okay?"

Into the following silence Gamble said gently, "We'll pay you."

She shrugged.

"Four hundred a day and expenses."

She didn't even bother to shrug this time.

The big man finished his coffee and motioned for the other man to do the same. He set both cups in the sink, standing next to her without looking at her. He worked the pump and rinsed them out and placed them upside down in the drainer. He dried his hands and pulled down his parka. Before shrugging into it, he reached into a deep pocket and pulled out a manila folder, which he tossed on the table. On his way out he paused at the door, glanced over his shoulder at Kate, up to her elbows in bread dough, and smiled to himself.

The woman's voice came out low and husky. "Jack."

He paused on the doorstep.

"Which investigator did you send in?" It was a question, but she didn't sound curious. She sounded as if she already knew.

He lifted the latch and opened the door. "Dahl went in." He paused, and added gently, "He had the most bush experience, you see. All that personal, one-on-one training you gave him." He stepped outside and said over his shoulder, "I left the ranger's file on the table. Get Bobby to call me when you have something."

Outside, Gamble looked at him and said, "Where'd she get that scar?" Jack busied himself with the starter on the engine, and Gamble repeated, "Morgan. Where did she get that scar?"

The other man sighed, and said flatly. "In a knife fight with a child molester."

Gamble stared at him. "Jesus Christ. That part of the story is true, then?"

"Yeah." The big man's eyes were bleak.

"Jesus Christ," Gamble repeated. "What happened?"

Jack unscrewed the gas cap and rocked the snow machine back and forth, peering inside the tank. "Somebody made an anonymous call to Family Services, reporting a father of five to be a habitual abuser of all five children. They called us. Kate went to check it out and caught him in the act with the four-year-old."

Gamble closed his eyes and shook his head. "You nail the perp?"

Morgan unhooked the jerry can from the back of the machine and emptied it into the gas tank. "He's dead."

Gamble's sigh was long and drawn out. "Uh-huh." He stared at the cabin. The sun was out by now, but he felt cold all the way through. "When did this happen?"

"Fourteen months, thirteen days." The big man thought for a moment, and added, "And seven hours ago."

Gamble stared at him. "You're sure about the time frame?"

The big man's ruddy cheeks darkened a little. It could have been the cold. He didn't answer.

Gamble thought for a moment. "That would have been about the time she left the D.A.'s office."

"About."

"Disability?"

"Nope. Quit." Morgan replaced the gas cap and gave it a final twist. He raised his eyes to stare at the closed cabin door, before which Mutt sat, alert, motionless, looking at them with her ears up and her yellow eyes unblinking. "She walked out of the hospital the next day and tacked a letter of resignation to my door with the knife she took off the perp."

"Jesus Christ," Gamble said for the third time.

"Yeah," Jack said. "Hell of a mess. His blood was still all over the blade." He shook his head disapprovingly. "Lousy crime scene inventory. APD should never have let her leave with it." The big man looked steadily at the cabin, as if by sheer will his gaze would penetrate the walls and seek out the woman inside. "She used to sing."

Gamble maintained a hopeful silence. It was the first remark Morgan had made all day that Gamble hadn't had to drag out of him.

"She knows all the words to every high sea chantey ever written down," Morgan said softly.

Gamble waited, but Morgan said nothing more. He started the engine and they climbed on the snow machine. Over the noise of the engine Gamble shouted, "Well?"

Morgan looked back at the cabin. "She'll do it."

Gamble snorted.

"She'll do it," the big man repeated. "Roll those snowsuit legs down or your feet'll get frostbite. And next time for chrissake bring some goddam boots." He pushed off with one foot and the machine began to slide forward.

"It's your call, Jack, but are you sure we shouldn't find someone else to do this job?" Gamble persisted. "You sure she'll look for them?"

"I'm sure," the big man said. His certainty did not sound as if it gave him any joy.

Jerking awake at three the next morning, fleeing dark dreams of an endless procession of frightened, bleeding children begging her not to hurt their parents, Kate, sweating, trembling, swearing loudly to drown out the blood pounding in her ears, came to the same conclusion. The hauntings would continue no matter what she did; she knew that already. But for a time, perhaps, the ghosts would take on a different shape, mouth different words, stare accusingly for different reasons. It was enough.

PART VII

Alaska as a Parable for the Future

FROM

THE FIRECRACKER BOYS

Dan O'Neill

 On July 14, 1958, Edward Teller, now director of the Lawrence Radiation Laboratory, and his entourage from Livermore landed unannounced in Juneau, the seat of the Alaska government and, according to guide books, perhaps the most beautiful of American capital cities. [...]

At his Juneau press conference, Teller said he had come to unveil a proposal known inside the AEC as "Project Chariot." The idea was to create an instant deepwater harbor at Cape Thompson in northwest Alaska by simultaneously detonating several thermonuclear bombs. Seventy million cubic yards of earth-moving would be accomplished instantly, as the sea rushed in to fill a keyhole-shaped crater. "We looked at the whole world—almost the whole world," he said, apparently forgetting his criterion that the site must be in U.S. territory, "and tried to pick a spot where we could most effectively demonstrate the peaceful uses of [nuclear] energy." On the basis of a preliminary study, Teller said, "the excavation of a harbor in Alaska, to open an area to possible great development, would do the job." [...]

At quarter to two on the afternoon of March 14, 1960, three men representing the AEC entered Browning Hall, a building so long and narrow that kids ran footraces there during the Christmas festivities. About 100 Eskimos sat, as they were accustomed to doing, on the floor, shoulder to shoulder against the two eighty-foot-long-walls. As the AEC men made their way to the head table

229

and the two now running tape recorders, it must have felt as if they were running a gauntlet.

David Frankson, the village council president, introduced the visitors in Inupiaq. They were Russell Ball, Rodney Southwick, and Robert L. Rausch.

Southwick took the floor. "Thank you, Mister Frankson. Ladies and gentlemen of Point Hope, we have come here as representatives of the United States Atomic Energy Commission. It is our purpose to tell you what the status is of the project at Ogotoruk Creek....I want to emphasize and repeat that the Commission has not approved any explosion. The Commission's decision on whether there should be an experiment up here will be based solely on these studies—if such an experiment can be conducted safely, and only if it can be conducted safely. The Commission, by safely, means no one would be hurt, no one would be moved, your normal means of hunting and fishing would not be interfered with."

It would be difficult to imagine a more effective way to get the attention of an Eskimo audience than to raise the possibility of risk to the animals upon which their economy depended, or the possibility of moving the people from their homeland. In 1960, the Inupiat people at Point Hope were both staunchly protective of their traditional lifeways and opportunistic when it came to incorporating those artifacts of American culture that appealed to them. The annual Christmas party featured both traditional Eskimo dancing and singing accompanied by the banged-out rhythms of the drum and the "Tikiraq Playboys" sporting Western shirts and scarves strumming guitars and crooning "Tom Dooley." They were deeply interested in Elvis. They still hunted sea mammals in skin boats, but they shot the animals with rifles, and outboard motors powered the boats. And they still ran dog teams, but often tucked away in the sled bag was a tape-recorded "letter" bound for friends in the next village. The people assimilated the white man's language as well; many could not only speak, but also read and write English.

Notwithstanding that the Inupiat of Point Hope lived in a hybrid culture, most of the people had difficulty with the AEC presentation: it was in English—and jargon-laden English at that; it dealt with technical matters such as the physics of cratering and the biological effects of radiation, subjects that would have presented a problem for most listeners at any American town-hall meeting; and the people simply had no affinity whatever for the technology proffered by the AEC.

After a brief power failure, Russell Ball was able to introduce the film *Industrial Applications of Nuclear Explosives*, which Livermore had produced and shown to the Second International Conference on Peaceful Uses of Atomic Energy in Geneva. "We now have available to show you a brief moving picture which describes several of the ways in which we think it will be possible to develop peaceful uses of these nuclear explosives. The first of these that will be in the movie has to do with the Cape Thompson project although it is not mentioned by that name....You will find that it talks about the creation of a harbor. And I would first point out that the film was made at a time when thought was being given to the creation of a much larger harbor than is now considered. Because of this, the explosive devices which the film mentions are much larger than the ones we now propose to use."

Council president David Frankson said a few words in Inupiaq, someone turned out the lights, and the film began. The first thing the Eskimos saw after the titled faded was a white flash followed by a churning, red fireball lifting off the earth. Over the quavering strains of the music track, they heard the smooth, euphonic tones of a narrator: "Now that man has learned to control a vastly greater force than chemical explosives, his thinking has turned to methods which will make effective use of this power within industry. The potential applications? Consider just one. The development of a harbor in the hard rock of a remote coastal area."

The still-growing mushroom cloud dissolved, and in its place appeared, in animation, the Ogotoruk Creek valley. The audience recognized the green, rolling hills where they hunted caribou, and the slanting limestone cliffs along the coast where they gathered crowbill eggs. Graphic overlays dissolved in to show the keyhole-shaped outline of a harbor and the location and depth of the nuclear explosives. "The procedure: bury an in-line series of four equally spaced one-hundred-kiloton shots at a depth of thirty meters, and a terminal shot of one megaton, fifty meters deep. All shots of minimum fission yield.

Depending on the nature of the surrounding medium, surround the devices with sufficient borated compounds to reduce neutron activation by several orders of magnitude. Detonate."

The green valley floor instantly heaved into a massive dome and blew apart in streamers of dark rocks and boiling dust. The audience cried "Yeeeee! Ahhhh!" Under the sound of the wailing, and as the screen showed the blue sea rushing in to fill the channel and crater, the narrator continued reassuringly: "Activity in the region of the crater would be washed out into the ocean rapidly and essentially removed from the biosphere. The activity on land near the crater would rapidly decay....In remote areas, where large yields can be safely used, and economic factors are favorable, such explosions are demonstrably feasible."

After the film, Russell Ball took questions. Keith Lawton, the Episcopal priest at Point Hope, stood up to speak. He had been cutting meat before the meeting and was still wearing bloody clothes and carrying a knife with a 13½-inch blade. Lawton asked several questions dealing with the suitability of the site's geology, the seismic effect of the blast, and the time of year of the detonation. He also wanted to know how long it would take for the various radionuclides in the fallout to decay to harmless elements. "Perhaps Dr. Rausch would answer that," said Ball.

Rausch was a slight, bespectacled and professional-looking scientist with the handshake of a blacksmith. He had a peculiarity of speech wherein he pronounced each word—each syllable—distinctly: "in-for-may-shun," he would say. Rausch forbore contractions. The whole effect was one of great precision, as if he took in the world in data bits, and processed them with robotic exactitude.

Rausch was not an employee of the AEC, but a parasitologist who had lived in Alaska since 1949. In connection with his work, he had traveled widely in northern Alaska, including to Point Hope, and was well known to the Eskimo people. That he was well liked is clear from an account of one trip Rausch took with four colleagues to Anaktuvuk Pass, a village in the central Brooks Range. A newspaper correspondent from the village filed a brief item noting the visit and describing the scientific party as including "four white guys and Bob Rausch."

When he traveled with people new to the Arctic, Rausch drew secret delight in supplying his companions with prosaic descriptions of the raw side of Northern life. With studied blandness, he might detail the pathology of some ghastly parasitic disease endemic to rural Alaska. Or he might casually recount the habit of Eskimo hunters, who, after downing a caribou, would rush to pull back the hide and expose hundreds of encysted warble fly larvae. The hunters would greedily pick off the thumb-sized grubs and pop them into their mouths. If his listener's jaw dropped and eyes widened, Rausch seemed not to notice. "They are quite delicious," he would say.

Bob Rausch had no particular problem with the Project Chariot experiment, though he did think some of the Livermore scientists were "like little boys" showing an almost "pathological glee" at setting off these explosions. Mainly, he considered Chariot "a very unusual opportunity to obtain some very good information." In any event, he had received the AEC's briefing from Allyn Seymour and Charles Weaver in Anchorage, and now found himself on the village tour explaining the Chariot environmental studies and the effects of radiation.

"According to the information that I have," Rausch began, in answer to Lawton's question about how long it would take the fallout to decay to harmless elements, "the amount that will escape, to begin with, will be a quite small part of the total yield. And the half life of the radioactive elements that are produced will be so short that some will be gone in a matter of hours, others will take longer." Here Rausch was speaking quite outside his area of training, and the impression he was leaving with the people was erroneous. Almost certainly Russell Ball knew that radiation with a half-life of many years would be released. But Ball said nothing. Nor did he correct him when Rausch told the people another thing he understood from AEC scientists: that "the amount of radiation that is likely to be released, according to the information that is available, will probably be so little [as] to make it impossible to detect the actual increase over the present amount of radiation that is there." Rausch had understood this to be true from the statements of the AEC's John Wolfe at the Anchorage meeting.

Returning to this topic later, Keith Lawton wanted to know what the AEC would do "if anything *did* happen...that some pocket of radioactivity due to a wind shift landed on a particular portion of Point Hope." Russell Ball replied, "At this distance the amount of airborne radioactivity which could reach here would be, could not *possibly* be enough to cause any injury to the people or the animals. There's just no chance of that." And at the crater site itself, Ball said that "after a short time—in terms of months, at least—it will be possible to remove all restrictions on access."

The effect of radiation on the animals was a matter of grave concern to the Point Hopers. When Lawton raised the question of radiation and fish that might swim into the crater, Ball tossed it to Rausch, saying, "Why don't you mention the experience from Eniwetok [the AEC's nuclear test facility in the Marshall Islands] with regard to fish."

Rausch had not been involved with the fish investigations at Eniwetok, and he qualified his information as coming from others, namely Allyn Seymour. "But," he said, "they found no evidence that fishes were destroyed or that there was any significant amount of radiation in them."

Ball added that "the amount of radioactive material released into the sea there was a thousand times greater than that which would be released here. And even there it was safe to eat the fish which were caught, even in that water."

At another point, again relying on information provided by the AEC's Seymour and Charles Weaver, Rausch added, "According to the tests that have been carried out in other places, there appears to be very little reason to believe that any of the animal life is likely to be harmed. In the Bikini tests that were carried on above ground, the amount of radioactive material in each was many times greater than will be the case here. And even then, there was no effect on the fishes in the sea. None were made radioactive and therefore really impossible for them to be eaten." Rausch said that the studies on fish after the detonations in the Pacific "did not show anything that was considered of any danger to anyone if those fishes were utilized."

Daniel Lisbourne, the previous village council president, raised the question of the project's interference with caribou hunting, and Lawton wondered if steps would be taken to keep the caribou away from Ogotoruk Creek. Rausch, again at Ball's prompting, mentioned the AEC's experience with a herd of cattle the government maintained on the Nevada Test Site. "Yes," he said, "they have been keeping cattle in the Nevada area, in the immediate vicinity where the shots have been made. That herd is maintained there and the animals are killed periodically and examined and tested in various detailed ways. And they have yet to find any evidence of any damage."

Ball added, tellingly, that the herd was brought in "to provide evidence to the farmers that it was safe."

Keith Lawton was beginning to see that the villagers' questions as to radiation safety were perhaps being asked of the wrong people. "Who is the radiation biologist who works with the AEC—who is the radiation biologist who is working on this program?"

Southwick perked up. "Dr. Allyn Seymour is a member of the committee."

"Dr. Allyn Seymour," repeated Lawton. "And he wasn't available for tours around the villages at all?"

"He was with us at the three-day meeting which the committee held at Anchorage," replied Ball. "But we didn't at that time consider it important enough to bring him up here."

"We didn't think it was necessary to pull him off the job he's on right now," said Southwick, hoping to put a slightly more polite spin on Ball's comment. Then, probably because he didn't want the session to become the sort of "donnybrook" he'd encountered in Juneau, Southwick moved to wrap up the meeting: "Are there any questions? If not, I would like to thank you very much Mr. Frankson, and the people who came here—"

He was interrupted by a woman's voice. Dinah Frankson, who had great influence in the village because she was an *umialik*'s wife, spoke in Inupiaq while Daniel Lisbourne translated. "Ah, the woman here mentioned, all of these people here, all these people, most of them are just silent right now and they have great fear in, in this detonation and the effects, and how the effects of it will be."

Southwick, who could be a little slow on the uptake, asked, "Internationally?"

"No, here," said Lisbourne.

"What?" asked Ball. "I don't quite get what her question was."

"The effect of the blast," explained Tommy Richards, the pilot.

"The effect of the blast to the people," echoed Lisbourne.

Dawn was breaking in Ball's mind. "On your own Eskimo people?" The audience looked back at him without speaking. "Oh, well, ah, I believe we've covered that already. Ah, I think we'll have to..." Ball's voice trailed off as he turned to Richards to discuss their return flight to Kotzebue.

"I don't think that's true," said Richards. "You haven't."

Many people then spoke at once, in Inupiaq. Daniel Lisbourne spoke for the people. "Ah, I think, Mr. Ball, that this, the majority of us here, right now, have no understand what you have said previously, having not know enough about the English language." Lisbourne said Dinah Frankson wanted to remind the AEC that she was a citizen of the United States and that she feared for the men who hunted in the Ogotoruk Creek area, especially the seal hunters who, in April, went out on the sea ice near the planned ground zero.

"All the way down there?" asked Ball.

"Yeah. All the way down there," said Lisbourne.

"And collect eggs," said Keith Lawton. The murre, known locally as the crowbill, laid a large, blue-green egg that was a favorite of the people. Crowbill eggs had a pronounced taper at one end so that they could roll only in a little arc, not waddle off the ledge. The people of Point Hope gathered them by the hundreds of dozens; they boiled them, peeled them, and preserved them in pokes of seal oil.

"When they do get them, they get them by boatloads from Cape Thompson," said Lisbourne.

"The eggs?" asked Ball.

"The eggs," said Lawton.

Dan Lisbourne said that last year the Point Hopers gathered 733 dozen, and that that was a low year.

"Ah," said Ball. He paused to think. "All I can say is, briefly, is that the studies we are conducting of your people, of your hunting, of your fishing, of your catching seals and so on, all of this will guide us in finding the right time of year for such an experiment. Only if these studies show that we can pick a time that will not be of harm to your people, only then would we do the experiment. We have your welfare at heart; we cannot afford to do you harm. This program is of great importance to us. This is one of many experiments we would like to do. If we do this carelessly, so as to bring harm to your village, the reaction would be to stop our whole program! We, we can't afford this! We can't afford to be careful—careless. We must be very careful not to injure your people or your way of life. So these studies we are conducting will tell us if there is a time when this can be done safely. If there is such a time, then we'll choose to do it and it will not harm you. If we cannot find a time to do it safely, we won't do it."

"I hope you don't," said Kitty Kinneeveauk to the laughter of the audience. "Once I read some news from magazines about Indians where you work on this too, blasting their town, and none of these atomic people help them. It didn't help them. Injure their food, their game and their water and their homes. And none of the atomic people help them, or turn back and see what's going on out there."

"We, ah, so…" began Ball.

But Kitty Kinneeveauk wasn't through. Kitty, all five feet of her, was well known in the village as a woman who would stand up to injustice wherever she found it. To the frequent alarm of her more reticent husband, Kitty did not hesitate to challenge white men at public meetings. […]

And Kitty had already had a run-in with the Chariot men at Ogotoruk Creek. When the construction workers put in the first airstrip, they bulldozed the sod house Kitty and her family used as a seasonal trapping base. On discovering the situation in the late fall, Kitty confronted the caretakers, as she remembers in a 1989 interview: "'How come you ripped our house off here? You didn't even ask! Didn't ask me, just working.' And my husband got scared, 'Dear, you are scared and we better go.'" But Kitty said, "I want to talk to them some more." She mentioned that the men now had built many houses, and pointing to them, she said, "Maybe you can replace it [with] one of these ones." When the men "didn't say nothing," Kitty told them, "You're just bad men." Though her claim for damages was ignored, Kitty had tried "to get action," she said, "because I pity my kids. And besides, we work hard."

Perhaps it was because of the bulldozing incident, or perhaps it was that Kitty's husband was finally resigned to her ways. In any event, when Kitty leaned over to him at the AEC meeting and said, "You talk," Mark Kinneeveauk wearily encouraged his outspoken wife, "Dear, you never be scared. You talk."

Interrupting Russell Ball, Kitty continued, "So, I've been thinking about we really don't want to see the Cape Thompson blasted because it our homeland. I'm pretty sure you don't like to see your home blasted by some other people who didn't live in your place like we live in Point Hope."

"Oh, I understand that thoroughly," said Ball. "We know this....What I'm saying is we will do the work only if it will *not* injure your home. If we cannot find a way to do it without injury to you, we will *not do it*....Now, in answer to your first question, ah, the testing we have done so far has had *no* effect on the Indian people anyplace. There are no Indian people within many, many miles of where we test. There are many, many, er, Americans, white people."

"I've read it on a book," insisted Kitty. "It happened while they blasted their homes."

"No, not by us," replied Ball. "I think you must have misunderstood the book because we have never done that to any people. Indian or otherwise, we have never done that."

"In the book they said it was done by white people," said Kitty.

"We have only tested weapons in two places," replied Ball. "In Nevada and *way out* in the Pacific."

"At Eniwetok," said Southwick.

"At Eniwetok," repeated Ball. "Now, er, at, ah," Ball turned to Southwick and quietly asked, "I wonder if she could have in mind the natives at Eniwetok?" Then, to the audience, "Perhaps you have in mind the native peoples of Eniwetok?"

Kitty was uncertain, but Daniel Lisbourne remembered. He asked about a detonation in the Pacific. Wasn't there a problem with a fishing boat?

"That's true, there was a fishing boat," said Ball.

"Seventy-five miles away, yeah," pressed Lisbourne.

"That's right and because they were where they were told not to be....They were within the danger—we had publicized around the world an area which we asked all shipping to stay out. They ignored that and were within the danger area."

Daniel Lisbourne turned up the heat on the AEC delegation by raising the issue of compensation. He said that Point Hope hunters brought in 175,000 pounds of meat as a result of hunting "every day of the week." What would the AEC do, he wondered, if the men were kept from hunting for several days. Would there be cash compensation?

"This is a question we'll have to take up," said Southwick.

"We don't really know the answer to that," said Ball.

"There's a method to do it," added Southwick, "by suit, *if* anything should go wrong."

"Yeah, *if*," said Lisbourne.

"What I mean is you can always sue, but that takes five years and it has to go through the courts and it is expensive—"

"I was not thinking about the sue at all," replied Lisbourne, "I was just asking if we should get laid up for a few days, that would cripple us, you know."

"We do not have an answer for that," said Southwick, "other than to say you can always sue. But we don't consider that satisfactory."

Don Foote, who had been silent throughout the long meeting, attempted to explain the Eskimos' position. "Mr. Ball, I think Daniel's question stems from the fact that there are many boys right here who don't have dog feed today and they have to get it. And *one day*, if kept in the village, can be serious and they want to know what—"

"Yeah, we know that," interrupted Southwick.

"...and what—" began Foote again.

"Yeah, we understand this thing," said Ball, cutting off Foote again.

"...and—" continued Foote.

"All I can give in the way of answer is..." said Ball.

"...the question is now under consideration for Plowshare," finished Southwick.

"But has not been acknowledged as such and—" said Foote, trying a fourth time to finish his sentence.

"We understand that, Don. What I was going to say was that, er..." said Ball.

"You're turning up a lot of these things," Southwick complained to Foote.

"This is obviously a question of great importance to your people," said Ball, "a matter which must be very carefully considered by us...it seems to me we would have to lay plans to assist you, perhaps lay in food ahead of time...we *must* work out a solution which protects your interests."

David Frankson had heard enough. "We council at the Point Hope that sent the protest letter to Atomic Energy Commission stating that we don't want to see the blast down there. And *when we say it, we mean it!*"

AFTERWORD

Project Chariot helps to illuminate a transitional period in environmental history and Alaska native history. And, as a study of one small episode in American nuclear history, it animates many themes of nuclear culture. But more important, Chariot raises ethical issues that we still face and that touch many of our central institutions.

Although antipathy toward the federal government was an established trademark of Alaska journalism, in the case of Chariot, editors told their readers simply to trust Uncle Sam to do right by Alaska. Editorial discussion was always predicated on the assumption that a desire for technological progress was the reality everyone shared. Of course, it was really an ideology, and one that everyone did not share.

While they are private sector entities, newspapers enjoy special protection under the constitution. In turn, the public has come to expect a measure of public responsibility from the press: a healthy skepticism—if not a vigorous search for contradictions—in the official story; the willingness to look at a wide variety of sources and give voice to a wide range of perspectives; a commitment to objectivity, rather than promotion of an ideology. It is a high expectation, and one rarely met in or outside Alaska.

Religious groups perennially wrestle with the question of militant involvement in social and political issues. Is the Church just another pillar of the establishment, with a vested interest in a stable, hierarchically organized social structure? Should it confine itself only to the periphery of political conflict? It would seem reasonable, if the Church is to provide credible leadership in matters of moral philosophy, that it also provide leadership in applying that philosophy to social issues. While some church leaders in Alaska apparently suppressed criticism of the government project, the Reverends Richard Heacock and Keith Lawton saw their public anti-Chariot advocacy as part and parcel of their ministry. They recognized that it cannot be sufficient simply to defer to the judgment of government officials in matters of social responsibility. For to do so is to tolerate ethnic cleansing, apartheid, genocide, slavery, and so on.

The reasons cited by the chambers of commerce and other business and labor leaders for embracing Project Chariot have a familiar ring to those who have followed the debates over economic development projects in rural areas: it will bring federal dollars to the area, create jobs for people, and put the area "on the map." Short-term economic contributions dominate the equation. Long-term, less visible, or noneconomic costs are seldom fully considered.

In many respects, science is big business, too. It is a fact of life that scientific research is expensive. And funding tends to come from large government agencies or large corporate entities, each of which can have strong, vested interests in the results. The Chariot case shows that it is not always possible to regard research opportunities from an apolitical, amoral, valueless vantage, especially when sponsors draw improper conclusions from the data. Les Viereck spoke to this issue in his letter of resignation from the University of Alaska: "A scientist's allegiance is first to truth and personal integrity and only secondarily to an organized group such as a university, a company, or a government." In a word, corporate and even scientific objectives must be subordinate to philosophical values. And a regard for human welfare must be the overarching canon of the scientific code of ethics.

The Western university is built on a concept of academic freedom—the opportunity to pursue any avenue of inquiry in an atmosphere of pure scholarship and freedom from political pressures. This special latitude allows a researcher to follow obstinately his or her own idea until its truth might ultimately be established. But throughout history, one ideology or another has infected the university: religious ideology in the Middle Ages, racist ideology in Germany, social ideology in communist Russia, and a mercantile ideology in America. During the 1950s and 1960s, the cold war came onto American campuses. In its 1955 annual report, the National Science Foundation framed the issue in frighteningly blunt language: "It is vital that this partnership of science and Government be strengthened in every way possible, and that elements tending to create conflict and distrust be eliminated." It is not surprising that the University of Alaska lost sight of its mission and yielded to the cold war political ambience by dismissing Pruitt and Viereck. What *is* surprising—and the lesson here—is that some scholars were able to hold strong to the principle of academic freedom and were willing to pay the highest professional cost in defense of that ideal.

A reverence for such ideals as justice and truth is understood to be among the philosophic underpinnings of democratic governments. Yet it has become a matter of record (since the Freedom of Information Act became law and a number of whistle-blowers within the agency have sounded off) that the U.S. Atomic Energy Commission and its successor agency, the Department of Energy, compiled a stunning record of willful manipulation of facts. "There is nothing comparable in our history," says former secretary of the interior Stewart Udall, "to the deceit and the lying that took place as a matter of official Government policy in order to protect [the nuclear arms] industry. Nothing was going to stop them and they were willing to kill our own people." At issue is the capacity and tendency of a government agency to circumvent the lawful administration of public affairs in order to advance its own agenda. Behind such institutional corruption may be a desire to save the country from a threat that, it is claimed, the citizenry does not fully appreciate. The fallacy, of course, is that, in the process, the zealots trample the very institutions they rush to protect. Rationalizations that bypass the public in matters of public policy threaten democracy in the most basic way; they usurp what Jefferson

called the "ultimate powers of society" from their only "safe reposi-
tory...the people themselves." It is not too exaggerated to say, as
Stewart Udall has done, that "the atomic weapons race and the secrecy
surrounding it crushed American democracy."

The Project Chariot story is a tale of conflict—even scandal—
involving passionate, radical, pioneering people. But it is more than
that. Chariot illustrates why the most cherished institutions of a free
society—a democratic government, a free press, the university, even the
Church—cannot necessarily be accepted as seats of objectivity and
candor. The lesson Project Chariot offers is that a free society must be
a skeptical one, that rigorous questioning and dissent protect, rather
than subvert, our freedoms.

THE WHALE AND THE SUPERCOMPUTER

ON THE NORTHERN FRONT OF CLIMATE CHANGE

Charles Wohlforth

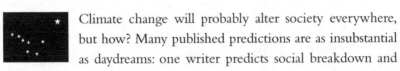 Climate change will probably alter society everywhere, but how? Many published predictions are as insubstantial as daydreams: one writer predicts social breakdown and world totalitarianism, another predicts a healthy boost in crop yields. You can predict anything you like by making choices on the many branching paths of uncertainty. But it is also possible, by discarding all but the most certain changes, to honestly estimate the basic challenges people will face. Sea level already has been rising since the last glacial period, when the Bering Sea floor was exposed and connected Alaska with Siberia. Sea level has been much higher in the past, too, as shown by ancient seashores far from the coast in the Arctic and many other places. Climate change accelerates the rise in sea level two ways: water expands when it warms, and melting continental ice increases runoff into the ocean (sea ice does not increase sea level when it melts, because it is already floating in the ocean). In the twentieth century, sea level rose four to eight inches, a rate ten times faster than the average for the previous three thousand years. Rising sea level, with increased erosion, storm damage, and flooding, will likely impose costs on many coastal communities. Each area's wealth will determine how it can respond. There will always be enough money to protect Manhattan Island, but most places will have hard choices to make, just like Barrow.

Ron Brunner, the University of Colorado public policy expert working on the Barrow study, saw these local decisions as the best avenue to a global climate change solution. When a town found ideas that worked, they would pass them on to other towns. Adaptation almost had to happen locally, and Ron thought carbon reduction could start there, too. Governor Jeanne Shaheen of New Hampshire signed carbon reduction legislation in 2002, noting that climate change "threatens skiing, foliage, maple sugaring, and trout fishing—all crucial to our state's economy." Many other U.S. states and local governments adopted carbon reductions based on local concerns, some more stringent than most national governments'. Companies such as BP and Johnson & Johnson were voluntarily cutting their carbon emissions for business reasons and because people wanted to do the right thing. If that seemed idealistic, Ron pointed out it might be the only real opportunity for progress. Social change could come either from coercion or from persuasion, and the top-down, coercive approach—scientists issuing reports and asking international organizations of governments to approve mandatory controls—wasn't working after decades of effort and $30 billion in research.

The problem wasn't that these scientists didn't understand the climate but that they didn't seem to understand people. Some climate modelers regarded their work as writing an "operator's manual...for Spaceship Earth." Ron wrote, "This implies a command center controlled by those few with the necessary technical expertise; the rest of us, presumably, are passengers along for the ride." But even if the scientists could produce the manual, no one was holding the steering wheel in the control center. That's not how the world works. In fact, there will be no operator's manual either, because the whole enterprise rests on a logical fallacy: events in an infinitely complex world, full of constantly adapting people and natural systems, cannot be predicted reliably by a mathematical code. Understanding climate change, as well as responding, must happen inside individual human beings, in their minds and in their bones, through judgment and trial and error, in the way the Iñupiat, and all people, learn the truth by living it. We needed modern science, Ron wrote, but we also needed a ten-thousand-year-old science based on the human experience of concrete places and events.

The solution was simpler than many people wanted to accept. Ron said, "Not enough people in the world, and particularly their leaders, want to do anything about this. So what do you do about it? You start with the easy cases, the people who already care and want to do something." Communities that felt compelled to act would influence one another. That, he hoped, would eventually lead to broad social change, a building of pressure upward from the towns and cities that would force governments to react nationally and globally to reduce carbon emissions. In the usual way social change occurs, ordinary people would communicate, their ideas and reactions spreading from one town to the next, to cities, to nations, and across cultures until the world was ready for action.

I asked if we had time for broad social change. Ron said, "No one can know that. But what's the alternative?"

Climate change that happens gradually is difficult for people to perceive. Even in Barrow, where the Iñupiat depended on wildlife, ice, and the timing of the seasons for their livelihood, and where scientific lectures were a popular form of evening entertainment, men like Oliver Leavitt and Richard Glenn became believers only during that terrible spring whaling season of 2002. Would a few cold winters revive their doubts? Most scientists weren't much help. Uncertainty was their daily bread. Not enough had Suki Manabe's ability to rank important certainties above trivial unknowns. The news media picked up this noise and amplified it, covering minor scientific controversies without context or scale and whipsawing readers back and forth in the same way they did with dietary advice: salt was bad for you, then it was good; the world was warming, then it wasn't.

The global profile of the problem was distant and depressing, like so many other environmental crises that came and went. (On New Year's Day of 2000, several of my friends shared a sense of relief that the world had survived; I wonder how many others who grew up amid the pessimism of the 1970s felt the same way that day.) Besides, said Amanda Lynch, any statement about the entire globe was fundamentally abstract—hard to quantify and, once quantified, hard to understand. On the other hand, she said, clear and specific statements could be made about particular places. She already had the tools to make firm predictions of the probability of different kinds of storms and the damage they would cause in Barrow over the next fifty years.

That was something that people could get their minds around.

Anne Jensen said, "People here see that things are changing, but I think that urban people don't—which is most of the people in the world—because they're so encapsulated. I think a lot of people are disconnected from climate because they're so insulated from it."

She had been away from Philadelphia and Bryn Mawr long enough that she sounded like an Eskimo in her disdain for people who ate veal but condemned hunting. Yet those were the people who would have to feel climate change coming and develop a personal and political desire to address it. Three-quarters of Americans lived in cities; any major social movement would have to be mainly urban. When that movement comes, perhaps the Iñupiaq worldview can help others to see. That is the dream implicit in Anne, Ron, and Amanda's work: a cultural transformation that allows many people, as one, to see the natural world as it really is.

MOONLIGHT AT MIDDAY

Sally Carrighar

 I went down to the beach, where the waves were casting up some of the ocean's discards. Before the sea froze, I wished to collect evidence of the life in its waters, for I would be writing about the marine animals and I needed to know what food these creatures were able to find in the depths. In a few minutes I had gathered sand dollars, clamshells, the carapaces of soft-shell crabs, and the egg cases made by marine worms, though I didn't know at the time what they were: little, pocked collar-shapes apparently fashioned of mud. The gold threads of purple-black mussels had tangled pieces of some of them into their colonies, which also included small shellfish, weighted down with sharp, stony barnacles.

An Eskimo came along the beach trundling a homemade wheel-barrow. He walked with an eager step, smiled as he passed, went on, and stopped a short distance farther. He too began picking up mussels. That was a delicate kind of approach, I thought: he went beyond where I was in case I did not want to talk, but only so far that my own collecting could make it natural for me to join him if I should wish. I worked up in his direction.

When I was near, he swept an arm towards the ocean.

"Pretty soon all ice out there. Interesting, to see how ice will be. Every year different." He spoke with vitality and with only a moderate accent. In the Eskimos' language, and also in ours when they speak it, there is a curious knobby effect, with the emphases like a series of vocal bumps. This man sounded almost as if he might be a European.

I asked if the sea would be frozen as far out as we could see.

"Maybe," he said. "Sometimes only two, three miles—to the bar. Sometimes twenty, twenty-five miles."

"Beyond that will there be open water?"

"Not much open water. Out beyond shore-ice will be big floating pack. Drifts around. When big wind blows in from the ocean, that pack-ice comes toward the shore fast. It hits edge of shore-ice, and BANG!" The man's arms flew up. "Edge of ice buckles way up like wall, higher than house sometimes. Pressure ridge, white people call it. Some years shore-ice gets heaved every place, all the way in to beach. Big jagged heaps. Then we have to cut trail out through ice. Lots of work, but we have to get our boats out to water."

"Do you go out to the open water to fish?" I asked.

"To get seals. We fish through the ice, close to beach, down through holes. Upriver we catch fish in traps."

All this sounded like cold, rugged work, but it was evident that the prospect of it was filling the man with zest. "Ice come pretty soon now," he finished gaily, with one of his frequent smiles.

Starting to gather his mussels again, the man darted in and out of the water. Most of his clothes had come from the States: a sweater and cords and a hunter's cap. But he wore Eskimo boots, and I asked him if they were waterproof. "Better than rubber," he said. "My wife make them. *Oogruk* skin rubbed with seal oil. Keep out water just fine. Threads are sinew. When they get wet, threads swell up, get bigger. No water can get through the stitches." At the top of the boots were hems with draw-strings pulling them tight around the man's knees.

Continuing work, he said,

"My grandsons like clams we buy in the store in cans. I like fresh mussels better. Besides, nice, picking them up." I said,

"In California some people have died from eating mussels during the summer. They may be poisonous then. In winter they are all right."

"Same here," said the Eskimo. "We never eat mussels till fall time."

"The white men, the scientists, didn't discover the poison until a few years ago. The news got to Unalakleet pretty fast."

"Eskimos always know," he replied. "When I was a boy my mother said, 'Never eat mussels till just before freeze-up.'" His manner in telling this was not boastful. It merely implied respect for his people's experience. I felt very humbled, however. This was the first of many times that something I'd say would reveal a white-person's ingrained assumption that our ways are superior, often to find that the Eskimos were ahead of me. "The white men discovered...The news got to Unalakleet..." Before civilized research chemists found that some toxic substance exists in mussels from May to September, white people in California thought that cases of mussel poisoning were due to the eating of mussels with broken shells, which had become contaminated. The Eskimos had known better. Why not suppose they might?

I asked the man if there were other poisonous foods on this coast. He said yes, the plant called beaver poison. "People die if they eat the root, but other parts of plant only make them little bit sick."

Many small clamshells were strewn on the sand, each with its fatal hole bored by a marine worm, through which the worm had sucked out the clam. That was one of the ecological factors that I was studying, and I asked where the clam beds were. The Eskimo said,

"I don't really know, but I think maybe off Tolstoy Point. That's about forty miles from here, toward St. Michael. When we catch white beluga whales here, lots of fresh clams in their stomachs. Whales swim pretty fast, though. Maybe clam beds not so near." I began to understand why I had been told that I could trust the observations of Eskimos. This man's conclusions, careful and skeptical, were like those of a scientist.

SHADOW OF THE HUNTER

STORIES OF ESKIMO LIFE

Richard K. Nelson

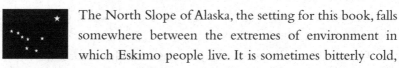

The North Slope of Alaska, the setting for this book, falls somewhere between the extremes of environment in which Eskimo people live. It is sometimes bitterly cold, but there are colder places; it is sometimes poor in game, but there are other places much poorer. In any case, the *Inupiat* do not judge the land around them as good or bad, hostile or friendly, rich or poor. It is the Land, and it is theirs...and that is all.

If anything dominates the Eskimos' environment it is the weather, and if any season dominates the weather it is surely winter. Temperatures in midwinter average close to minus twenty and sink to minus forty or fifty with chilling regularity. During the coldest months it is rare indeed for the temperature to climb above zero. But even this would seem comparatively mild were it not for the winds. Pounding gales rake the tundra and the coast throughout the winter, as storms pass over in monotonous succession. These high winds greatly intensify the bitter cold, blind travelers in clouds of blown snow, move and crush the pack ice, and imprison hunters in their dwellings. For seventy days the sun remains below the horizon, though twilight always appears for several hours around noon.

The Arctic summer provides a brief period of respite and revitalization. Along the coast, midsummer temperatures average in the low forties, and in rare heat waves they reach the sixties or seventies. Constant cloudiness and sea winds add to the coolness of summer, but still it is warm enough so that the snow disappears for several months.

Compensating for winter's darkness, there is perpetual sunlight and twilight from May to August; and for seventy days the sun never sets.

Anyone who has seen the North Slope understand why it is a place of winds. Over most of its length and breadth, an area of some seventy thousand square miles, the tundra prairie is nearly flat. There is nothing higher than a rounded knoll or deeper than a shallow ravine. Sometimes the plain is so level that even an upturned rock stands out as a dominant feature on the landscape.

No trees grow this far north. The nearest stunted spruces are found across the distant mountains. On the North Slope there are only willow bushes, tall as a man's head near the mountains but barely ankle-high along the coast. And beneath the willows is the tundra, a potpourri of grasses, mosses, and tiny flowering plants that burst with color during their moment of summer.

The mat of tundra vegetation provides a livelihood for a variety of small animals and a single large one—the caribou. This graceful member of the deer family wanders in great herds over the North Slope and is food for wolves, grizzly bears, wolverines, and the predatory Eskimo. Recently, the large and ungainly moose has spread northward onto the Slope, adding an entirely new animal to the fauna. In addition to these creatures, there are abundant waterfowl in summer, nesting on thousands of lakes and ponds. And, in the rivers, great runs of fish swim each year to spawning places at the headwaters.

Far out across the Slope, away from the flanking wall of mountains, the thin veneer of land finally ends against the Arctic Ocean. To the north it is called the Beaufort Sea and to the west, the Chukchi Sea. The demarcation between these bodies of water means little to the Inupiat, however, who refer to it all as *Tareoq*.

In winter the sea is hidden beneath a limitless expanse of ice, a continent unto itself, a forbidding moonscape of upthrown ridges, frozen plains, and open cracks that steam in the cold. This is the Arctic pack, ice continuously in motion at the will of wind and current. Only along its edges, where it becomes grounded in the shallows near land, is it immobile. This shelf of quiet ice, only a few miles wide, is the margin of safety that Eskimos depend on when they hurry out to hunt at the pack's fringe.

During the cold months, only seals and polar bears live on or beneath the ice. But in summer the pack thaws and loosens, finally becoming a mass of fragmented floes adrift on the frigid sea. With the turn of seasons, animals arrive in profusion—migrating whales, abundant waterfowl, increasing numbers of seals, and great herds of walrus. Using skin-covered boats, the Eskimos hunt ceaselessly until the pack drifts away to the north. After this the open water is empty of game, and so they await the return of winter before venturing onto the sea again.

This, briefly described, is the environment in which the *Inupiat* and their ancestors have lived for thousands of years. Over the long passage of time, they have gradually perfected an adaptation to the extraordinarily difficult conditions surrounding them. Many facets of this adaptation are widely known, so captivating have they been to the outsider's imagination.

Before they saw white men, the Eskimos had developed a technology so masterly that it would bewilder an engineer. They paddled far out to sea in kayaks, nautical perfection to the last miniscule detail, designed for maximum speed with minimum effort, able to be capsized and righted again without peril or discomfort to the paddler. They glided swiftly over the snow on sleds pulled by harnessed dogs. They built snug houses with blocks of snow carved from the drifts underfoot. They hunted the mightiest of polar animals, whales and walrus, with harpoons almost as complex and deadly as the rifles that replaced them. And they met the inhabited world's most extreme temperatures with animal-hide clothing so efficient that Western man has never produced its equal.

But there is far more to the Eskimos' ingenious response to the challenge of their environment. Implements, after all, are only the tangible results of human thought. The most powerful tool used by the *Inupiat* was, and still is, knowledge. Throughout the long succession of generations, they have sought to increase their understanding of the world around them and to devise new methods for dealing with it. As a result, the Eskimos have a great body of traditional knowledge surrounding every significant plant, every animal, and every feature of landscape, of the sea, of the atmosphere, and even of the heavenly bodies.

All this existed before the white man came, and the *Inupiat* spread and prospered. The inland people lived in tiny camps strewn widely across the tundra, following caribou on their nomadic wanderings, trading hides for seal oil with their coastal neighbors. The coast people built larger villages, a few families in each, at the best places for hunting seal or whale or walrus, according to the season. When scarcity arose in one place, the people moved. Such were the freedoms and the demands of life.

Then a sail appeared on the horizon, and a floating village of strange white men hove to off the shore. Soon more of them followed, chasing bowhead whales along the coast, trading for furs, bargaining for women, leaving behind sacks of flour, bottles of whiskey, rifles, and bits of cloth. Later there were still more; the white men came to live, and they were named *Taniks* by the Eskimos. They brought stores to be filled with goods, schools to be filled with children, churches to be filled with salvation. The missionary-teachers imposed new taboos no *Inupiat* had ever dreamed of, even a day of the week when one could not hunt because the Lord required that one rest instead.

Today there are frame houses, cloth shirts, eyeglasses, blue jeans, radios, strawberry soda pop, outboard engines, iron stoves, comic books…and whatever else can be loaded aboard the annual supply ship or the weekly airplane. The *Inupiat* have left their nomadic camps and crowded together in a few villages, places with names in English and in Eskimo, places where the two worlds intermingle to produce a new culture that is neither fully one nor fully the other.

Yet the people still hunt and fish and travel across land and sea. They still share that enormous body of knowledge that is essential to their traditional livelihood. The knowledge is passed on in the same Eskimo language that was used by forgotten ancestors. Personality, world view, social interaction, instruction, and authority—much of it remains as before. The trappings are changed, but underneath it all the people who have not forsaken their villages remain *Inupiat*.

This modern society of Eskimo hunters is the one I entered in 1964, fresh from a beginning semester of graduate school, ready to spend my first year away from home. I had been in Alaska before, working two summers as an assistant for zoological and archaeological researchers. These experiences, combined with a great deal of reading and much stimulation from teachers, led to my deep fascination with Eskimos. Above all, I was impressed by their ability to understand their environment and make a living from it.

I had chosen to become a cultural anthropologist, to study the ways of living people outside the sphere of Western culture. And I planned to focus on human ecology, the relationships between people and their environments. I suppose it was inevitable that I would eventually go to study Eskimos, but when the chance came I was reluctant and afraid rather than excited. I was twenty-two years old, and the thought of spending a year alone with strange people in that hard land was in some ways unattractive. But I had always believed in the value of new experiences, and so the decision came almost automatically.

The study would focus on Eskimo methods of hunting, traveling, and surviving on the sea ice. It was funded by the Air Force, with the practical aim of gathering information for survival manuals. My personal goal was to observe these activities, then write ethnographic accounts of them. Perhaps these would later become my thesis—I scarcely let the thought of a book enter my mind, though I had often dreamed of writing one.

After many months of preparation, I was finally ready to head north. It was muggy August weather when I left Madison, Wisconsin; when my plane landed at Barrow, Alaska, it was dark, windy, and snowing. The prospect of the year ahead suddenly appeared dismal, and homesickness swept over me. But it was replaced by excitement a few days later as I flew down the coast in a light plane piled high with my gear.

An hour after we left Barrow a little group of houses appeared along the sea cliff ahead. We circled once, then made a bumpy landing on the soft sand of the beach. My heart was pounding, but the crowd of friendly children that surrounded the plane made me feel somewhat at ease. Older people, perhaps fifty of them, stood along the top of the cliff and watched quietly. Minutes later my gear was on the beach and the plane flew off, leaving me behind in a cloud of sand.

It did not take me long to settle into the small house that had been prearranged for me and to begin meeting the people. They were kind and friendly, though reserved and uncertain of my reason for being there. Nearly everyone spoke English, so I could explain my interests and ask that I be allowed to live among them as a hunter. With a great deal of help from the people, and from two schoolteachers who had spent several years in the village, I soon had my own dog team and was participating in the daily activities of village life.

In the months that followed I devoted myself to becoming an apprentice hunter. My goal was to write accurate descriptions of methods for subsisting on the sea ice, and so it seemed essential that I learn them myself. The common anthropological method of gathering information through interviews and conversations simply would not be adequate for this undertaking. And of course it was infinitely more exciting to hitch up my dog team, head out onto the sea ice, and spend the day hunting with the other men.

My routine in the village centered on daily hunting activities. In the course of a year I participated in hundreds of hunts and shared experiences so profound that I cannot begin to measure the changes they wrought in me. But I was too busy to philosophize at the time. I was almost continuously exhausted from the long days of hunting, from cooking meals and maintaining my house, from endless rounds of visiting, and from late nights spent writing down what I had learned.

There were times when I could scarcely contain my enthusiasm for what I was doing; but there were also times when I felt the opposite. The Eskimos correct foolish errors by teasing, and I made many errors. On occasion I grew impatient with this and became sullen. Or I felt lonely and homesick and retreated from their kindness.

But as time passed I began to see that my Eskimo companions were giving me the most important lessons of my life. I developed tremendous respect and admiration for them, feelings I still hold strongly. They taught me to become self-sufficient, to live off the land and sea, to think practically, to respect the wisdom of the old, to appreciate the knowledge of other people, to persevere in all endeavors, to laugh when things go wrong, and to find deep pleasure in sharing.

The year I spent with Eskimos changed the course of my life and made me a very different person. I can only hope that what I have written of them shows that I watched carefully and learned well.

THE LAST WOLF

Mary TallMountain

The last wolf hurried toward me
through the ruined city
and I heard his baying echoes
down the steep smashed warrens
of Montgomery Street and past
the few ruby-crowned highrises
left standing
their lighted elevators useless

Passing the flicking red and green
of traffic signals
baying his way eastward
in the mystery of his wild loping gait
closer the sounds in the deadly night
through clutter and rubble of quiet blocks
I heard his voice ascending the hill
and at last his low whine as he came
floor by empty floor to the room
where I sat
in my narrow bed looking west, waiting
I heard him snuffle at the door and
I watched

He trotted across the floor
he laid his long gray muzzle
on the spare white spread

and his eyes burned yellow
his small dotted eyebrows quivered

Yes, I said.
I know what they have done.

TWO IN THE FAR NORTH

Margaret E. Murie

 In the diary I kept on that trip [with Mildred Capron in the summer of 1967]: "We were not long on the ferry out of Prince Rupert before getting the 'feel' of a new Alaska. There was a fascinating mixture of people onboard. Going through Wrangell Narrows, quiet, under a slow bell, at dusk, everyone watching the very close shores, a young man, a piledriver operator in the timber business, was talking quietly: 'Never a dull moment in the new state of Alaska if you keep your eyes and ears open for what's around you; and we don't have much artificial amusements up here, so we keep our eyes and ears open for what's around us.'

"The new Alaskans—the young men love the life; some of the wives do, some don't. The young mechanic who was towing us in for repairs at Tok said: 'I love hunting in the fall, snowshoeing all over in winter, but my wife hates it.'

"In Fairbanks a taxi driver told Mildred: 'I came up here twelve years ago for two weeks. Never been back. No desire to go back.'

"At a cannery near Haines, a young fisherman was mending his nets: 'I wouldn't live anywhere else. Always something beautiful to look at. Wake up in the morning, look out the window—always something nice to look at.'

"Why do they love it? Most of all the land itself I think, even though some of them are busy altering it, busy killing the thing they love, making it like all other states. But most of Alaska's new people love it. Will there be enough who care? The struggle will be between these two, both new: one group thinking of a whole life, the other of making money and getting out. As for the old-timers, the sourdoughs, they live in nostalgia, and can they be blamed? There were, in spite of hardships, so many charming things about the old life; dog teams, sternwheel steamers, absolute freedom. If a prospector didn't strike it in one creek, there were plenty of others to try. At Fortymile we stopped to take movies at the roadhouse, where they were raising Siberian Huskies. One of the partners said: "So where is there to go any more? Up at Barrow they say there's only two dog teams left; everybody's got those Ski-Doos, and natural gas piped into their houses. So where is there to go any more? Fortymile is the only place left I guess; the folks there don't *want* all that new stuff."

"My own overriding thought is: while all this is going on, what is being left for the one industry which can be most lucrative, nonde-structive, self-perpetuating, for all time—a commodity in short supply in other world markets—the industry of simply letting people come, look, and enjoy Alaska?

"We talked to so many tourists, and what were they looking for? Size, vastness, magnificence, naturalness, informality of life, happy people, enthusiasm about Alaska, mountains, glaciers, waterfalls, great trees, whales, seals, porpoises, birds, all the other wildlife? Yes, but also glimpses of old Alaska and of everyday life of people. I saw tourists stopping to look at a garden in Fairbanks, admiring the cabbages, the peas, the flowers, and talking to the white-haired sourdough working in it. At Miller House on the Steese Highway, we stopped in to see if they served breakfasts. The old proprietor said: 'No, we don't do that any more, but come on in and light your pipe and set and visit awhile anyway.'

"I hope there will be an Alaska for the young mechanic at Tok, for the old sourdough who doesn't want the new stuff, for the young student who wants to explore glaciers, for the Indian or Eskimo who still wants to live in his village, for the young university professor and his wife who merely want to live simply, in the woods, and for the young fisherman who wants to keep on fishing in his own small boat, and 'look out every morning at something nice.'"

FROM

TALES OF ALASKA'S
BUSH RAT GOVERNOR

THE EXTRAORDINARY AUTOBIOGRAPHY OF JAY HAMMOND,
WILDERNESS GUIDE AND RELUCTANT POLITICIAN

Jay Hammond

Numerous issues have pitted Alaskan against Alaskan over the years, cacophonic conflicts that have compelled politicians to dance with alacrity between warring factions to seem in step with each. By contrast, being tone deaf and fumble footed, I seemed to step on the toes of both sides. Unlike the consummate politician who can convince both advocates and opponents he is with them, I convinced each we were at odds.

The pitched battle between "developers" and "conservationists" provided a showcase for my political shortcomings. Nowhere are such conflicts more easily triggered than in Alaska. This is understandable. After all, the two types of persons most inclined to come to the Greatland assure it.

One type are folks who, fed up with environmental degradation and people pressures found elsewhere, flee to Alaska believing it the last redoubt of pristine wilderness and broad horizons. Here they can indulge in lifestyles which, if not long since lost elsewhere, are at least suppressed in their native states. These people have read Robert Service and Thoreau. They arrive with romantic notions of life in a remote homestead cabin away from the urban rat race.

Along with these would-be rustics, however, comes another type of "pioneer" no less determined to find a different kind of "good life." Jobless or discouraged by conditions "back home," and hearing tales of common, unmonied folk striking it rich in Alaska, they flood north intent upon exploitation. It's inevitable that the shovels and picks of these treasure seekers often bruise environmentalists' toes.

Empathizing a bit with both factions, often I placed a foot in each camp, only to find I'd stepped into a campfire. Inability to see but one side of an issue compounded political pain. How I envied those who saw issues in clear black or white rather than unfocused gray.

At first, I naively attributed this to greater sensitivity or intellect, and pondered both sides of a conflict in public. Only after much punishment did I learn more astute politicians ponder such questions in private. The most successful learn more quickly than I how voters want their leaders to take strong, unequivocal positions with absolute confidence in their omniscience. The electorate does not suffer lightly one who admits he may be as confused as they are.

Until I learned this lesson, opponents happily bombed me with charges of inconsistency. Although I might be in accord with them ninety percent of the time, that ten percent deviation enraged extremists on both sides. Some conservationists believed I should do all in my power to stifle growth and development; some developers were certain I aspired to "zero growth" and would return Alaska to a howling wilderness.

Since my heart, if not always my head and gut, was more green than gold, I took perverse but imprudent delight in outraging developmental extremists who were convinced my policies on Alaska's natural resources were a conspiracy to propel Alaska back to pre-Gold Rush conditions. I did not sit down to a standing ovation when I told the Anchorage Chamber of Commerce:

"Now I know there is some apprehension in the business community that Hammond, with his perceived environmentalist views, will somehow stifle economic development, hurl Alaskans out of work, create a mass exodus and devastate the economy. Some have asserted if I have my way I'd make the entire state one huge, national park; fence it in and throw away the key. That's not only untrue, it's absolutely ridiculous. You have nothing to fear in that regard. It could not happen here. *Your city does not merit park status. It has already degenerated beneath acceptable environmental eligibility requirements."*

I confess to more empathy with environmentalists than with rabid developers. Except for those most extreme, I often found them better prepared to back their positions with factual data and intelligent argument. By contrast, their opponents' arguments were too often more visceral than cerebral. This seemed especially true, of course, when an environmentalist position conformed to my own. Getting my head to modify the environmental bent of my heart, took a bit of doing. After all, I was a boy who lamented he'd not been born a hundred years earlier and able to pursue the life of the legendary mountain men.

To this day I can empathize with those two old mountain men in A. B. Guthrie's classic, *The Big Sky*. Riding through a vast western grassland, backdropped by the shining spires of the Rockies, one grizzled oldtimer reins up. Squinting into the setting sun beneath his horny palm, he sees, far away, a lone, covered wagon. Turning to his companion he sadly laments, "By God, she must have been pretty once!"

Likewise, I hold a deep respect for the colorful and out-spoken cowboy artist, Charlie Russell, whose finest hour perhaps came when a group of Montana boosters asked him to address them. Introduced as "one of Montana's true pioneers," old Charlie rose and glowered at his audience.

"I ain't no pioneer. In my book, a pioneer is a man who comes to a virgin country, traps off all the fur, kills off all the wild meat, cuts down all the trees, grazes off all the grass, plows the roots up and strings ten million miles of bob wire. A pioneer destroys things and calls it Civilization. I wish to God that this country was just like it was when I first saw it, and that none of you folks were here at all!"

Charlie probably got even less applause than I did from the Anchorage Chamber of Commerce.

A REQUIEM
FOR THE ARCTIC REFUGE

John Haines

No sign of life, no bird calls,
no mating cries from the tundra...

Only the strewn wreckage of a passing
illness—the discards of metal
and trash left behind by those
who write sorrow on the earth,
and leave to renew their plunder.

I remember, and so must you,
the lost sweetness of this land,
and far to the south a people
for whom it was home, driven to
forage your crime-cemented streets.

I hear a voice from another age
that would speak to us now:
"Forests precede civilization,
and deserts follow..."

Tell me, citizens in your lighted
houses:
       Is this what you wish
for our loaned and borrowed future?
When your houses are darkened

and your stations shut down,
your thousand-year dreampipe emptied...

And of our lost earth-bound refuge,

only a broad sheet of white paper
once held by an official hand—
now certified and fingerprinted,
smudged and stained with oil.

NEXT CHAPTER

Howard Weaver

In the past couple of years, I've learned to do a relaxation exercise that involves imagining the most special place I've ever been. I knew without reflection which to choose: a spot beside a driftwood fire on the beach at Aurora Lagoon on Kachemak Bay. In memory the time is late on a summer evening, sunlight slanting in from an improbable angle, falling without warmth but leaving buttery light on the stalks of grass that grow up through the sand.

It's a specific recollection, selected from a deep catalog of days and nights on the bay. I don't expect to find a more beautiful spot in this life, or spend a more contented evening than that night in magical memory. But I haven't been back for more than five years now.

I left Alaska against all expectations—my own and those of nearly everybody else who knew me. Anchorage born, Muldoon reared, Alaska seasoned, I was a lifer if ever there was one. I had a great answer for folks who asked if I'd lived in Alaska all my life: "Not yet," I always replied.

But I can't use that line any more. I rolled into Sacramento, California, on Halloween in 1995 and haven't spent a whole week back in Alaska since. Two quick personal visits—a sick friend, and a brother graduating from the University of Alaska Anchorage—and a short business trip have been all the Alaska I've needed. I expect that to change, but honest appraisal forces me to admit that it hasn't, yet.

I guess I'd been gone a couple of years before I realized I had left Alaska because it broke my heart. Some people get tired of winter; I got tired of the cold-hearted attitudes that were taking over the place I loved so well.

At the time I thought I left for opportunity. After more than twenty years at the *Anchorage Daily News*, battling the *Anchorage Times*, they finally quit. I knew there was still a lot of valuable newspaper work to do in Alaska, but I was forty-five years old and the feeling of finishing up a chapter and turning the page was powerfully upon me. The corporate job exploring Internet publishing in California felt like a damned good chance to start writing a new one.

A couple of years into my new narrative, a friend asked me to write a preface for his book of Alaska oil history. I wrote a thousand words about the state's relationship with Big Oil and showed them to my wife, Barbara. She read it through quietly and said, "You know, this is awfully bitter." I toned it down considerably—I've learned over the years to trust her solid advice—and sent the piece on to the publisher.

"You know," he told me a few weeks later, "this is awfully bitter." I toned it down again, and still ended up with a piece that sometimes occasions comment.

I didn't realize how I felt until I wrote that. I can't find my original draft—Awfully Bitter Number One—but I remember the overwhelming emotion was of loss and mourning. Somewhere between Swanson River and Bligh Reef, the pioneers who settled Alaska became colonists. The homesteaders became company men, the prospect of a paycheck and a Permanent Fund dividend replacing the self sufficiency and community spirit that knitted together earlier generations through so many long, dark winters. Though there was a brief rebellion after the *Exxon Valdez* oil spill, a few months later Alaska's body politic rolled over again and renewed its bargain with the industry: Take what you want; leave money.

I don't blame the big oil companies for acting like big oil companies; they sometimes make me mad, but I expect no better of them. My aching disappointment came from watching Alaska's character change so profoundly.

Over decades in the writing game in Alaska, I suppose I encountered every one of the 6,743 cliches available to describe the place, and none was truer than this: The real Alaska isn't so much a state as a state of mind. Therein lies my problem; while the landscape and the scenery have survived reasonably well over the past thirty years, the collective "state of mind" has deteriorated faster than a spawned-out humpy in fresh water.

Alaskans who used to be routinely generous and optimistic have become selfish. Oh, not everybody, of course not; and not *you*, gentle reader. But far too many of your neighbors.

In a society with no income tax, no sales tax and a two thousand dollar payment from the state for every man, woman and child, they pushed a tax cap. Public services and public facilities inexorably starve to death; bright new landmarks like the Alaska Center for the Performing Arts already look worn around the edges, and public dollars to fund assistance for the less fortunate have been unapologetically eroded, as well.

The growing selfishness is particularly virulent when it comes to relations between the new majority culture and Alaska Natives—never more evident than in the endless, ugly debates over subsistence hunting and fishing. Yeah, sure, some guy in a Wasilla four-plex has just as much claim on the fish and game as a family on a roadless stretch of the Yukon whose culture has revolved around hunting for 5,000 years. Think Native suicides and alcoholism might be connected to missionaries and the cash economy? "Hey, *I* never did anything to 'em," he might reply.

Alaskans' unwillingness to recognize the unique needs and rights of Native people amount to the continuing rejection of a rare opportunity to blend dominant and indigenous cultures in ways that could have strengthened both. Instead, unconditional surrender is demanded, engulfment *uber alles*.

Hand-in-hand comes the steady deterioration of the authentic in Alaska. Yes, February is still dark and sometimes chilly, but there's often little else to distinguish Anchorage from Akron, strip mall alongside franchise next to themed restaurant. Far too little of Alaska's art or music springs from northern soil; it is far more likely to be derivative, a country-cousin copy of something being done Outside. The tourist trade is most often an entirely packaged experience these days, industrial recreation delivered aboard self-contained floating cities.

Alaska is no worse than many places in such matters—but I never expected much of the other places. Alaska was supposed to be special;

my affection flagged as I discovered the many ways in which it is not. California's legislature can be as cynical and venal as Alaska's (though seldom as boneheaded), but it doesn't pain me nearly so much to watch them screw up here. I like my new life here and living in California just fine, thank you—but I truly love Alaska.

As a journalist, I still sometimes miss the security of working in my hometown, of knowing the political landscape as intimately as the natural scenery, of feeling sure-footed while navigating the community. About seven months after leaving, a friend wrote with lots of detailed, inside news about the Alaska legislature. Reading his letter and understanding all the nuances, I realized, with some sadness, that I would never again in this life understand anything as fundamentally as I had understood Alaska. The realization came with a distinctly bittersweet twinge.

But I knew that wasn't all bad, either. Being so fluently aware of Alaska was part of what fueled the imperative to leave—to learn something new, to live something different. As Shakespeare said, "Things won are done; soul's joy lies in the doing."

And so I left.

I write about this now with some reluctance, for I know that leaving Alaska feels like betrayal to the folks who stay behind. I know that because I felt it so often myself over those many years. (If you doubt that observation, turn it around and look from the other side: Ever feel anything more satisfying than talking with somebody who left and then moved back, full of stories about how bad things are Out There?)

Aboard the MV *Columbia*, well away on our journey out of Alaska, a woman came across the aisle in the snack bar and stopped at our table. "You don't know me, but I wanted to tell you that we're going to miss you in Anchorage," she said.

I'd heard that a few times before departing; the people who were glad to see me go mainly had the good grace not to say so to my face. I smiled and told her I knew I was going to miss Alaska, too.

My wife first noticed the woman's husband—a trim seventy-year-old with a neat white goatee and a Levis jacket: Keith Miller, third governor of Alaska. They were en route back to their winter home in Florence, Oregon, after a summer in Girdwood.

"You'll be back," he told us.

And who am I to argue with that?

FOR THE SAKE OF THE LIGHT

Tom Sexton

The lantern cleaned and put away
after a long winter, I sit by the window
writing about the last snow
turning to mist beneath the alders.
Long before dawn, I can see
the glacial mountains to the west
flecked with blue and braided silver.
Soon bog candle will bloom in the marsh.
For all our sadness, melancholy and regret,
at times it is possible, even necessary,
to believe we are here for the sake of the light.

CONTRIBUTORS

John Active, a Yup'ik Eskimo from the Bethel area, has been recognized by the Alaska Humanities Forum for his contributions to the understanding of Native cultures.

Jean Anderson moved to Fairbanks in 1966 from St. Louis. A story from her collection *In Extremis* was a PEN Syndicated Fiction Selection.

Alan S. Boraas, an anthropologist, was teaching at Kenai Peninsula College when he began working with Peter Kalifornsky, one of the last speakers of Dena'ina.

Sally Carrighar was a naturalist writing about a marsh in the Tetons when Olaus Murie convinced her to write about the Arctic Coast. *Moonlight at Midday*, about her experiences in Unalakleet, was published in 1958.

Jerah Chadwick directs the University of Alaska's Extension Program in Unalaska, where he has lived for twenty-five years. He is the Alaska Writer Laureate 2004-2006. He first beheld the "Woman of Ounalashka" when she came "home" to the Museum of the Aleutians in 2000. James Webber, the artist for Captain James Cook's expedition, made a quick pencil sketch of her in 1778.

Ann Fox Chandonnet came to Alaska from rural Massachusetts in 1965. She has worked as a journalist, publicist, editor, and teacher.

Marjorie Kowalski Cole moved to Fairbanks with her family when she was thirteen. In 2004 her first novel, *Correcting the Landscape*, won the Bellwether Prize for Fiction.

Kimberley Cornwall grew up on a ranch in British Columbia. She works with people with disabilities in Fairbanks.

Nora Marks Dauenhauer is a Tlingit linguist. Born in Juneau, she grew up living on her family's fishing boat for most of the year. She has published many volumes of Tlingit oral history as well as several books of her own poetry.

June McGlashan Dirks, an Aleut from Akutan in the Aleutian Islands, now lives in Unalaska. She enjoys cooking traditional food at the Qugaayux Culture Camp.

Joseph Enzweiler is an Ohio native who came to Alaska in 1975. He works as a carpenter and stone mason in the summer and writes in the winter. He has published four books of poetry.

Jill Fredston is an avalanche expert and long-distance rower. She and her husband, Doug Fesler, are co-directors of the Alaska Mountain Safety Center in Anchorage.

James Greiner was a pilot and outdoorsman. *Wager with the Wind* tells the story of his friend, bush pilot Don Sheldon, who made legendary air rescues of climbers off of Mt. McKinley.

John Haines homesteaded at Richardson, seventy-five miles south of Fairbanks, in 1947. He has written more than ten books of poetry and essays and has received numerous awards. He is a former Alaska Poet Laureate.

Jay Hammond was born in Troy, New York. He served as a Marine fighter pilot in the South Pacific during World War II. He moved to Alaska in 1946, where he became a bush pilot, a commercial fisherman, and served as governor of Alaska from 1974–1982.

Anne Hanley, a playwright, screenwriter, and poet, has a biweekly column on Alaskan writing in two newspapers. She has lived in Fairbanks since 1976 and served as Alaska State Writer Laureate 2002-2004.

Sidney Huntington is the son of Gold Rush pioneer James S. Huntington and Anna, a Koyukon Athabascan. He grew up hunting and trapping along the Koyukuk River. In 1972 he was appointed to the Alaska Board of Fish and Game.

Jennie Masruana Jackson, an Inupiaq Eskimo, was born in 1893 in Noorvik, where she passed away in 1987. She was a subsistence gatherer. The story she tells dates back to at least the mid-1800s.

Nick Jans is an Alaskan photographer and the author of several nonfiction books. His friend, the internationally known photographer Michio Hoshino, was killed by a brown bear in 1996 near Kurilskoya Lake in the Russian Far East.

Arlitia Jones was born in Pasco, Washington, and moved with her family to Anchorage in 1972 when she was seven. Her first book of poetry, *The Bandsaw Riots*, won the Dorothy Brunsman Poetry Prize in 2001.

Peter Kalifornsky was born in 1911 near the mouth of the Kasilof River in the Cook Inlet region. One of the last speakers of the Kenai dialect of the Dena'ina language (Athabascan), he passed away in 1993.

Seth Kanter was born in a sod igloo near the Kobuk River in northwest Alaska. His parents were college graduates from Ohio who wanted to live a subsistence lifestyle.

Carolyn Kremers moved from Colorado to Western Alaska in 1986 to teach in the village of Tununak. Her book *Place of the Pretend People: Gifts from a Yup'ik Eskimo Village* was inspired by that experience. She writes literary nonfiction and poetry, and lives in Fairbanks.

Natalie Kusz moved to Alaska from California with her parents and three siblings when she was six. She has received several grants for her writing, including the prestigious Whiting Award.

Jack London was born in San Francisco. He came north for the Gold Rush in 1897. His most famous tales of adventure are set in the Yukon.

Nancy Lord came to Alaska from New Hampshire in 1973. She fishes commercially for salmon and teaches creative writing. She has published four nonfiction books and three collections of short stories.

Robert Marshall, a naturalist and forester, made several expeditions to the Central Brooks Range for the U.S. Forest Service in the 1930s. His books, *Arctic Village* and *Alaska Wilderness*, raised public awareness of the wilderness values of this area.

John McPhee is a former staff writer for *The New Yorker*. His book, *Coming into the Country*, depicts changes brought about by resource development in Alaska in the 1970s.

John Morgan taught for many years in the English Department at the University of Alaska Fairbanks. He is the author of three books of poetry.

John Muir first came to Alaska in 1879 when he was forty-one. He did not compile *Travels in Alaska* until thirty years later. The book was published in 1915, one year after his death.

Margaret E. Murie and her biologist husband, Olaus Murie, worked for conservation of Alaska's wild lands. This entry from her diary was written in 1967.

Richard K. Nelson is a writer, naturalist, and anthropologist who lives in Sitka. His books include *The Island Within, Hunters of the Northern Ice*, and other works of nonfiction influenced by his experiences with Athabascan and Inupiaq people.

Phoebe Newman moved to Ketchikan in 1994. During National Poetry Month, she produces *One Poem a Day Won't Kill You* for Ketchikan's public radio station.

Sheila Nickerson lived in Juneau for twenty-seven years before retiring in Washington state. She worked for the Alaska Department of Fish and Game and was Alaska Poet Laureate from 1977-1981. She writes nonfiction, fiction, and poetry.

Dan O'Neill is a writer and historian. In *The Firecracker Boys*, he describes how Edward Teller planned to create a harbor in northern Alaska in 1958 by detonating thermonuclear bombs and how a few Alaskan scientists and Inupiaq Eskimos stopped him.

Semyon Pan'kov was an Aleut from Unalaska who acted as an interpreter for the Russian Orthodox priest and missionary Ivan Veniaminov during the nineteenth century. In 1846, Pan'kov wrote down twelve Eastern Aleut song texts and helped translate them into Russian.

Kim Rich was a reporter for the *Anchorage Daily News*. Her memoir of growing up in Alaska's underworld, *Johnny's Girl*, was made into a movie starring Treat Williams.

Linda Schandelmeier grew up on a homestead in what is now part of Anchorage. She teaches elementary school in Fairbanks.

Robert Service was born in England in 1874. He is best known for his narrative poems celebrating the Klondike Gold Rush in Canada.

Tom Sexton is a former Alaska Poet Laureate. He came to Alaska in 1959 and taught creative writing and literature for many years at the University of Alaska Anchorage. He is the author of three books of poetry.

Peggy Schumaker moved to Alaska in 1985 to teach at the University of Alaska Fairbanks. She retired in 1999 and is the author of several books of poetry.

Sherry Simpson moved to Juneau with her family when she was seven. She teaches creative writing and literature at the University of Alaska Anchorage. Her book of essays, *The Way Winter Comes*, is about living in Alaska.

Frank Soos was born and raised in Pocahontas, Virginia. He moved to Alaska in 1986 and taught in the English Department at the University of Alaska Fairbanks. He is the author of two collections of short stories and a book of essays.

Dana Stabenow is the author of nineteen mystery novels, including ten featuring Kate Shugak and three featuring Alaska State Trooper Liam Campbell. A winner of the Edgar Award, she lives in Anchorage.

Mary TallMountain, an Athabascan born in Nulato in 1918, was taken away from her family and her village at age six when her mother contracted tuberculosis. She did not return to Nulato until fifty years later.

Spike Walker crewed for nine seasons on a crab boat during the boom years of Alaska crab fishing (1976-1984). "Working on the edge" is crewman's lingo for fishing in the dangerous outer waters of the Bering Sea.

Velma Wallis is a Gwich'in Athabascan from Fort Yukon. She is the sixth in a family of thirteen children. Her book, *Two Old Women*, was an international bestseller.

Howard Weaver was born in Anchorage, where he worked as a newspaperman for twenty-five years until moving to California in 1995.

James Wickersham was a U.S. District Judge in Alaska from 1900–1908. He often traveled by dog sled to preside at trials.

Charles Wohlforth was an investigative reporter for the *Anchorage Daily News* immediately following the *Exxon Valdez* oil spill. He served on the Anchorage Municipal Assembly for six years. He describes *The Whale and the Supercomputer* as "an adventure story about climate change."

PERMISSIONS

Active, John. "Why Subsistence Is a Matter of Cultural Survival: A Yup'ik Point of View." *Alaska Quarterly Review* 17 (Spring/Summer 1999). **Reprinted by permission of John Active.**

Anderson, Jean. "Snobs." *Prairie Schooner* 74, no. 1 (Spring 2000). **Reprinted from the *Prairie Schooner*, volume 74, number 1 (Spring 2000) by permission of the University of Nebraska Press. Copyright 2000 by the University of Nebraska Press.**

Boraas, Alan S. *Peter Kalifornsky: A Biography by Alan S. Boraas*. Fairbanks: Alaska Native Language Center, 1991. **Copyright 1991, Alaska Native Language Center. Reprinted by permission of Alaska Native Language Center, College of Liberal Arts, University of Alaska Fairbanks and Peter Kalifornsky.**

Carrighar, Sally. *Moonlight at Midday*. New York: Alfred A. Knopf, 1958. **From *Moonlight at Midday* by Sally Carrighar, copyright © 1958 by Sally Carrighar. Used by permission of Alfred A. Knopf, a division of Random House, Inc.**

Chadwick, Jerah. "*Nawalaskam Agagaa*: Woman of Ounalashka." *Ice-Floe* 3, no. 1 (Summer Solstice 2002). **© 2002 by Ice-Floe Press. Reprinted by permission of Ice-Floe Press, Anchorage, Alaska.**

Chadwick, Jerah. "Not to Talk Bad of the Weather." *Ice-Floe* 2, no. 1 (Summer Solstice 2001). **© 2001 by Ice-Floe Press. Reprinted by permission of Ice-Floe Press, Anchorage, Alaska.**

Chandonnet, Ann Fox. "Entering the Surroundings." *Auras, Tendrils*. Manotick, Ontario, Canada: Penumbra Press, 1984. **"Entering the Surroundings" by Ann Fox Chandonnet originally appears in *Auras, Tendrils* (1984) and is reproduced here with permission of the author.**

Cole, Marjorie Kowalski. *Correcting the Landscape*. New York: Harper Collins, 2005. **Chapter One from *Correcting the Landscape* by Marjorie Kowalski Cole. Copyright © 2005 by Marjorie**

Pan'kov, Semyon. "Love Song." In *Unangam Ungiikanginkayux Tunusangin—Unangam Uniikargis ama Tunuzangis: Aleut Tales and Narratives.* Collected by Waldemar Jochelson. Fairbanks, Alaska: Alaska Native Language Center, University of Alaska, 1990. **Reprinted by permission of the Alaska Native Language Center, Fairbanks, Alaska. © 1990 Alaska Native Language Center, College of Liberal Arts, University of Alaska Fairbanks; ed. Knut Bergsland and Moses L. Dirks.**

Rich, Kim. *Johnny's Girl: A Daughter's Memoir of Growing Up in Alaska's Underworld.* New York: William Morrow and Company, 1993. ***Johnny's Girl*, by Kim Rich © 1993, with the permission of Alaska Northwest Books®, an imprint of Graphic Arts Center Publishing Company.**

Schandelmeier, Linda. "Fire." In *Listening Hard among the Birches.* Fairbanks: Vanessapress, 2002. **© 2002 by Vanessapress. Reprinted by permission of Vanessapress, Fairbanks, Alaska.**

Service, Robert. "The Quitter." In *Collected Poems of Robert Service.* New York: Dodd, Mead & Company, 1907.

Sexton, Tom. "Rowing toward the Spirit World" and "For the Sake of the Light." In *Autumn in the Alaska Range.* Cliffs of Moher, County Clare, Ireland: Salmon Publishing, 2000. **© 2002 by Tom Sexton. Reprinted by permission of Salmon Publishing, Cliffs of Moher, County Clare, Ireland.**

Shumaker, Peggy. "Braided River." In *Underground Rivers.* Los Angeles: Red Hen Press, 2002. **© 2002 by Peggy Shumaker. Reprinted by permission of Red Hen Press, Granada Hills, California.**

Simpson, Sherry. "A Man Made Cold by the Universe." Anchorage: Anchorage Press, 2003. **© 2003. Reprinted by permission of the Anchorage Press, Anchorage, Alaska.**

Soos, Frank. *Bamboo Fly Rod Suite: Reflections on Fishing and the Geography of Grace.* Athens, Ga.: University of Georgia Press, 1999. **From *Bamboo Fly Rod Suite: Reflections on Fishing and the Geography of Grace.* Text copyright 1999 by Frank Soos. Illustrations copyright 1999 by Kesler Woodward. Reprinted by permission of the University of Georgia Press.**

Stabenow, Dana. *A Cold Day for Murder.* New York: Berkley Publishing Group, 1992. **From *A Cold Day for Murder* by Dana Stabenow, copyright © 1992 by Dana Stabenow. Used by permission of Berkley Publishing Group, a division of Penguin Group (USA) Inc.**

TallMountain, Mary. "The Last Wolf" and "There Is No Word for Goodbye." In *The Light on the Tent Wall*. Los Angeles: American Indian Studies Center, UCLA, 1993. **Reprinted from *Shadow Country* by permission of the American Indian Studies Center, UCLA. © 1982 Regents of the University of California.**

Walker, Spike. *Working on the Edge: Surviving in the World's Most Dangerous Profession: King Crab Fishing on Alaska's High Seas.* New York: St. Martin's Press, 1991. **From *Working on the Edge* by Spike Walker. Copyright © 1991 by the author and reprinted by permission of St. Martin's Press, LLC.**

Wallis, Velma. *Raising Ourselves: A Gwich'in Coming of Age Story from the Yukon River.* Kenmore, Wash.: Epicenter Press, 2002. **© 2002 by Velma Wallis. Reprinted by permission of Epicenter Press, Kenmore, Washington.**

Weaver, Howard. "Next Chapter." In *Our Alaska: Personal Stories about Living in the North.* Edited by Mike Doogan. Kenmore, Wash.: Epicenter Press, 2001. **© 2001 by Mike Doogan. Reprinted by permission of Epicenter Press, Kenmore, Washington.**

Wickersham, James. *Old Yukon: Tales–Trails–and Trials.* Washington, D.C.: Washington Law Book Co., 1938.

Wohlforth, Charles. *The Whale and the Supercomputer: On the Northern Front of Climate Change.* New York: North Point Press, 2004. **Reprinted by permission of North Point Press, a division of Farrar, Straus and Giroux, LLC: Excerpt from *The Whale and the Supercomputer* by Charles Wohlforth. Copyright © 2004 by Charles Wohlforth.**